A Tale of Two Cultures

# A Tale of
# Two Cultures

*Qualitative and Quantitative*
*Research in the Social Sciences*

Gary Goertz and James Mahoney

PRINCETON UNIVERSITY PRESS

PRINCETON AND OXFORD

Copyright © 2012 by Princeton University Press

Published by Princeton University Press, 41 William Street, Princeton, New Jersey 08540

In the United Kingdom: Princeton University Press, 6 Oxford Street, Woodstock,
Oxfordshire OX20 1TW

press.princeton.edu

Library of Congress Cataloging-in-Publication Data

Goertz, Gary, 1953–
A tale of two cultures : qualitative and quantitative research in the social sciences / Gary Goertz and
James Mahoney.
   p. cm.
Includes bibliographical references and index.
ISBN 978-0-691-14970-7 (hardcover : alk. paper) — ISBN 978-0-691-14971-4 (pbk. : alk. paper)
1. Political science—Research—Methodology.   2. Political sociology—Research—Methodology.
3. Social sciences—Research—Methodology.   I. Mahoney, James, 1968–   II. Title.
  JA86.G56 2012
  301.072—dc23
                                   2012010983

British Library Cataloging-in-Publication Data is available

This book has been composed in Times and Helvetica


Typeset by S R Nova Pvt Ltd, Bangalore, India


10 9 8 7 6 5 4 3 2 1

# Contents

## IV. RESEARCH DESIGN AND GENERALIZATION

# Preface

This book analyzes quantitative and qualitative research in the social sciences as separate cultures. We arrived at this "two cultures" view in the course of carrying out teaching and research over the last decade. We repeatedly discovered ways in which qualitative and quantitative researchers vary in their methodological orientations and research practices. We also observed misunderstandings and constrained communication among qualitative and quantitative researchers. As we tried to make sense of these facts, it became clear to us that the qualitative and quantitative traditions exhibit all the traits of separate cultures, including different norms, practices, and tool kits.

Our goal in writing this book is to increase scholarly understanding of the ways in which these cultures are different as well as the rationales behind those differences. In order to do this, we cover a large range of methodological topics. These topics concern key research design and data analysis questions that nearly all social scientists must face. Many of the topics covered here are not addressed in research methods textbooks and cannot be found together in any convenient book on methodology, qualitative or quantitative. Hence, one way to read and use this volume is as a guide to the range of questions that any social scientist might consider when designing and carrying out research.

We first learned about each other's research while teaching at the Institute for Qualitative and Multi-Method Research, and we would like to express our gratitude to the many students who attended this Institute and gave us feedback on our two cultures argument over the years. We owe the Institute's leader, Colin Elman, special thanks for making room for our work in the annual program. We are also grateful to the Organized Section on Qualitative and Multi-Method Research of the American Political Science Association, which provided newsletter and conference outlets for early drafts of several chapters.

The first version of our argument was an article published in *Political Analysis* in 2006. We are grateful to Robert S. Erikson, who was editor of *Political Analysis*, for going forward with that early piece. Without its publication, we might not have been inspired to continue to find and explore differences in quantitative and qualitative research.

We discussed parts of this manuscript while teaching graduate courses on methodology at the University of Arizona and Northwestern University. It was in interacting with our graduate students—quantitative and qualitative—that many of the topics rose to the top of our list of important methodological issues. In addition, much of this material has been presented in workshops and short courses in the United States, Europe, and Latin America. We express our thanks to the graduate students in all of these courses, workshops, and short courses for their insights. We especially acknowledge the contribution of Khairunnisa Mohamedali and Christoph Nguyen, who carried out the survey of articles reported in the appendix. We also thank the professors and students who offered comments on presentations of this material at Northwestern University, the University of Wisconsin, and Yale University.

At Princeton University Press, Chuck Myers helped to secure reviewer reports from which we benefited. Chuck also worked to speed the production process along. We are grateful to Glenda Krupa for copyediting the manuscript. We acknowledge Sage Publications Inc. for granting permission to publish the epigraph at the beginning of Chapter 13, which originally appeared in *Applied Regression Analysis and Generalized Linear Models* (Second Edition) by John Fox (Los Angeles, CA: Sage Publications, 2008).

Finally, we received insightful comments from a number of colleagues: Michael Baumgartner, Nathaniel Beck, Andrew Bennett, Janet Box-Steffensmeier, Bear Braumoeller, David Collier, Thad Dunning, Colin Elman, John Gerring, Jack Levy, Diana Kapiszewski, Charles C. Ragin, Carsten Schneider, Jason Seawright, David Waldner, and Sebastian Zaja. We know that not all of these colleagues agree with everything that we say in this book. But we hope that engaging and debating the ideas presented here will itself help to move forward both quantitative and qualitative research in the social sciences.

A Tale of Two Cultures

# Chapter 1

# Introduction

In this book, we explore the relationship between the quantitative and qualitative research traditions in the social sciences, with particular emphasis on political science and sociology. We do so by identifying various ways in which the traditions differ. They contrast across numerous areas of methodology, ranging from type of research question, to mode of data analysis, to method of inference. We suggest that these differences are systematically and coherently related to one another such that it is meaningful to speak of distinct quantitative and qualitative research paradigms.

We treat the quantitative and qualitative traditions as alternative cultures. Each has its own values, beliefs, and norms. Each is associated with distinctive research procedures and practices. Communication within a given culture tends to be fluid and productive. Communication across cultures, however, tends to be difficult and marked by misunderstanding. When scholars from one tradition offer their insights to members of the other tradition, the advice is often viewed as unhelpful and inappropriate. The dissonance between the alternative cultures is seen with the miscommunication, skepticism, and frustration that sometimes mark encounters between quantitative and qualitative researchers. At its core, we suggest, the quantitative–qualitative disputation in the social sciences is really a clash of cultures.

Like all cultures, the quantitative and qualitative ones are not monolithic blocks (see Sewell (2005) for a good discussion of the concept of "culture"). They are loosely integrated traditions, and they contain internal contradictions and contestation. The particular orientations and practices that compose these cultures have changed over time, and they continue to evolve today. The two cultures are not hermetically sealed from one another but rather are permeable and permit boundary crossing. Nevertheless, they are *relatively* coherent systems of meaning and practice. They feature many readily identifiable values, beliefs, norms, and procedures.

By emphasizing differences between qualitative and quantitative research, this book stands in contrast to King, Keohane, and Verba's work, *Designing Social Inquiry: Scientific Inference in Qualitative Research*. They famously argue that "the differences between the quantitative and qualitative traditions are only stylistic and are methodologically and substantively unimportant" (1994, 4). They believe that the two traditions share a single logic of inference, one that can be largely summarized in terms of the norms of statistical analysis. The differences between the two traditions that they identify concern surface traits, especially the use of numbers versus words.

We reject the assumption that a single logic of inference founded on statistical norms guides both quantitative and qualitative research. Nor do we believe that the quantitative-qualitative distinction revolves around the use of numbers versus words. Instead, we see differences in basic orientations to research, such as whether one mainly uses within-case analysis to make inferences about individual cases (as qualitative researchers do) or whether one mainly uses cross-case analysis to make inferences about populations (as quantitative researchers do). We even suggest that the two traditions are best understood as drawing on alternative mathematical foundations: quantitative research is grounded in inferential statistics (i.e., probability and statistical theory), whereas qualitative research is (often implicitly) rooted in logic and set theory. Viewing the traditions in light of these contrasting mathematical foundations helps to make sense of many differences that we discuss in this book.

In pointing out basic divergences, our goal is not to drive a wedge between the quantitative and qualitative research paradigms. To the contrary, we seek to facilitate communication and cooperation between scholars associated with the different paradigms. We believe that mutual understanding must be founded upon recognition and appreciation of differences, including an understanding of contrasting strengths and weaknesses. We advocate boundary crossing and mixed-method research when questions require analysts to pursue goals characteristic to both the qualitative and quantitative paradigms. At the same time, we respect and do not view as inherently inferior research that stays within its own paradigm. There is a place for quantitative, qualitative, and mixed-method research in the social sciences.

One lesson that grows out of this book is that asking whether quantitative or qualitative research is superior to the other is not a useful question. King, Keohane, and Verba (1994, 5–6) also state that "neither quantitative nor qualitative research is superior to the other." However, they arrive at this conclusion only because they believe qualitative methods must be used as a last resort when statistical analysis is not possible.[1] By contrast, we believe that quantitative and qualitative techniques are appropriate for different research tasks and are designed to achieve different research goals. The selection of quantitative versus qualitative techniques is not a matter of the data that happen to be available. Rather, for some research goals, quantitative methods are more appropriate than qualitative techniques, and qualitative methods are more appropriate than quantitative methods for other research questions. Depending on the task, of course, it may well be the case that the analyst must draw on *both* kinds of techniques to achieve his or her goal. Mixed-method research that combines quantitative and qualitative techniques is essential for many complex research projects whose goals require analysts to draw on the orientations and characteristic strengths of both traditions.

Like some anthropologists who study other cultures, we seek to make sense of research practices while maintaining a kind of neutrality about them. Our goals are mainly descriptive, not primarily normative or prescriptive. Certainly, the methods of the two traditions are not beyond criticism. However, we believe that the critique and reformulation of methods works best *within* a given tradition. Thus, statistical methodologists are the scholars most qualified to improve statistical methods, whereas qualitative methodologists are the scholars best positioned to improve qualitative methods. We find that many existing "cross-cultural" criticisms, such as critiques of quantitative research by qualitative scholars, are not appropriate because they ignore the basic goals and purposes of research in that tradition. What appears to be problematic through one set of glasses may make good sense through the lenses of the other tradition.

In telling a tale of these two cultures, we often end up considering how lesser-known and implicit qualitative assumptions and practices differ from well-known and carefully codified quantitative ones. This approach is a by-product of the fact that quantitative methods, when compared to qualitative methods, are more explicitly and systematically developed in the social sciences. Quantitative methods are better known, and the quantitative culture is, no doubt, the more dominant of the two cultures within most social science fields. As such we devote more space to a discussion of qualitative methods. Yet the approach throughout remains clarifying what is distinctive about *both* traditions while avoiding invidious comparisons.

---

[1] As they put it, "Since many subjects of interest to social scientists cannot be meaningfully formulated in ways that permit statistical testing of hypotheses with quantitative data, we do not wish to encourage the exclusive use of quantitative techniques" (King, Keohane, and Verba 1994, 6).

## Why Two Cultures?

King, Keohane, and Verba suggest that there is a single logic of inference—one basic culture—that characterizes all social science, both quantitative and qualitative. An alternative, "many cultures" view might hold that the quantitative and qualitative traditions are heterogeneous groups with many variants and subcultures within each. Indeed, each paradigm—like any culture—features big divisions as well as smaller ones. For example, historically within the statistical paradigm, one big division was between the classical, frequentist school and the Bayesian approach to statistical analysis (e.g., see Freedman 2010 and Jackman 2009). Other smaller divisions—over issues such as the utility of fixed effect models or the number of independent variables that should be included in a statistical model—exist among scholars who may agree on larger issues such as the frequentist versus Bayesian debate.

Likewise, the qualitative paradigm includes many divisions. Perhaps the biggest split concerns the differences between scholars who work broadly within the behavioral tradition and who are centrally concerned with causal inference versus scholars associated with various interpretive approaches. These two big tents each have their own subdivisions. For example, qualitative scholars who embrace the goal of causal inference may disagree on the relative importance of specific tools, such as counterfactual analysis or Qualitative Comparative Analysis (QCA). Likewise, within the interpretive camp, there are differences between scholars who embrace interpretive analysis à la Clifford Geertz (1973) and scholars who advocate critical theory and poststructural approaches.

Our two cultures approach shares certain similarities with King, Keohane, and Verba's one culture approach, especially in that we focus on research that is centrally oriented toward causal inference and generalization. The methods and techniques that we discuss are all intended to be used to make valid scientific inferences. The employment of scientific methods for the generation of valid causal inferences, above all else, unites the two research traditions discussed in this book.

One consequence of our focus on causal inference is that important currents within the qualitative paradigm drop out of the analysis. In particular, interpretive approaches are not featured in our two cultures argument. These approaches are usually less centrally concerned with causal analysis; they focus more heavily on other research goals, such as elucidating the meaning of behavior or critiquing the use of power. The interpretive tradition has its own leading norms and practices, which differ in basic ways from the quantitative and qualitative paradigms that we study in this book. One could certainly write another book focusing on the ways in which the interpretive culture contrasts with the "causal inference" cultures that we discuss. Such a book would bring to light fundamental clashes over epistemology and ontology that exist within parts of the social sciences. In this book, however, we focus on scholars who agree on many basic issues of epistemology and ontology, including the centrality of causal analysis for understanding the social world.[2]

There are various reasons why it makes sense to focus on these two traditions of research. For one thing, the qualitative–quantitative distinction is built into nearly everyone's vocabulary in the social sciences, and it serves as a common point of reference for distinguishing different kinds of work. Nearly all scholars speak of qualitative versus quantitative research, though they may not understand that contrast in the same way. Even scholars, such as ourselves, who feel that the labels "quantitative" and "qualitative" are quite inadequate for capturing the most salient differences between the two traditions still feel compelled to use this terminology.

Furthermore, social scientists have organized themselves—formally and informally—into quantitative and qualitative research communities. In political science, there are two methodology sections, the Section on Political Methodology, which represents quantitative methodology, and the newer Section on Qualitative and Multi-Method Research. In sociology, the Section on Methodology stands for mainly quantitative methods, whereas the kinds of qualitative methods that we discuss are associated with the Section on Comparative and Historical Sociology. Leading training institutes reflect the two culture division as well: the Interuniversity Consortium for Political and Social Research (ICPSR) provides almost exclusively quantitative training, whereas the Institute for Qualitative and Multi-Method Research (IQMR) focuses on qualitative and mixed-method research.

Our goal in this book is not to turn quantitative researchers into qualitative researchers, or vice versa. However, we do seek to increase the number of scholars who understand the norms and practices—and their rationales—of both cultures of research. We believe that overcoming the quantitative-qualitative division in the social sciences is significantly a matter of better understanding the methodological differences between these two traditions along with the reasons why those differences exist.

---

[2] Our decision to not treat interpretive approaches in this book should not be taken as evidence that we see no place for these approaches in the social sciences. In fact, our two cultures argument is, broadly speaking, an exercise in description and interpretation. We seek to elucidate the practices and associated meanings of two relatively coherent cultures of research. Thus, while interpretive analysts will not find their tradition of research represented in the qualitative culture that we describe, they nonetheless will find many of the tools of their tradition put to use in our analysis.

## Characterizing and Comparing the Two Cultures

In discussing the quantitative and qualitative traditions, we draw on various data sources and focus on certain kinds of practices and not others. In this section, we briefly describe our approach to characterizing and comparing the two cultures.

### Types of Data

Our characterizations of research practices derive from three kinds of data. First, we rely on the literature concerning quantitative and qualitative methodology. Methodologists often do an excellent job of making explicit the research techniques used in a given tradition and the rationale behind these techniques. For the quantitative paradigm, we make much use of textbooks written by prominent scholars in the fields of statistics, econometrics, and quantitative social science. Our presentation draws heavily on literature concerning the Neyman-Rubin-Holland model and the associated "potential outcomes" framework (e.g., Angrist and Pischke 2009, Berk 2004, Freedman 2010, and Morgan and Winship 2007). We also reference the literature on experimental research in the social sciences when relevant. For the qualitative paradigm, our discussion is grounded in the "classic cannon" of work associated with scholars such as Giovanni Sartori, Alexander George, and David Collier. In addition, we utilize many insights from the work of Charles Ragin. At the end of each individual chapter, we recommend books and articles that one might read to explore further the differences discussed in the chapter.

Second, we use exemplary quantitative and qualitative studies to illustrate the distinctions that we discuss in the individual chapters. These studies are not only useful as examples, but also as sources of insight about characteristic practices in the two cultures. Some of these exemplars engage topics that are important to both research cultures, such as the study of democracy. Looking at the same topic as treated in exemplary studies from each culture allows us to illustrate more vividly the different kinds of questions and methods that animate the two cultures. At the same time, however, one of our key points is that some topics are more easily addressed in one culture than the other. Hence, some of our examples do not extend across both cultures.

Third, we also sampled and coded a large number of research articles from leading journals in political science and sociology. The items coded and the results are summarized in the appendix. This large-N sample was intended to be representative of good work—as defined by appearance in major journals in political science and sociology. The sample provides a further basis for generalizing about leading research practices. For example, when we make assertions such as the claim that quantitative researchers often include several control variables in their statistical models, it is based on results from our survey.

## Explicit and Implicit Practices

Our discussion focuses on the dominant methodological practices in the quantitative and qualitative paradigms. In general, when discussing quantitative research, we focus on *explicit* practices that follow well-established advice from the methodological literature. Quantitative research methods and procedures are often clearly specified, and quantitative researchers often quite explicitly follow these well-formulated methodological ideas.

At many points, nevertheless, we discuss assumptions and procedures in the quantitative tradition that are usually implicit. The comparison of quantitative research to qualitative research calls attention to underlying norms and practices in both traditions that otherwise might go unnoticed. For example, by considering the asymmetry assumptions of many qualitative methods, the extent to which most quantitative methods implicitly assume symmetric relationships becomes more visible. Systematic comparison of the paradigms helps bring to light research practices that are often taken for granted.

Our treatment of qualitative research focuses more heavily on a set of *implicit* procedures and techniques. In general, qualitative methods are used far less explicitly when compared to quantitative methods. At this stage, in fact, the implicit use of methods could be seen as a cultural characteristic of qualitative research. To describe this research tradition, we must reconstruct the procedures that qualitative researchers use when doing their work. Our reconstruction draws on a broad reading of qualitative studies, including an effort at systematically coding qualitative research articles. In addition, the practices that we describe are consistent with other methodological texts that have worked to make explicit and codify qualitative research practices (e.g., Brady and Collier 2010; George and Bennett 2005; Ragin 1987). Nevertheless, because qualitative methods are often used unsystematically, certain characterizations of this tradition will inevitably be controversial. In the text, we try to indicate areas where our description of dominant practices in qualitative research might be contested.

## Typical Practices, Best Practices, and Possible Practices

For any research tradition, there may be a tension between typical practices and so-called best practices (e.g., as identified by leading methodologists). Within the social sciences, the identification of a "best practice" is usually quite contested. Methodologists within a given tradition debate the pros and cons of particular research procedures. These debates point to the presence of different subcultures within qualitative and quantitative methodology. For example, within the field of quantitative methodology, scholars who advocate experiments hold serious reservations about most work that attempts to make causal inferences using observational data.

In this book, we do not weigh in on these methodological controversies about what constitutes best practice. Instead, given our interest in describing what researchers are actually doing, we focus on typical research practices—defined as published work appearing in influential outlets—in the quantitative and qualitative traditions. The practices that we examine are standard tools for conducting social science analysis. They are widely though not universally regarded as acceptable and appropriate for making descriptive and causal inferences. Indeed, from the point of view of the larger scholarly community, these typical practices are "good practices" in that the work that uses them is influential (in the positive sense) and routinely appears in the very top peer-reviewed journals and in books published by the most respected presses. Our analysis thus focuses on those practices that scholars often carry out when producing what is regarded by the overall scholarly community as the very best work.

In discussing differences in practices across the two cultures, we do not deny that it may be possible for quantitative researchers to mimic qualitative practices and vice versa. However, we are concerned here with real practices, rather than what might be called "possible practices." For example, the Neyman-Rubin-Holland model of statistical research might be reconfigured to address issues that are salient in qualitative research, such as the analysis of necessary and sufficient conditions. Yet studying necessary and sufficient conditions is not a natural thing to do in the quantitative culture and it is virtually never done in practice. Likewise, mathematical modes of set-theoretic analysis, which are associated with the qualitative paradigm, might be used to analyze average causal effects in a population. But no researcher in the social sciences of whom we are aware has used these methods for that purpose. Our point is simply that certain sets of tools make it natural to carry out certain kinds of practices and not others. While one might conceive ways of extending the tools of one culture to do what is easily accomplished in the other culture, these extensions are unnatural and usually purely hypothetical.

Characterizing the practices used in highly regarded research is more straightforward for the quantitative paradigm because its methods are laid out rather explicitly in prominent textbooks. Applied researchers learn their methods from these textbooks, and often work openly to follow their rules as closely as possible. Of course, textbooks do not always agree with each other and change over time. Nevertheless, they provide a basis for many shared norms and practices in the quantitative tradition.

The situation is more fluid on the qualitative side. While it is easy to talk about cookbook statistics, we have never heard anyone use the expression "cookbook qualitative analysis." Despite the existence of many qualitative methods (text)books, there is no single, core set of techniques that students can expect to learn in their qualitative methods classes. Part of the reason why is the division within qualitative research between scholars who are centrally concerned with causal inference versus scholars who use interpretive methodologies. It is also the case that the implicit use of methods in qualitative research makes the field far less standardized than the quantitative paradigm.

Nevertheless, if we focus on the causal inference school of qualitative research, a set of implicit but quite common practices can be identified and discussed. These practices are found in the work of many prominent qualitative scholars and described in the influential methodological works on qualitative research, such as Brady and Collier (2010), George and Bennett (2005), Gerring (2007), and Ragin (1987).

Our hope is that by examining typical practices as they appear in highly respected journals and books, scholars may develop new ideas for doing better research. This could happen in different ways. One possibility is that scholars of a given tradition may discover certain ideas from the other tradition that can help inform practices within their own tradition. For instance, the qualitative approach to concept formation might offer fresh insights to quantitative researchers about how to enhance measurement validity. Conversely, qualitative researchers may benefit by drawing on ideas from the extensive statistical literature on measurement error when making their own descriptive inferences. These observations suggest the possibility of cross-cultural learning, a topic to which we return at various points in this book.

Another possibility is that scholars may be surprised that a given practice is common within their tradition because it does not accord with their view of best practices. For example, quantitative methodologists who advocate the Neyman-Rubin-Holland model may be surprised to learn the limited extent to which this model influences social science research as actually practiced. On the qualitative side, advocates of medium-N QCA work may find it interesting to learn that within-case analysis remains the central basis for causal inference in most qualitative research. We believe that endorsing, criticizing, and improving prevailing research practices requires having a good understanding of those practices. This book provides a basis for developing this understanding.

## What Is Distinctive about Qualitative Research?

Because qualitative methods are often used implicitly, we wish to signal up front two of the main kinds of tools that we believe characterize this tradition and that set it apart from quantitative research. The first are techniques of *within-case analysis*, such as process tracing, emphasized in many leading works on qualitative methods in political science, including perhaps most notably Alexander L. George and Andrew Bennett's *Case Studies and Theory Development in the Social Sciences* and Henry E. Brady and David Collier's edited book, *Rethinking Social Inquiry: Diverse Tools, Shared Standards*. The second set of tools is logic and set theory, which informs nearly all major qualitative techniques (including within-case analysis) and is often associated with the work of Charles Ragin (2000; 2008).

## Within-Case Analysis

One common way of distinguishing quantitative versus qualitative research is to focus on the size of the N. It is natural to associate "large-N" studies with statistical research and "small-N" studies with qualitative research. In their discussion of qualitative research, King, Keohane, and Verba (1994) devote much attention to the "small-N problem" of qualitative research, or the difficulty of making inferences in the absence of enough cases to use conventional statistical methods. This approach follows a long line of research that thinks about qualitative methodology in terms of a degrees of freedom problem (Lijphart 1971; Campbell 1975).

Yet some studies with a relatively large N are regarded as qualitative, and other studies with a fairly small N use mainstream statistical methods (see Collier, Brady, and Seawright 2010, 178–79, for examples). This fact suggests that while a small N is correlated with qualitative research, it does not *define* such research. Far more important in defining qualitative research is the use of within-case analysis. Within-case analysis requires broad knowledge of specific cases, and thus its usage helps to explain why most qualitative studies have a small N. Qualitative scholars may select a small N because their central method of inference—within-case analysis—requires a kind of case-oriented analysis that is difficult to achieve with a large N.

If one focuses on within-case analysis as a core trait of qualitative research, the idea of linking qualitative research to a small-N problem tends to fall out of the discussion. It becomes clear that qualitative research embodies its own approach to causal analysis. Within-case analysis involves the use of specific pieces of data or information to make inferences about the individual case. These within-case observations may be "smoking guns" that decisively support or undermine a given theory. In this context, it is not helpful to think about qualitative methodology in terms of a degrees of freedom problem.

In contrast to qualitative research, statistical methods are virtually by definition tools of cross-case analysis. We can see this with the experimental method, which is often held up as the gold standard for causal inference in the quantitative paradigm. An experiment involves contrasting subjects who receive a treatment with those who receive the control. Causal inference is fundamentally built around this cross-case comparison. One is not trying to explain, for example, what happens to specific individuals who receive the treatment. The method is not designed to tell us whether the treatment caused the outcome for any particular subject. Although observational analyses differ from experiments in many important ways (e.g., research design), they share with experiments a fundamentally cross-case approach to causal inference.

## Logic and Set Theory

When qualitative scholars formulate their theories verbally, they quite naturally use the language of logic. We refer to this as the "Monsieur Jourdain"[3] nature of the relationship between qualitative scholarship and logic. Qualitative researchers speak the language of logic, but often are not completely aware of that fact. To systematically describe qualitative research practices, however, it is necessary to make explicit and formalize this implicit use of logic.

Ideas concerning necessary conditions and sufficient conditions are at the core of qualitative research practices. These kinds of conditions are implicitly used in the formulation of countless hypotheses in the qualitative tradition. They are central components of qualitative methods of concept formation, qualitative approaches to case selection, and nearly all qualitative methods of hypothesis testing. The qualitative methods of hypothesis testing that are built around necessary and sufficient conditions include Mill's methods of agreement and difference, major process tracing tests such as hoop tests and smoking gun tests, and all modes of QCA. Our view is that qualitative research and methodology cannot be fully codified and understood without taking into consideration ideas of necessity and sufficiency.

A long list of terms directly or indirectly indicates that the researcher is formulating hypotheses using the resources of logic. To express the causal idea that $X$ is necessary for $Y$, scholars use terms and expressions such as "only if," "is essential, indispensable, requisite, necessary for," "blocks, vetos, prevents," "is sine qua non of," and "enables, permits, allows." Some of these expressions are quite explicit and direct about using logic to express the nature of the causal relationship: "$Y$ only if $X$." Others are less explicit though still clear: "$X$ is requisite for $Y$" or "Not $X$ prevents $Y$."

---

[3] Moliere's M. Jourdain was very impressed to learn from his poetry teacher that he spoke in prose.

Analogously, various terms suggest that the scholar understands $X$ to be *sufficient* for $Y$. In this case, the scholar uses words and expressions such as "ensures, guarantees," "is always followed by," "inevitably leads to," and "yields, generates, produces." Again, some of these terms more directly suggest a sufficiency relationship (e.g., "$X$ is always followed by $Y$") than others ("$X$ yields $Y$").

Once one is sensitized to the use of the natural language of logic, one sees it everywhere in the social science literature. It is completely unexceptional for qualitative researchers (or any researcher, for that matter) to formulate a verbal theory using one or more of the expressions listed above. We have come across literally hundreds of examples of hypotheses about necessary conditions or sufficient conditions.[4] These hypotheses are not incidental to the scholarly works in question; they are, instead, at the heart of the claims being put forward (for 150 examples of necessary condition hypotheses, see Goertz 2003).

The use of logic and set theory extends well beyond the formulation of hypotheses. To define a concept using the classical approach of qualitative methods associated with Giovanni Sartori (1970), one works to construct a list of conditions that are individually necessary and jointly sufficient for membership in the concept. Qualitative scholars in the tradition of Sartori have "naturally" adopted logic as a framework to think about issues of conceptualization.[5] Likewise, when one uses Mill's method of agreement to "eliminate" a hypothesis, one is implicitly assuming that the hypothesis posits a necessary condition. Even major process tracing tests—such as "hoop tests" and "smoking gun tests"—are predicated on ideas of necessity and sufficiency, as we shall see.

The ways in which procedures and methods in qualitative research draw on logic will be discussed throughout the book. In fact, since mathematical logic and its set theory cousin are not well known in the social sciences, we offer a short introduction to them in the prelude of this book. For now, we wish to emphasize that logic and ideas of necessity and sufficiency are not only tools used in QCA techniques developed by Charles Ragin. Rather, they are the resources that qualitative scholars have implicitly been using for decades in many aspects of their research.

---

[4] This list includes famous comparative sociologists such as Skocpol (1979, 154), Moore (1966, 418), and Rueschemeyer, Stephens, and Stephens (1992, 270) as well as the best known comparativists from political science such as O'Donnell and Schmitter (1986, 65), Linz and Stepan (1996, 61), and Levi (1988, 144). In international relations, nearly all leading scholars (implicitly) develop these kinds of hypotheses, including (neo)realists such as Waltz (1979, 121; see Levy and Thompson (2010) for an extended discussion), liberal institutionalists such as Keohane (1980, 137) and Young and Osherenko (1993), and social constructivists such as Wendt (1992, 396) and Finnemore (1996, 158).

[5] Of course, Sartori himself was quite aware of the logical foundations of his approach.

## Conclusion

By the end of this volume, we hope that the reader will be dissatisfied with the terms "quantitative" and "qualitative." We will have discussed a large number of important differences between the two paradigms, but they are not identified particularly well by these terms, especially if those terms are understood to mean numbers versus words.

In the conclusion, we summarize many of the contrasts made in the book. We offer checklists with a total of about 25 differences between the two cultures. Although some differences such as within-case versus cross-case analysis and statistics versus logic are at the center of our argument, we do not argue that any single contrast drives all others. Instead, our conclusion is that each culture is made up of many different norms and practices that all work together relatively coherently.

Looking ahead, there are different ways to read this book. Although we have tried to group the chapters into coherent parts, it is not necessary to read the chapters in any particular order. Each chapter is intended to stand on its own as a separate and complete essay. Thus, readers can pick and choose topics of interest and skip around the book without difficulty. The mathematical prelude provides a selective introduction to logic and set theory for readers without a background in methods that use ideas of necessary and sufficient conditions. Already with this prelude we shall consider how the two cultures see and interpret the same data in quite different—though equally legitimate—ways.

## References

Angrist, J. D., and J.-S. Pischke. 2009. *Mostly harmless econometrics: an empiricist's companion.* Princeton: Princeton University Press.

Berk, R. 2004. *Regression analysis: a constructive critique.* Newbury Park: Sage Publications.

Brady, H. E., and D. Collier, eds. 2010. *Rethinking social inquiry: diverse tools, shared standards*, 2nd edition. Lanham, MD: Rowman Littlefield.

Campbell, D. 1975. Degrees of freedom and the case study. *Comparative Political Studies* 8:17–93.

Collier, D., H. E. Brady, and J. Seawright. 2010. Sources of leverage in causal inference: toward an alternative view of methodology. In *Rethinking social inquiry: diverse tools, shared standards*, 2nd edition, edited by H. E. Brady and D. Collier. Lanham, MD: Rowman Littlefield.

Finnemore, M. 1996. Constructing norms of humanitarian intervention. In *The culture of national security: norms, identity, and world politics,* edited by P. Katzenstein. New York: Columbia University Press.

Freedman, D. 2010. *Statistical models and causal inference: a dialogue with the social sciences.* Cambridge: Cambridge University Press.

Geertz, C. 1973. *On the interpretation of cultures.* New York: Basic Books.

George, A. L., and A. Bennett. 2005. *Case studies and theory development in the social sciences.* Cambridge: MIT Press.

Gerring, J. 2007. *Case study research: principles and practices.* Cambridge: Cambridge University Press.

Goertz, G. 2003. The substantive importance of necessary condition hypotheses. In *Necessary conditions: theory, methodology, and applications*, edited by G. Goertz and H. Starr. New York: Rowman & Littlefield.

Jackman, S. 2009. *Bayesian analysis for the social sciences.* New York: Wiley.

Keohane, R. 1980. The theory of hegemonic stability and changes in international regimes, 1967–1977. In *Changes in the international system*, edited by O. Holsti, R. Siverson, and A. George. Boulder: Westview.

King, G., R. Keohane, and S. Verba. 1994. *Designing social inquiry: scientific inference in qualitative research.* Princeton: Princeton University Press.

Levi, M. 1988. *Of rule and revenue.* Berkeley: University of California Press.

Levy, J., and W. Thompson. 2010. Balancing at sea: do states ally against the leading global power? *International Security* 35:7–43.

Lijphart, A. 1971. Comparative politics and the comparative method. *American Political Science Review* 65:682–93.

Linz, J., and A. Stepan. 1996. *Problems of democratic transition and consolidation: Southern Europe, South America, and post-communist Europe.* Baltimore: Johns Hopkins University Press.

Moore, B. 1966. *Social origins of dictatorship and democracy: lord and peasant in the making of the modern world.* Boston: Beacon Press.

Morgan, S., and C. Winship. 2007. *Counterfactuals and causal inference: methods and principles for social research.* Cambridge: Cambridge University Press.

O'Donnell, G., and P. Schmitter. 1986. *Transitions from authoritarian rule: tentative conclusions about uncertain democracies.* Baltimore: Johns Hopkins University Press.

Ragin, C. 1987. *The comparative method: moving beyond qualitative and quantitative strategies.* Berkeley: University of California Press.

Ragin, C. 2000. *Fuzzy-set social science.* Chicago: University of Chicago Press.

Ragin, C. 2008. *Redesigning social inquiry: fuzzy sets and beyond.* Chicago: University of Chicago Press.

Rueschemeyer, D., E. Stephens, and J. Stephens. 1992. *Capitalist development and democracy.* Chicago: University of Chicago Press.

Sartori, G. 1970. Concept misformation in comparative politics. *American Political Science Review* 64:1033–53.

Sewell, Jr., W. H. 2005. The concept(s) of culture. In *Logics of history: social theory and social transformation*, by W. H. Sewell, Jr. Chicago: University of Chicago Press.

Skocpol, T. 1979. *States and social revolutions: a comparative analysis of France, Russia, and China.* Cambridge: Cambridge University Press.

Waltz, K. 1979. *Theory of international relations.* Boston: Addison-Wesley.

Wendt, A. 1992. Anarchy is what states make of it: the social construction of power politics. *International Organization* 46:391–425.

Young, O., and G. Osherenko. 1993. Polar politics: creating international environmental regimes. In *Polar politics: creating international environmental regimes*, edited by O. Young and G. Osherenko. Ithaca: Cornell University Press.

# Chapter 2

# Mathematical Prelude: A Selective Introduction to Logic and Set Theory for Social Scientists

My underlying complaint is that political scientists eminently lack
(with exceptions) a training in logic—indeed in elementary logic.
—*Giovanni Sartori*

## Introduction

In this prelude, we discuss some key ideas from logic and set theory that inform our discussion of qualitative research in the chapters to come.[1] We do not pretend to offer any kind of comprehensive introduction to the field of logic and set theory, which would require a book in its own right. Instead, our discussion is a selective treatment focused on ideas connected to qualitative methodology, especially ideas concerning necessary and sufficient conditions.

This prelude is merited because the dominant mathematical orientation underlying qualitative research—logic and set theory—is not well known to most social scientists (including most qualitative researchers who implicitly use it). Although there are numerous books on logic and set theory from other academic fields (e.g., philosophy, systems engineering, mathematics, artificial intelligence, and computer science), there are virtually none for the

---

[1] Throughout the book we shall consider "logic" and "set theory" to refer to basically the same mathematics. Sometimes it seems more natural to talk about and use the notation of logic; sometimes it is easier to use the resources of set theory. On the different metaphorical underpinnings of logic and set theory, see Lakoff and Núñez 2000.

social sciences.[2] Simply put, we need a mathematical prelude to this book because the mathematical orientation of qualitative research is almost never taught in the social sciences.

The discussion also presents a first major contrast between qualitative and quantitative research: they are grounded in different mathematical traditions. Quantitative research draws on mathematical tools associated with statistics and probability theory. These tools are familiar to most social scientists because they are widely taught in courses on research methods and explicitly used in quantitative research. One might even say that most social scientists assume that statistics–probability theory is *the* math of the social sciences. Yet, we believe that qualitative research is often based, explicitly or implicitly, on set theory and logic, and these mathematical tools must be comprehended in their own right if one wishes to compare qualitative and quantitative research.[3]

Of special importance to our discussion is the mathematical logic used in fuzzy-set analysis. Although philosophers are required to learn logic— just like social scientists are required to learn statistics—fuzzy-set analysis is not a major topic in philosophy textbooks on logic. Instead, it figures prominently in applied fields such as engineering, computer science, and expert systems. Expert systems designers use fuzzy-set math to build "smart" machines ranging from washing machines to elevators to video cameras (McNeill and Freiberger 1994). Despite its proven practical utility in the real world, fuzzy-set math has only recently been brought into the social sciences as a formal tool of data analysis (e.g., Smithson 1988; Ragin 2000; 2008).

This prelude is directed at both quantitative and qualitative researchers. For quantitative researchers, it describes the mathematical underpinnings of a nonstatistical research culture. Just as a course on logic offers tools not found in any course on statistics, the procedures discussed in this chapter are distinct from leading statistical methods. For qualitative researchers, this prelude uncovers a mathematical orientation that they often use only implicitly.

## Natural Language and Logic

When qualitative scholars formulate their theories verbally, they quite naturally use the language of logic. In the introduction, we referred to

---

[2] The work of Charles Ragin and others (e.g., Schneider and Wagemann forthcoming) in the Qualitative Comparative Analysis (QCA) tradition explicitly discusses logic and set theory. However, there is still no widely used textbook providing an introduction for social scientists.

[3] The contrast between statistics and set theory is a popular topic in technical journals such as *Fuzzy Sets and Systems*.

the "Monsieur Jourdain" nature of the relationship between qualitative scholarship and logic. Qualitative researchers speak the language of logic but often are not completely aware of that fact.[4]

A theory stated in terms of logic and set theory normally has two components. First, the theory treats concepts as sets or categories in which cases (or observations) can have membership, including perhaps partial degrees of membership. In ordinary language, concepts such as democracy, development, and war are treated as categories in which particular cases may or may not have membership, or have a certain degree of membership (cf., Lakoff 1987). As we explore below, logic and set theory retain much of this ordinary language approach to concepts.

Second, the hypothesized associations between two or more concepts are conceived in logical terms using ideas of necessity and/or sufficiency— or, equivalently, superset/subset relationships. Although notions of necessity and/or sufficiency may immediately strike some researchers as inappropriate for social science research, this volume suggests that this is not the case. As we noted in the introduction, a wide range of scholars use ideas of necessity/sufficiency when formulating hypotheses, constructing concepts, selecting cases, and testing hypotheses.

We can contrast the natural language of logic in the qualitative culture with the language of probability and statistics in the quantitative culture. This latter language is familiar to nearly all because almost everyone learns it in statistics classes and knows it from the journal articles using statistical methods. For example, well-known formulations include:

- The probability of $Y$ occurring increases (or decreases) with the level or occurrence of $X$.

- The level of $Y$ increases (or decreases) on average with the level or occurrence of $X$.

The functional form of the relationship between $X$ and $Y$ can vary a great deal, depending on the particular statistical model used. For example, the functional form is linear with OLS regression, S-shaped with probit or logit, and log-linear for other statistical models (e.g., gravity models of trade). When probabilistic models are used, the functional form may remain unspecified: $P(Y|X) \neq P(Y|\neg X)$.

Within both cultures, scholars sometimes fail to notice any difference between statistical hypotheses and logic-based ones. They may even go back

---

[4] Formal modelers also speak the language of necessary and sufficient conditions. It is common in mathematical theorems, e.g., in economics or game theory, to provide necessary and/or sufficient conditions (see Goertz 2003b for some examples). However, when it comes to empirical testing, the statistical paradigm takes over.

and forth between the two when stating their own hypotheses, treating them as if they were interchangeable. For example, while Waltz mainly states hypotheses using the natural language of logic, he says at one point that "the smaller the group ... the likelier it becomes that some members—the larger ones—will act for the group interest ... the greater the relative size of a unit the more it identifies its own interest with the interest of the system" (1979, 198). Here we see the classic language of the quantitative culture. Yet, in his concluding chapter, he moves back to logic and argues that "extensive international cooperation is *only possible* under current conditions under the leadership of the United States" (1979, 210).

A basic issue throughout empirical social science is precisely how verbal theories should be formalized in order to subject them to testing. Can one translate a verbal theory expressed in terms of logic into a form consistent with conventional statistical methods without a loss of meaning? By the same token, can one recast a theory stated in terms of probability and statistics into one that is built around necessary and sufficient conditions? These questions raise what can be called the *translation problem*. To see why translating across paradigms is a problem, we need to examine logic and set theory more closely.

## Necessary Conditions and Sufficient Conditions with Binary Categories

### Set Theory and Venn Diagrams

Whereas logical terminology involving necessity and sufficiency is sometimes used explicitly by qualitative analysts, it is quite rare to see these same researchers explicitly employ set-theoretic terminology. Nevertheless, propositional logic and set theory are intimately related and often can be used interchangeably. The translations work as follows:

- "$X$ is a necessary condition for $Y$" is equivalent to "$Y$ is a subset of $X$."

- "$X$ is a sufficient condition for $Y$" is equivalent to "$X$ is a subset of $Y$."

Figure 2.1 illustrates this idea with Venn diagrams. To add content to these figures, simple examples of categories might be useful. In figure 2.1a, let $Y$ stand for the set of students who fail Logic 101. Let $X$ stand for the set of students who skip the final exam for Logic 101. Being a member of the set of students who skip the final exam is *sufficient* for being a member of the set of students who fail the class. $X$ is sufficient but not necessary because there are other ways to fail the class (e.g., receiving a failing grade

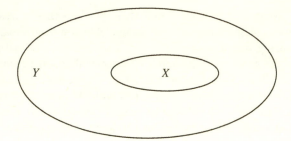

Figure 2.1a: Sufficient condition

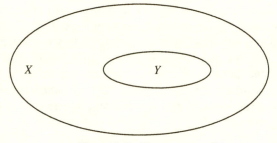

Figure 2.1b: Necessary condition

**Figure 2.1.** Illustration of necessary and sufficient conditions using Venn diagrams

on course work). This idea of multiple paths to the same outcome is known as "equifinality."

To add simple content to figure 2.1b, let $Y$ stand for the set of all individuals who are pregnant. Let $X$ stand for the set of all individuals who are female. Being a member of the set of females is *necessary* for being a member of the set of pregnant individuals. $X$ is not sufficient for $Y$ because many female people are not pregnant, as the Venn diagram clearly shows.

One way in which set-theoretic language appears implicitly in data analysis is via descriptions of the form "All $X$ are $Y$." If the scholar says, "All $X$ are $Y$," then she is also saying that $X$ is a subset of $Y$. Conversely, if she says, "All $Y$ are $X$," then $Y$ is a subset of $X$. From the perspective of set theory, there is a big difference between "All $X$ are $Y$" and "All $Y$ are $X$." But how would one translate this idea into the quantitative culture? Both statements imply a relationship between $X$ and $Y$; for both there would normally be a solid correlation between $X$ and $Y$. But it is not immediately clear how to translate the set-theoretic statement into the language of probability or statistics. In principle, one can probably make

**Table 2.1**

Illustration of Necessary and Sufficient Conditions Using $2 \times 2$ Tables

Table 2.1a: Necessary Condition

|   |   | X | |
|---|---|---|---|
|   |   | 0 | 1 |
| Y | 1 | 0 | $N_2$ |
|   | 0 | $N_3$ | $N_4$ |

Table 2.1b: Sufficient Condition

|   |   | X | |
|---|---|---|---|
|   |   | 0 | 1 |
| Y | 1 | $N_1$ | $N_2$ |
|   | 0 | $N_3$ | 0 |

such a translation (e.g., for some translations see Goertz 2003a, chapter 10, Cioffi-Revilla 1998, Seawright 2011), but it is not naturally or easily accomplished.

This translation problem is analogous to the difficulty qualitative scholars face when attempting to recast a linear correlation or statistical association into the language of necessary and sufficient conditions. While there are ways to make such translations (e.g., Eliason and Stryker 2009), they are constrained and unnatural. As our two cultures metaphor suggests, what is obvious and easy in one culture is often problematic and difficult (though not impossible) in the other.

### Two-by-Two Tables

Perhaps the most common way that scholars depict necessary or sufficient conditions is via 2×2 tables. Tables 2.1a and 2.1b illustrate how these conditions appear for binary categories. To help remember the difference between necessary and sufficient conditions, we can use the same examples presented earlier: being female ($X = 1$) is necessary for being pregnant ($Y = 1$) in table 2.1a, and skipping the final exam ($X = 1$) is sufficient for failing the class ($Y = 1$) in table 2.1b.

When expressed in terms of 2×2 tables, to say that $X$ is necessary for $Y$ means three related things: (1) "No $Y = 1$ are $X = 0$," (2) "All $X = 0$ are $Y = 0$," and (3) "All $Y = 1$ are $X = 1$." Thus, in terms of our example,

**Table 2.2**

Example of a Sufficient Condition: The Democratic Peace

|  | Not democratic dyad | Democratic dyad |
|---|---|---|
| Peace | 1045 | 169 |
| War | 36 | 0 |

*Source:* Russett 1995, 174.

it means: (1) No pregnant people are not female (i.e., male), (2) All not-females (i.e., males) are not pregnant, and (3) All pregnant people are female.[5] The key feature of the $2 \times 2$ table is that the cell $(\neg X, Y)$ is empty (note that $\neg X$ reads "not-$X$"). In fact, one can call this cell the necessary condition cell of a $2 \times 2$ table. Similarly, in table 2.1b, the sufficient condition cell is $(X, \neg Y)$ because this cell must be zero for a sufficient condition to be present.

To ground this discussion in the social sciences, let us examine the data concerning the democratic peace given in table 2.2. When assessing the democratic peace theory, the cases are dyads (i.e., pairs) of countries. The main outcome of interest is peace, which is treated as a dichotomous category, with the opposite of peace being war (an idea that we will contest in the chapter "Conceptual Opposites and Typologies," but which is fine for current purposes). The causal factor is "democratic dyad," which is also a dichotomous category. A dyad is democratic only if both states are democracies. Dyads in which one or both states are not democracies are coded as "not democratic dyad."

From the perspective of logic, the data in the $2 \times 2$ table are an excellent example of a sufficient condition. Specifically, democratic dyad, $X$, is sufficient for peace, $Y$. One can see this clearly in the table, where the cell for democratic dyad and war is empty, and all the cases of democratic dyad are in the peace cell.

Certainly, one can calculate statistics for $2 \times 2$ tables such as table 2.2. The results would vary depending on the statistics used. For example, the $\chi^2$ statistic for the data in table 2.2 has a value of 5.80 with a significance level of 0.02. Spearman and Pearson correlational statistics along with $\tau_b$ have a value −0.07 that is statistically significant at .006.[6] More revealing is the odds ratio: it is extremely significant at .08 (an odds ratio of 1.00 means no relationship, such that values close to zero or much greater than one indicate

---

[5] Some researchers would assert that not-female is not identical to male. As we explore in chapter 13, the negation of a category is not equal to the opposite of the category.

[6] Strictly speaking, one cannot calculate many $2 \times 2$ measures of association, e.g., $\chi^2$, when there are zero cells. However, most statistical packages have standard fixes which allow these statistics to be calculated.

very significant results). Thus, the odds ratio calculated with logit analysis shows that democratic dyads are substantially more likely to be at peace than nondemocratic dyads. None of these standard statistics, however, pick up the fact that the data are fully consistent with a relationship of sufficiency.

Statements about necessary conditions can always be converted into statements about sufficient conditions (and vice versa). One can make this conversion by simply negating the categories under analysis when shifting from necessity to sufficiency (or from sufficiency to necessity). For example, if $X$ is sufficient for $Y$, then $\neg X$ is necessary for $\neg Y$. In the case of the democratic peace, one can formulate the key finding as follows: the absence of a democratic dyad is a necessary condition for war.

While in logic one would not normally confuse a necessary condition with a sufficient condition, with statistical methods the relationships appear the same. In fact, if you calculate $2\times2$ measures of association, you can arrive at *exactly* the same results regardless of whether the data are distributed as a necessary condition or a sufficient condition. This is true because standard methods of association assume symmetric relationships and are not designed to detect and summarize asymmetric relationships.

Of course, many $2\times2$ datasets have cases distributed in a way that makes it useful to use symmetric measures of association. This is true for bivariate correlations in which cases are concentrated in two diagonal cells (e.g., with a positive correlation, cases are concentrated in the lower left and upper right cells). When a scholar armed with the tools of logic and set theory confronts such a symmetric dataset, she or he may view it as having some properties of necessity and some properties of sufficiency. There is nothing wrong with this interpretation of the data. The point is that it is less natural (though not impossible) to think about relationships in terms of symmetric correlations when using logic and set theory.

This discussion of $2\times2$ tables illustrates what might be called the Rorschach Principle. Rorschach tests present ambiguous images to people and ask for their interpretation. Data can play the same role for social scientists. After all, a core principle of science is that data underdetermine theory. One can look at the same data and legitimately see different things. No single way of viewing the data is uniquely right (though not all ways of viewing the data are equally useful). $2\times2$ tables illustrate how one can look for different patterns in the data, depending on one's research purposes.

## Truth Tables

The truth tables used in logic-based approaches resemble the datasets analyzed in statistical analysis, though they also differ in interesting ways. Table 2.3 presents a truth table. As in a quantitative rectangular dataset, the variables are represented by the columns. Since this is an "empirical" truth

**Table 2.3**

Empirical Truth Table

| $X_1$ | $X_2$ | $Y$ | $N$ |
|---|---|---|---|
| 1 | 1 | 1 | 5 |
| 1 | 1 | 0 | 0 |
| 1 | 0 | 1 | 3 |
| 1 | 0 | 0 | 10 |
| 0 | 1 | 1 | 0 |
| 0 | 1 | 0 | 7 |
| 0 | 0 | 1 | 0 |
| 0 | 0 | 0 | 12 |

table, it also includes a final (fourth) column for the empirical observations that correspond to each configuration of truth values (see Ragin 1987, chapter 7).

While most of the columns look similar to a rectangular dataset in statistical analysis, the rows are quite different. In a statistical dataset, the rows are *observations*. By contrast, the rows in a truth table are *configurations* of truth values. All logically possible configurations are listed, such that the number of variables determines the number of rows. The number of rows has nothing to do with the number of observations. A row, say row 1, is the logical statement: $X_1 = 1$ AND $X_2 = 1$ AND $Y = 1$. The data may, or may not, be consistent with this claim (the data in table 2.3 are consistent and without contradiction).

Qualitative Comparative Analysis (QCA) is a methodology for describing and analyzing the logical relationships embedded in truth tables like this one (Ragin 1987; 2000). It uses the mathematics of Boolean algebra (e.g., Boolean minimization and implication) to reduce logical expressions to simpler forms. The point we wish to emphasize is that the *configurations of variable values*—not the individual variables—form the core of the analysis.

Typically, a configuration is a combination (or set intersection) of values for two or more variables that is jointly sufficient for an outcome. The individual variable values that compose a configuration are connected together with the logical AND. These individual variable values are often "INUS conditions" (alternatively, they could be necessary conditions; Mackie 1965; 1980).[7] INUS conditions are variable values that are neither individually necessary nor individually sufficient for an outcome of interest. Instead, they

---

[7] The acronym INUS is derived by Mackie (1965, 246) as follows: "The so-called cause is, and is known to be, an *insufficient* but *necessary* part of a condition which is itself *unnecessary* but *sufficient* for the result."

are essential (i.e., non-redundant) components of an overall configuration of variable values that is sufficient for the outcome. Thus, when a combination of variable values is sufficient to produce an outcome, the individual variable values are either necessary conditions or INUS conditions. If the latter, "equifinality" is always present—i.e., there is more than one path to the same outcome.

One could analyze the data in table 2.3 using statistical methods. But the data would not be analyzed as given. For example, the rows would need to be converted into observations. Since there are 37 observations, the statistical dataset would have 37 rows. In making this move, the logical configurations with no cases in the truth table (i.e., rows 2, 5, and 7) would, in effect, be removed from further consideration. A statistical analyst might explore the covariation between each independent variable ($X_1$ and $X_2$) and $Y$. A scholar using QCA, by contrast, might summarize the interesting patterns in the data as:

1. $X_1 = 1$ is a potentially necessary condition for $Y = 1$.

2. $X_1 = 1$ AND $X_2 = 1$ is a potentially sufficient combination for $Y = 1$.

Thinking about the statistical covariation between $X_1$ and $Y$, and between $X_2$ and $Y$, is not at all incorrect. It is neither more right nor more wrong than summarizing the results using logic-based approaches. It simply brings to light a different aspect of the data. Ideally, one would have the tools and inclination to examine the data from multiple perspectives in order to call attention to the most relevant features of the data, given one's research question and objective.

## Necessary Conditions and Sufficient Conditions with Fuzzy Sets

In Aristotelian logic and what is known as crisp-set theory, concepts or variables are treated as dichotomies in which cases are either members or nonmembers. Membership in the category is normally represented with a value of 1 (i.e., $X = 1$), whereas the absence of membership is represented by a value of 0 (i.e., $X = 0$). A distinctive feature of fuzzy logic is that cases are allowed to have partial degrees of membership in categories. Full membership is still denoted with a value of 1, and full nonmembership receives a value of 0. But cases can also have any value between 0 and 1 (e.g., $X = .75$, $X = .33$, $X = .10$), depending on the extent to which they are members of the category of interest. Thus, a given case could have a membership score of .5 for the category of "war," which suggests that the case is as much in the category as it is outside of it.

Just as we can talk about necessary and sufficient conditions in the context of 2×2 tables, we can discuss necessary and sufficient conditions for continuous scatterplots between $X$ and $Y$. This is possible and natural with fuzzy-set analysis because case membership in sets is measured continuously from 0 to 1. When plotting fuzzy-set scores for two categories, one must allow the X- and Y-axes to range continuously from 0 to 1.

While most scholars can interpret 2×2 tables in terms of necessary and sufficient conditions without any specific training, such is not the case for fuzzy-set scatterplots. In the 2×2 case, we called attention to the empty cells associated with necessary conditions and sufficient conditions. What does one do with continuously coded fuzzy sets?

Figures 2.2a and 2.2b illustrate, respectively, what a necessary condition and a sufficient condition look like when cases are plotted on a fuzzy-set scatterplot (see Ragin 2000). They appear as "triangular" scatterplots. The lower-right triangular scatterplot is a necessary condition, while the upper-left triangular scatterplot is a sufficient condition. One can think about the scatterplots as an extension of our analysis of 2×2 tables. In those tables, three of the four cells have data. The three cells with data form a triangle-like shape. Thus, if one were to stretch the tables, one would arrive at the scatterplots in figure 2.2.

More formally, the fuzzy logic rule for a *necessary* condition ($X$) is that all cases' fuzzy-set values on $X$ must be equal to or greater than their values on $Y$:

$X$ is necessary condition for $Y$: $x_i \geq y_i$ for all $i$,   $x_i, y_i \in [0, 1]$.

The underlying idea is that with a necessary condition, a case must have at least as much membership in $X$ as in $Y$, otherwise it makes no sense to say that $X$ is necessary for $Y$. For example, if a case has only slight membership in $X$ (e.g., 0.1 membership), but full membership in $Y$ (i.e., 1.0), it is not correct to say that its membership in $X$ was essential for its membership in $Y$ (unless other special assumptions are made).

With a *sufficient* condition in fuzzy logic, by contrast, all cases' fuzzy-set values on $X$ will be equal to or less than their values on $Y$:

$X$ is sufficient condition for $Y$: $x_i \leq y_i$ for all $i$,   $x_i, y_i \in [0, 1]$.

Here the idea is that a case must have at least as much membership in $Y$ as in $X$ if the latter is sufficient for the former. For example, if a case has full membership in $Y$ (i.e., 1.0), but only slight membership in $X$ (e.g., 0.1), it is not problematic to say that its membership in $X$ was potentially sufficient for its membership in $Y$.

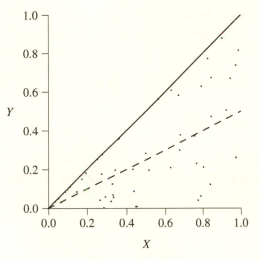

Figure 2.2a: Necessary condition

Note: Dashed line is the OLS line

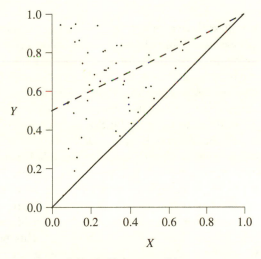

Figure 2.2b: Sufficient condition

Note: Dashed line is the OLS line

**Figure 2.2.** Fuzzy logic: illustration of a necessary condition and a sufficient condition

If one goes back to the Venn diagrams discussed earlier, i.e., figure 2.1, we see the following consistency between the crisp-set (i.e., binary) and fuzzy-set relationships:

Necessary condition: $Y \subseteq X \equiv y_i \leq x_i$.

Sufficient condition: $Y \supseteq X \equiv y_i \geq x_i$.

It is not an accident that even the symbols look similar.

It is useful to take the Rorschach test with the scatterplots, adopting a statistical perspective. What are the features of these scatterplots that would leap out to someone having just taken a regression class or two?

1. Modest fit. One would draw a line through the data and find that there was a clear but modest relationship between $X$ and $Y$.

2. Slopes. The OLS slope in figure 2.2a is the same as in figure 2.2b.

3. Heteroskedasticity. The variance around the OLS line is clearly not constant.

Let us consider these three points in turn from a two cultures perspective. First, from the perspective of fuzzy logic, the scatterplots in figure 2.2 would be viewed as *perfect fits*. A perfect fit for a necessary condition occurs when all the observations lie on or below the 45-degree diagonal (according to the definition of a necessary condition above). Similarly, a perfect fit for a sufficient condition occurs when the observations all lie on or above the 45-degree diagonal. By contrast, in an OLS regression model, a perfect fit occurs when all the points lie exactly on the OLS line.

Second, from the point of view of statistics, the relationship between $X$ and $Y$ in the scatterplots in figure 2.2 is basically the same. The intercepts are different, but those parameters are rarely of interest. In contrast, with fuzzy-set analysis one would not conclude that scatterplots represent similar associations: the finding that $X$ is necessary for $Y$ is considered completely different from the finding that $X$ is sufficient for $Y$. This point parallels exactly what we saw for 2×2 tables. The qualitative culture saw one table as a necessary condition and then another as a sufficient condition, whereas the quantitative culture interpreted the two tables as representing the same relationship.

Of course, these are asymmetric scatterplots from a set-theoretic point of view, and thus they are particularly useful for illustrating the potential utility of a set-theoretic approach. If one starts with two symmetric scatterplots in which points are randomly scattered around straight lines, however, the quantitative perspective can emphasize nuances and differences that are not easily expressed using set-theoretic tools. Again, our point is not that one approach is right and the other is wrong. Rather, our point is that the approaches notice and call attention to different features of the data. Set-theoretic tools are especially useful for the analysis of asymmetric relationships (though they can be used to study symmetric relationships as well).

Third, a standard statistical reaction when faced with heteroskedastic data is to transform the variables to achieve constant variance. This transformation may be essential for valid statistical inference in the quantitative tradition. By contrast, qualitative researchers do not usually make such transformations. For them, transforming a variable often entails changing its meaning. Such transformations are not appropriate unless one can show that they increase the meaning of the underlying concepts being analyzed (see the chapter "Semantics, Statistics, and Data Transformations").

## Aggregation

Choices about aggregation are basic issues in methodology. For illustrative purposes, let us define aggregation as the function one uses to combine $X$s in order to get $Y$: $Y = f(X_1, X_2, \ldots)$. The function $f$ could assume many different forms, depending on one's approach and assumptions. Logic and statistics each have their own distinctive, default assumptions about aggregation procedures.

Within statistics, a common aggregation technique is the weighted sum. The general linear model is a good example:

$$Y = w_0 + w_1 X_1 + w_2 X_2 + \ldots . \tag{2.1}$$

Here $Y$ is the weighted sum of the $X$s. The mean is of course a special case of weighted aggregation where the weights are $1/N$.

Another common form of statistical aggregation involves an interaction term: $X_1 * X_2$. Typically the interaction term would be part of a larger weighted linear aggregation such as equation (2.1). However, it is not impossible to have a pure interaction aggregation model:

$$Y = X_1^{w_1} * X_2^{w_2} * X_3^{w_3} * \ldots . \tag{2.2}$$

In practice, this kind of equation would be converted into a log-linear model as in equation (2.1). The quantitative culture is certainly not limited to addition or multiplication when pursuing aggregation. But for good practical and statistical reasons, most statistical models are weighted sums or log-linear weighted sums.

What are the standard aggregation techniques used by scholars who implicitly or explicitly draw on logic and set theory? Our discussion of the truth table in table 2.3 gives a number of examples, one per row, all of the same basic form. For example, row 1 reads as follows:

$$X_1 = 1 \text{ AND } X_2 = 1 \text{ AND } Y = 1. \tag{2.3}$$

The logical AND connects together the conditions into an overall combination of conditions. In Boolean algebra, the logical AND is often written with the multiplication symbol ($*$).

If one wants to stress the analogy between logic and statistics, one can try to *translate* between the logical AND and statistical multiplication. The two mathematical operations can be written in the same way: $Y = X_1 * X_2$. This analogy works well if $X_i$ are dichotomous variables. The analogy of AND with multiplication begins to break down when we move away from dichotomous variables. For example, we can ask about the aggregation procedure for equation (2.3) if the variables are understood to be continuously [0,1] coded fuzzy sets. In logic, the standard rule for calculating a case's membership with the logical AND (i.e., the multiplication symbol in Boolean algebra) is to use the *minimum* value of the $X$s:

$$Y = \min(X_1, X_2, X_3, \ldots), \quad X_i \in [0, 1]. \tag{2.4}$$

Thus, with the logical AND, a case's membership in $Y$ is equal to its minimum score in the sets $X_i$. For example, if the lowest fuzzy-set value among the $X$s is 0.1, then the case receives a score of 0.1 for $Y$. Using the minimum with the logical AND also works perfectly well for dichotomous variables.

To state the very obvious:

Multiplication is not the same as using the minimum.

Differences such as this are at the heart of our two cultures argument. Multiplication in statistical analysis and the logical AND in set-theoretic analysis are analogous, but they are not the same mathematical procedure. Moreover, one procedure is not somehow inherently superior to the other. They are merely different ways to aggregate data. In certain theoretical or substantive contexts, scholars might have reasons to prefer one mode of aggregation to the other. But there is no a priori reason to believe that one aggregation model *should* be preferred.

The two cultures metaphor also allows that one *could* use the other culture's aggregation technique. There is nothing in principle that prevents the statistical culture from using the model: $Y = \beta_0 + \beta_1 X_1 + \min(X_2, X_3)$. Similarly, weighted sums and multiplication are possible within fuzzy-logic systems. In both cases, however, they are not natural and are not often used, in the social sciences at least.

We have discussed the relationship between multiplication and the logical AND; is there something similar for addition? The logical OR plays the role of addition in aggregation using logic. With Boolean algebra, the logical OR is written with the plus (+) sign, which again emphasizes the analogy. The general rule for calculating case membership with the logical OR is to use the *maximum* value of a case's membership in the $X$s:

$$Y = \max(X_1, X_2, X_3, \ldots), \quad X_i \in [0, 1]. \tag{2.5}$$

For example, if the highest fuzzy-set value among the $X$s is .85, then the case receives a score of .85 for $Y$. This formula also works for dichotomous variables, so we can consider it the general aggregation procedure for the logical OR.

To again state the obvious, addition is not the same thing as using the maximum value. While they can potentially generate the same results, they often will not. We emphasize once more that our claim is not that one mathematical procedure is better than the other. We merely seek to call attention to their differences, given that they are standard aggregation procedures in their respective research cultures.

## Confronting Models with Data

A basic scientific activity is assessing the "fit" between empirical data and theories, models, and hypotheses. Within the social sciences, this assessment is often carried out with statistical analysis. For example, in terms of overall model fit, $R^2$ is a classic measure (though measures of overall fit are no longer considered very important in contemporary quantitative social science). In terms of the fit of an individual variable, one asks whether the data "support" a hypothesis about that variable. One looks at, for example, the causal effect and statistical significance of the individual variable.

But how does the assessment of a model or causal factor work with logic or set theory? What are the criteria for assessing the "fit" of the model or the "importance" of a given causal factor? In this section, we address these questions. The ideas that we discuss are relevant to qualitative studies regardless of whether QCA is used or not.

## Fit and Consistency

To assess the fit of a theory or model, the basic requirement is that the theory or model make a clear prediction about the data (the prediction itself can assume many different forms). If the prediction is clear, one can ask: how consistent are the data with the model? With a statistical model, data that are highly consistent lie near or on the line described by the model (assuming a parametric model). In their first statistics course, students normally learn how to eyeball bivariate scatterplots and see if there is any line or curve that fits the data.

In set-theoretic analysis, the term "consistency" is used by scholars as a measure of fit for hypotheses about necessary or sufficient conditions (Ragin 2008). Either measured dichotomously or with fuzzy-set coding, necessary and sufficient condition hypotheses make clear predictions about data patterns. To take the simple example of 2×2 tables (see table 2.1), a necessary condition hypothesis predicts that there should be no cases in the $(\neg X, Y)$ cell. One can imagine various scenarios in which that cell does not have zero cases, but rather a small proportion of them. These cases are the "counterexamples" to the hypothesis. In table 2.1 if $N_2, N_3, N_4$ are reasonably large, then a "few" cases in the $(\neg X, Y)$ cell mean that consistency is not 100 percent, but still high enough to support the hypothesis. The data might show that 95 percent, to choose a popular standard in statistics, of the cases in the $Y = 1$ row are in the $(X, Y)$ cell (recall that one definition of a necessary condition is that all $Y = 1$ are $X = 1$). Given this, one might claim that the data are quite consistent with the necessary condition hypothesis.

The same basic idea applies to fuzzy-set hypotheses. As illustrated in figure 2.2, if the data are perfectly consistent with a sufficient condition hypothesis, they must all lie on or above the 45-degree diagonal. Consistency decreases as observations move below the diagonal. The trick (see Ragin 2008) is to devise a formula for summarizing the degree to which these observations are inconsistent. This is analogous to what the sum of squared deviation divided by total variation does for OLS regression: it summarizes how inconsistent the observations are vis-à-vis the OLS line.

In short, there are well-specified ways to assess how well logic-based hypotheses and models fit with data. While the exact formulas for doing this differ from those used in statistics, the principle is the same: compare the predictions of the model with the data. If they are close, then the model or theory is generally supported by the data.

## Assessing Importance: Coverage and Trivialness

One concern sometimes raised about hypotheses formulated in terms of necessary conditions is that a factor may be necessary for an outcome, but it is nevertheless a trivial cause.[8] George Downs provides a good statement of this concern: "There are an infinite number of necessary conditions for any phenomenon. For example, it is true that all armies require water and gravity to operate, but the contribution of such universals is modest" (1989, 234).

Contained within this trivialness critique is the notion that necessary (or sufficient) conditions vary in their "importance." With statistical models, there are several means for determining the importance of a given variable. For example, the slope of the line is one indication of a variable's importance: steeper slopes generally mean more important variables. Rigorous criteria can also be developed for measuring the relative importance of necessary conditions and sufficient conditions. In fact, Downs's argument offers a useful point of departure. He implies that certain necessary conditions are trivial because they are always present. This observation suggests that the relative frequency of necessary conditions might be related to their importance.

We can think about the issue systematically with the tools of set theory (Ragin 2008; Goertz 2006). With a necessary condition, $X$ is a superset of $Y$ (equivalently, $Y$ is a subset of $X$). This definition does not tell us about the *relative size* of the set of $X$ in relationship to the set of $Y$. As a rule, a necessary condition $X$ becomes more important as it becomes a smaller superset in relationship to $Y$; that is, $X$ becomes more important as it approaches a perfect overlap with $Y$.

Another way to think about the issue is to ask what is the opposite of a "trivial" or unimportant necessary condition. The obvious answer is a necessary condition that is also sufficient for the outcome. In terms of set theory, the extent to which a necessary condition is close to also being a sufficient condition can be expressed as the extent to which subset $Y$ "covers" or fills up the superset $X$. At the limit, when the sets $X$ and $Y$ are identical, $X$ is necessary and sufficient for $Y$ and its importance is at its maximum.

As an example, consider the finding that the presence of gravity and an authoritarian regime are necessary conditions for a social revolution (i.e., in the absence of either gravity or an authoritarian regime, a society cannot experience a social revolution). Of these two necessary conditions, the authoritarian regime factor is obviously the more important one. But how can we express that fact using set theory? As figure 2.3 suggests, we can do it by showing that the set of cases with gravity contains the full population of all societies; thus, the extent to which the set of $Y$ "covers" the set of $X$ is as minimal as possible for a necessary condition (i.e., there are no not-$X$ cases). By contrast, the set of cases with an authoritarian regime is not nearly

---

[8] Interestingly, while these concerns are commonly made for necessary conditions, scholars do not raise them very often or at least explicitly for sufficient conditions.

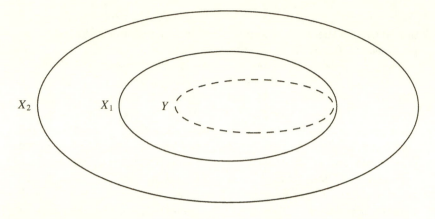

$X_2$: cases of gravity

$X_1$: cases of authoritarianism

$Y$: cases of social revolution

**Figure 2.3.** Trivial necessary conditions: a set-theoretic example

the full population. As a result, the extent to which the set of $Y$ "covers" the set of $X$ is much greater. If one generalizes the idea, one can say that when multiple necessary conditions are present, the less frequently present ones (i.e., the ones that are rarer or abnormal within the relevant population) are the more important ones.

The assessment of the importance of a sufficient condition (or a combination of factors that are jointly sufficient) works in a similar way. In this case, $X$ is a subset of $Y$. The sufficient condition $X$ will become more important as its coverage of $Y$ increases; that is, the subset $X$ becomes more important as it approaches a perfect overlap with $Y$. Importance thus varies depending on how close the sufficient condition is to also being necessary for the outcome. Highly important sufficient conditions are ones that approach being necessary for the outcome. A fully trivial sufficient condition is one that *would* produce an outcome if it were present, but the condition is never present, and thus it never generates the outcome. If one generalizes this idea, one can say that when multiple sufficient conditions are identified for a given kind of outcome, the more frequently present ones are the more important ones.

The democratic peace again provides a good illustration. As noted above, the democratic peace can be formulated as "a democratic dyad is sufficient for peace."[9] With this hypothesis, $X$ (the set of democratic dyads) is a subset

---

[9] In fact, as noted above, this formulation is potentially problematic, in that non-war is not equal to peace.

All peaceful dyads

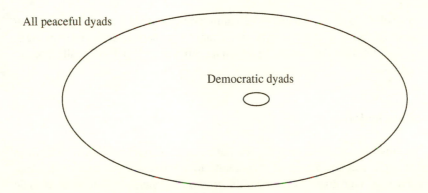

Figure 2.4a: Hypothetical democratic peace in 1820: trivial sufficient condition

All peaceful dyads

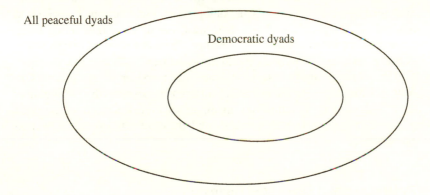

Figure 2.4b: Hypothetical democratic peace in 2000: nontrivial sufficient condition

**Figure 2.4.** Trivial versus nontrivial sufficient conditions: the democratic peace

of $Y$ (the set of peaceful dyads). However, the relative size of this subset has varied over time. In figure 2.4a, we have a hypothetical depiction of the situation as of 1820. At that time, there were few democracies in the world, and thus very few democratic dyads. The set of $X$—democratic dyads— was a small subset of peaceful dyads, i.e., $Y$. If we fast-forward to 2000, illustrated in figure 2.4b, more than half the countries of the world are now democracies. This means that $X$ as a subset of $Y$ has increased dramatically, constituting a reasonable proportion of $Y$. With data from 1820, one could plausibly claim that the theory of a democratic peace is a true but fairly trivial finding. In our times, however, one cannot say that the democratic peace is trivial, because democratic dyads make up a sizable subset of all peaceful dyads.

## Conclusion

In this mathematical prelude, we have sketched out some basic principles of logic and set theory as they relate to empirical research in the social sciences. Our goal has not been to provide a general introduction to logic and set theory. Instead, we have focused on ideas from logic and set theory that implicitly animate the field of qualitative research. In doing so, we have also started our two cultures analysis, for we have contrasted logic–set theory with probability–statistics. We have seen that there are many analogies between the two; these analogies are simultaneously useful and misleading. They are useful as a first start, but they are misleading when viewed as exact equivalents of one another. There is a problem of translation between logic–set theory and probability–statistics.

The initial contrasts discussed here will reappear in the chapters to follow. Ultimately, the mathematical differences between the two cultures have wide-ranging ramifications in all areas of research, from research goals, to causal models, to concepts and measurement, to case selection procedures.

## References and Suggested Readings

There are many good introductions to logic in the philosophy literature. A classic one useful for social scientists is Copi, Cohen, and McMahon (2010). Other good surveys include Hausman, Kahane, and Tidman (2010), Gensler (2002), and Suppes (1999). A comprehensive mathematical introduction to fuzzy-set logic is Klir and Yuan (1995). See also Zadeh (1965), which is the original fuzzy-set article. Many of the ideas discussed in this chapter draw on the work of Ragin (1987; 2000; 2008); see also Schneider and Wagemann (forthcoming) and Rohlfing (forthcoming). For a bibliography of works that use logic and set theory in the social sciences, see the COMPASSS website http://www.compasss.org/.

Braumoeller, B. 2004. Hypothesis testing and multiplicative interaction terms. *International Organization* 58:807–20.
Braumoeller, B., and G. Goertz. 2000. The methodology of necessary conditions. *American Journal of Political Science* 44:844–58.

Cioffi-Revilla, C. 1998. *Politics and uncertainty: theory, models and applications.* Cambridge: Cambridge University Press.

Copi, I. M., C. Cohen, and K. McMahon. 2010. *Introduction to logic,* 14th edition. Upper Saddle River, NJ: Prentice Hall.

Downs, G. 1989. The rational deterrence debate. *World Politics* 41:225–37.

Eliason, S. R., and R. Stryker. 2009. Goodness-of-fit tests and descriptive measures in fuzzy-set analysis. *Sociological Methods and Research* 38:102–46.

Gensler, H. J. 2002. *Introduction to logic.* London: Routledge

Goertz, G. 2003a. *International norms and decision making: a punctuated equilibrium model.* New York: Rowman & Littlefield.

Goertz, G. 2003b. The substantive importance of necessary condition hypotheses. In *Necessary conditions: theory, methodology, and applications*, edited by G. Goertz and H. Starr. New York: Rowman & Littlefield.

Goertz, G. 2006. Assessing the trivialness, relevance, and relative importance of necessary or sufficient conditions in social science. *Studies in Comparative International Development* 41:88–109.

Hausman, A., H. Kahane, and P. Tidman. 2010. *Logic and philosophy: a modern introduction*, 11th edition. Boston: Wadsworth.

Kam, C., and R. Franzese. 2008. *Modeling and interpreting interactive hypotheses in regression analysis: a brief refresher and some practical advice.* Ann Arbor: University of Michigan Press.

Klir, G. J., and B. Yuan. 1995. *Fuzzy sets and fuzzy logic: theory and applications.* Upper Saddle River, NJ: Prentice Hall.

Lakoff, G. 1987. *Women, fire, and dangerous things: what categories reveal about the mind.* Chicago: University of Chicago Press.

Lakoff, G., and R. E. Núñez. 2000. *Where mathematics comes from: how the embodied mind brings mathematics into being.* New York: Basic Books.

Mackie, J. L. 1965. Causes and conditions. *American Philosophical Quarterly* 2:245–64.

Mackie, J. L. 1980. *Cement of the universe: a study of causation.* Oxford: Clarendon Press.

McNeill, D., and P. Freiberger. 1994. *Fuzzy logic.* New York: Simon and Schuster.

Ragin, C. 1987. *The comparative method: moving beyond qualitative and quantitative strategies.* Berkeley: University of California Press.

Ragin, C. 2000. *Fuzzy-set social science.* Chicago: University of Chicago Press.

Ragin, C. 2008. *Redesigning social inquiry: fuzzy sets and beyond.* Chicago: University of Chicago Press.

Rohlfing, I. Forthcoming. *Case studies and causal inference: an integrative framework.* New York: Palgrave Macmillan.

Russett, B. 1995. The democratic peace: "and yet it moves." *International Securtiy* 19:164–75.

Schneider, C., and C. Wagemann, Forthcoming. *Set-theoretic methods in the social sciences.* New York: Cambridge University Press.

Seawright, J. 2011. Matching quantitative case selection procedures with case-study analytic goals. Manuscript, Northwestern University.

Smithson, M. 1988. Fuzzy set theory and the social sciences: the scope of applications. *Fuzzy Sets and Systems* 26:1–21.

Suppes, P. 1999. *Introduction to logic.* Mineola, NY: Dover.

Waltz, K. 1979. *Theory of international relations.* Boston: Addison-Wesley.

Zadeh, L. A. 1965. Fuzzy sets. *Information and Control* 12:338–53.

# PART I

Causal Models and Inference

# Chapter 3

# Causes-of-Effects versus Effects-of-Causes

**Cause**: [Middle English from Old French from Latin *causa*, reason, purpose] n. 1.a. The producer of an effect, result, or consequence. b. The one, such as a person, an event, or a condition, that is responsible for an action or a result.
—*The American Heritage Dictionary of the English Language*

## Introduction

Let us distinguish two different ways to ask and address causal questions. One can begin with an outcome, i.e., $Y$, and then work backward to the causes, i.e., $X$s. The second option works in the other direction; one starts with a potential cause and then asks about its impact on $Y$. The former procedure is often called the "causes-of-effects" approach, whereas the latter is known as the "effects-of-causes" approach. If one asks about the causes of global warming, one is pursuing a causes-of-effects question; if one asks about the impact of carbon emissions on global temperatures, one is pursuing an effects-of-causes question. Good science is concerned with both kinds of questions. Yet, in the social sciences, the two approaches have tremendous downstream methodological consequences, and many of the topics we cover arise because of these differences.

The quantitative and qualitative cultures differ in the extent to which and the ways in which they address causes-of-effects and effects-of-causes questions. Quantitative scholars have clearly come down as a group in favor of the effects-of-causes approach as the standard way to do social science. In particular, they have come down in favor of estimating the *average effects* of particular variables within populations or samples. In this tradition, scholars view the controlled experiment as the gold standard for research. In an experiment, one seeks to estimate the average effect of a treatment. Analogously, in statistical research with observational data, one seeks to estimate the average effect of an independent variable of interest. While occasionally a quantitative researcher might seek to explain $Y$ by maximizing variance explained (e.g., a high $R^2$), this kind of practice has declined significantly in contemporary quantitative research. In our survey (see the appendix), only 6 percent of quantitative articles discussed explicitly the $R^2$ statistic.

In the qualitative culture, by contrast, scholars are interested in explaining outcomes in individual cases as well as studying the effects of particular causal factors within individual cases. These scholars often start with events that have occurred in the real world and move backwards to ask about their causes. Much like other scholars in the historical sciences, including natural history, geology, and cosmology, they develop causes-of-effects models and use methods to identify the causes of particular occurrences in the past. These models ideally identify combinations of conditions, including all non-trivial necessary conditions, that are sufficient for outcomes.

Answering a causes-of-effects question almost always requires a *multivariate* explanation. The causal analysis of outcomes in specific cases involves a variety of factors. In contrast, with the average effect approach of statistical research, it is easy and normal to focus on just *one* independent variable. Of course, outside of an experimental setting, the researcher will almost always need to include other "control" variables in the statistical model to estimate the effect of interest. But these other variables are included to deal with the problem of confounding causes, not because the analyst is interested in their effects or contribution to the outcome under study.

Qualitative scholars also examine the effects of individual causes, either as part of a causes-of-effects approach or for their own sake. However, they do not equate an analysis of the effects of causes with the analysis of average causal effects. Instead, causal effects are analyzed by asking whether factors are necessary or jointly sufficient for specific outcomes in particular cases. Thus, when qualitative researchers study the effects of causes, they implicitly or explicitly conceptualize those effects in ways that are consistent with set theory and logic.

These differences are closely related to the extent to which researchers are interested in populations versus individual cases. Quantitative analysts, almost by definition, are centrally concerned with population analysis but not interested in individual cases. This naturally leads them to view the effects of causes in terms of averages that apply to populations. By contrast, while work in the qualitative tradition involves generalizations across cases, there is always a strong concern for explaining individual cases. This leads qualitative scholars to be far less concerned with average effects and to focus centrally on the causes that produce outcomes in specific cases.

## Type of Research Question

Both quantitative and qualitative researchers are interested in addressing questions that have the generic form: "What causes $Y$?" However, they translate this question differently. Quantitative researchers translate the question using their version of the effects-of-causes approach: "What is the average effect of $X$ on $Y$ within a population of cases?" Only rarely would these researchers translate the question into their version of the causes-of-effects approach: "What are the various $X$s that explain $Y$ for a population of cases?" By contrast, qualitative researchers often translate the question using their causes-of-effects approach: "What $X$s explain $Y$ for one or more specific cases?" Qualitative researchers may also translate the question using their version of the effects-of-causes approach: "Did $X$ cause $Y$ in one or more specific cases?"

Statistical methodologists have recognized the differences between the causes-of-effects versus effects-of-causes approaches. For example, the statistician Holland (1986, 970) argues that there is an "unbridgeable gulf" between the two approaches:

> Both wish to give meaning to the phrase "$A$ causes $B$." [The causes-of-effects approach] does this by interpreting "$A$ causes $B$" as "$A$ is *a* cause of $B$." [The effects-of-causes] model interprets "$A$ causes $B$" as "the *effect* of $A$ is $B$."

While Holland's quote emphasizes a single causal factor, causes-of-effects questions lend themselves quite naturally to a multivariate explanation designed to "fully" account for an outcome. With the causes-of-effects approach, one starts with the outcome, $Y$, and then tries to develop a causal model that identifies conditions that explain $Y$.

Although they recognize the two approaches, contemporary quantitative researchers embrace the effects-of-causes approach. As Morton and Williams (2010, 35) write:

> A lot of political science quantitative research—we would say the modal approach ... focuses on investigating the effects of particular causes. Sometimes this activity is advocated as part of an effort to build toward a general model of the causes of effects, but usually if such a goal is in a researcher's mind, it is implicit.

For instance, when quantitative researchers ask, "What causes democracy," they normally inquire about the effects of particular independent variables of interest. They ask whether variables such as economic development (Londregan and Poole 1996), political parties (Mainwaring 1993), and presidential systems (Cheibub 2007) have some effect on democracy. The point of these studies is precisely to learn whether development, parties, or presidentialism exert an effect on democracy within a population.

The basic experimental paradigm that underpins quantitative research makes it hard for these analysts to truly embrace the causes-of-effects tradition. It is more natural to downplay work on the causes of effects. For example, some quantitative methodologists argue that causes-of-effects research is only "descriptive" (Sobel 1995) or cannot produce general causal knowledge (Beck 2006). According to Angrist and Pischke (2009, 5), "Research questions that cannot be answered by any experiment are FUQs: fundamentally unidentified questions." Analysts have pointed out that the influential Neyman-Rubin-Holland model of causality "is purely a model of the effects of causes. It does not have anything to say about how we move from a set of effects to a model of the causes of effects" (Morton and Williams 2010, 99). When the statistician Dawid (2000) proposed a causes-of-effects approach as a special case of causation, he was mostly ignored. In his response to a series of comments from several distinguished statisticians, he expressed surprise that his analysis of causes-of-effects provoked so little discussion. "I am surprised at how little of the discussion relates to my suggestions for inference about 'causes of effects,' which I expected to be the most controversial" (Dawid 2000, 446).

One might ask how a statistical researcher would address a causes-of-effects question. One way to pursue the goal of "explaining $Y$" is to try to maximize variance explained. In early statistical practice, variance explained, i.e., maximizing the $R^2$, was a major goal of research and a key criterion for evaluating statistical models. With this approach, one has explained $Y$ if the model has an $R^2$ close to 1.00. There are many examples of statistical articles from earlier decades in which the researcher is interested in: (1) how much variance of $Y$ is explained by each individual $X_i$, and (2) how much of the variance of $Y$ is explained by the whole model.

Starting around the mid-1980s in political science and sociology, however, statistical researchers began to reject the "$R^2$ model" and adopt the effects-of-causes approach. Leading quantitative methodologists became quite skeptical about the variance explained goal:

> If your goal is to get a big $R^2$, then your goal is not the same as that for which regression analysis was designed ... The best regression model usually has an $R^2$ that is lower than could otherwise be obtained. The goal of [generating] a big $R^2$ ... is unlikely to be relevant to any political science research question. (King 1986, 677; see also King 1991)

King and others show how the inclusion of variables close to the dependent variable (e.g., lagged values of $Y$) can easily inflate the $R^2$. Also the search for a high $R^2$ encourages the inclusion of many independent variables, which can be problematic for a variety of reasons (Achen 2005). In sum, few quantitative researchers now use the $R^2$ statistic as a basis for evaluating causal models. It is completely possible to publish highly regarded research with an $R^2$ of less than .10.

It is also worth noting that an earlier generation of statistical researchers often developed quantitative path models in the effort to more or less comprehensively explain outcomes (e.g., Blalock 1964). These scholars used techniques such as structural equation models to specify how multiple independent variables located at different points within a sequence worked together to generate the outcome of interest (Bollen 1989). While quantitative path models are still occasionally discussed in work on statistical analysis mostly outside the social sciences (e.g., Pearl 2000; Morgan and Winship 2007), they have largely dropped out of empirical research as actually practiced in the social sciences.

On the qualitative side, by contrast, researchers still develop causal arguments that are intended to specify factors jointly sufficient for outcomes. For example, qualitative researchers attempt to identify the causes of World War I, exceptional growth in East Asia, the end of the Cold War, the creation of especially generous welfare states, and the rise of neopopulist regimes. A central purpose of this research is to develop a comprehensive explanation of the specific outcome for each and every case within the scope of the investigation (e.g., Levitsky and Way 2010).

Qualitative researchers also study and analyze the effects of individual causes. Often they do so in conjunction with trying to comprehensively explain an outcome. To focus on explaining $Y$ (i.e., analyzing the causes of an effect) requires showing how various $X$s have causal effects (i.e., analyzing the effects of causes). Sometimes qualitative researchers are interested in a particular cause and its effect for its own sake. For example, Collier and Collier's (1991) *Shaping the Political Arena* is focused on understanding the effect of variations in labor incorporation periods on long-run political dynamics in Latin America. A major goal of the analysis is to show how similarities and differences in labor incorporation periods are essential to the explanation of major political similarities and differences among the individual cases.

When qualitative researchers use an effects-of-causes approach, however, they do not estimate average causal effects, even when they are generalizing about a population of cases. Instead, they typically study conditions whose effects are understood to be necessary for an outcome that has actually occurred in one or more cases. Thus, when a qualitative researcher asserts that $X$ exerted a causal effect on $Y$, he or she usually believes that if $X$

had not occurred (or occurred differently), then $Y$ would not have occurred (or occurred differently) in the specific case or cases under analysis.[1] For example, Collier and Collier's (1991) study is built around the idea that different types of labor incorporation periods left distinctive legacies. Although labor incorporation periods did not fully determine political outcomes, they were necessary ingredients for many important political dynamics that did occur in the individual countries under study.

## Individual Cases

Qualitative researchers are drawn to general questions about the causes of important outcomes, such as democracy, war, economic growth, and institutional change. At the same time, they seek to develop explanations that can account for these outcomes in individual cases. The causes-of-effects approach leads them to explanations that simultaneously apply to a group of cases *and* to each individual case within that group. In the qualitative culture, to provide a convincing general explanation is at the same time to provide a convincing explanation of individual cases.

Hence, qualitative scholars espouse the following basic principle:

A good general explanation of $Y$ is also a good explanation of individual cases of $Y$.

For instance, a good qualitative explanation of social democracy in interwar Europe entails identifying the causes of social democracy in Sweden, Norway, and Denmark. In the case of Luebbert's (1991) famous work, the same factors (divided middle classes, weak liberals, and an alliance between socialists and farmers parties) that cause social democracy in general in interwar Europe also cause it in the specific cases of Sweden, Norway, and Denmark. A general explanation of an outcome that does not do a good job of accounting for individual cases is not a good general explanation. To take another popular example, Skocpol (1979) proposes an explanation of social revolution among historical agrarian states that were not subject to colonialism. Her explanation is general, in the sense that it is intended to apply to all positive cases of social revolution within this (limited) scope. At the same time, the explanation is designed to offer an adequate account of each of the positive cases within the scope, i.e., France, Russia, and China.

---

[1] The exception is a situation where the outcome in the particular case is overdetermined by multiple sufficient conditions. In this situation the individual factor $X$ may not be necessary for $Y$ in that specific case.

If the explanation fails at accounting for social revolution for one of these cases, it cannot be considered a successful overall explanation.

Qualitative scholars thus need to be sure that their causal model is operative in their individual cases. They want to verify that the causal model works as an explanation of $Y$ in *all*—or at least almost all—cases under investigation (within what is normally a modest scope). As such, they do not view the estimation of a significant average effect as the goal, but they rather try to make a causal argument that works almost all the time in explaining their $Y = 1$ cases.

By contrast, in quantitative effects-of-causes analyses, the intensive study of individual cases and their causes plays at most a minor role. The reasons why can be understood by considering the place of individual observations in a typical experiment, such as the famous Milgram (1974) obedience experiment. Individuals are randomly assigned to treatment and control groups through the manipulation of experimental conditions (e.g., spatial proximity to the "teacher"). While the experiment may tell us something important about the effect of spatial proximity to an authority figure on obedience, it is not designed to explain why any *particular* individual subject behaved the way that he did. Experiments tell us about effects in general, not about the causes of outcomes for particular individuals. In an experiment, there may not even be a way to debate about individual cases because the larger research community may not know the identity of the individuals.

In quantitative research, likewise, the focus is not on explaining any one case. Rather, the focus is on the average effect of an independent variable within a population. That average may or may not apply to particular cases. The question of whether an independent variable exerts its usual effect in a particular observation is beside the point. One can learn about the usual effect of $X$ on $Y$ in the population without knowing how $X$ affects $Y$ in any single case.

One can, in principle, ask about individual cases in a large-N effects-of-causes analysis: did $X$ have a causal effect for individual $i$ who was in the treatment group? However, without any information from within cases, it is difficult to answer this question in practice. In fact, standard statistical approaches assume it is impossible to estimate a causal effect for the individual $i$, which is precisely why one estimates an average causal effect for a population of cases (e.g., King, Keohane, and Verba 1994).

To be sure, information about average causal effects can be usefully applied to individual observations. For instance, doctors routinely make recommendations to individuals based on large-N experimental and/or observational studies. If they prescribe medicine and certain symptoms go away, they may *infer* that the medicine exerted a causal effect in the individual patient (of course, it could have been the placebo effect). However, without analyzing the causal pathway through which the medicine affected the symptom, it is difficult for this inference to be anything more than informed speculation.

## Conclusion: Complementarities and Mixed-Method Research

The decision to adopt a causes-of-effects versus effects-of-causes approach revolves in large part around contrasting research orientations and goals: studying individual cases through within-case analysis versus analyzing central tendencies in populations through cross-case analysis. Qualitative scholars use within-case analysis to make inferences about the specific events and processes that generate outcomes. Within-case analysis goes hand in hand with the effort to say something about the factors that caused outcomes in the specific cases studied. By contrast, quantitative scholars use cross-case analysis to make inferences about populations. Here it is natural to ask and answer questions about the typical effects of specific variables of interest within the population as a whole. But it is unusual to say something about the effect of a variable for any specific case.

The utility of each approach is suggested by the fact they can and sometimes do complement one another. When qualitative researchers seek to explain their specific outcomes, they often begin with existing knowledge, including prior statistical research on the effects of particular causes. Analogously, good quantitative research often takes into consideration the results of work on the causes of outcomes in particular cases. These qualitative findings may be subjected to further evaluation in a statistical analysis.

Thus, there are sound reasons to believe that both qualitative and quantitative approaches are valuable and complement one another. A good qualitative explanation of an outcome in a small number of cases leads one to wonder if the same factors are at work when a broader understanding of scope is adopted, stimulating a larger-N analysis in which the goal is less to explain particular cases and more to estimate average effects. Likewise, when quantitative results about the effects of causes are reported, it seems natural to ask if these results make sense in terms of the history of individual cases; one wishes to try to locate the effects in specific cases. These kinds of complementarities make mixed-method research possible, and they point toward the value of cross-cultural communication and cooperation.

## References and Suggested Readings

The distinction between the causes-of-effects and effects-of-causes approaches is discussed in Holland (1986), Dawid (2000), and Morton and Williams (2010). Although with research in political science and sociology (as actually practiced) these approaches are closely associated with the qualitative and quantitative paradigms, they need not always be. For discussions of the ways in which experiments and statistical approaches could be used to help test large-N cause-of-effect models, see Heckman (2005) and Morton and Williams (2010, 33–41 and chapter 6). For discussions of the ways in which qualitative research can help estimate average effects, see Gerring (2007). On the role of individual cases in qualitative research, see Collier, Brady, and Seawright (2010), George and Bennett (2005), and Mahoney and Rueschemeyer (2003).

Achen, C. H. 2005. Let's put garbage-can regressions and garbage-can probits where they belong. *Conflict Management and Peace Science* 22:327–39.

Angrist, J. D., and J.-S. Pischke. 2009. *Mostly harmless econometrics: an empiricist's companion.* Princeton: Princeton University Press.

Beck, N. 2006. Is causal-process observation an oxymoron? *Political Analysis* 14:347–52.

Blalock, H. M., Jr. 1964. *Causal inferences in nonexperimental research.* Chapel Hill: University of North Carolina Press.

Bollen, K. A. 1989. *Structural equations with latent variables.* New York: Wiley.

Cheibub, J. A. 2007. *Presidentialism, parliamentarism, and democracy.* Cambridge: Cambridge University Press.

Collier, D., H. E. Brady, and J. Seawright. 2010. Sources of leverage in causal inference: toward an alternative view of methodology. In *Rethinking social inquiry: diverse tools, shared standards*, 2nd edition, edited by H. E. Brady and D. Collier. Lanham, MD: Rowman & Littlefield.

Collier, R. B., and D. Collier. 1991. *Shaping the political arena: critical junctures, the labor movement, and regime dynamics in Latin America.* Princeton: Princeton University Press.

Dawid, A. P. 2000. Causal inference without counterfactuals (with discussion). *Journal of the American Statistical Association* 95:407–48, 450.

George, A., and A. Bennett. 2005. *Case studies and theory development in the social sciences.* Cambridge: MIT Press.

Gerring, J. 2007. *Case study research: principles and practices.* Cambridge: Cambridge University Press.

Heckman, J. J. 2005. The scientific model of causality. *Sociological Methodology* 35:1–97.

Holland, P. 1986. Statistics and causal inference (with discussion). *Journal of the American Statistical Association* 81:945–60.

King, G. 1986. How not to lie with statistics: avoiding common mistakes in quantitative political science. *American Journal of Political Science* 30:666–87.

King, G. 1991. "Truth" is stranger than prediction, more questionable than causal inference. *American Journal of Political Science* 35:1047–53.

King, G., R. Keohane, and S. Verba. 1994. *Designing social inquiry: scientific inference in qualitative research.* Princeton: Princeton University Press.

Levitsky, S., and L. A. Way. 2010. *Competitive authoritarianism: hybrid regimes after the Cold War.* New York: Cambridge University press.

Londregan, J., and K. Poole. 1996. Does high income promote democracy? *World Politics* 49:1–31.

Luebbert, G. 1991. *Liberalism, fascism, or social democracy: social classes and the political origins of regimes in interwar Europe.* Oxford: Oxford University Press.

Mahoney, J., and D. Rueschemeyer, eds. 2003. *Comparative historical analysis in the social sciences.* Cambridge: Cambridge University Press.

Mainwaring, S. 1993. Presidentialism, multipartism, and democracy: the difficult combination. *Comparative Political Studies* 26:198–228.

Milgram, S. 1974. *Obedience: an experimental view.* New York: Harper & Row.

Morgan, S., and C. Winship. 2007. *Counterfactuals and causal inference: methods and principles for social research.* Cambridge: Cambridge University Press.

Morton, R., and K. Williams. 2010. *Experimental political science and the study of causality: from nature to the lab.* Cambridge: Cambridge University Press.

Pearl, J. 2000. *Causality: models, reasoning, and inference.* Cambridge: Cambridge University Press.

Skocpol, T. 1979. *States and social revolutions: a comparative analysis of France, Russia, and China.* Cambridge: Cambridge University Press.

Sobel, M. 1995. Causal inference in the social and behavioral sciences. In *Handbook of statistical modeling for the social and behavioral sciences*, edited by G. Arminger. New York: Plenum Press.

# Chapter 4

## Causal Models

As to causal models, these must have different forms depending
on what they are to be used for and on what kinds of systems are
under study.
                    —*Nancy Cartwright*

### Introduction

In this chapter, we compare an additive, linear causal model, which is
common in the statistical culture, to a set-theoretic causal model based
on logic, which is often used (implicitly) in the qualitative culture. In
subsequent chapters, we explore the ramifications of the choice of one or
the other causal model, since they imply different views about causation,
causal asymmetry, counterfactuals, and the like.

We first introduce and illustrate via example the two causal models. The
next sections then describe core differences between them. We suggest that
while these causal models are quite different, neither is a priori correct. They
are both potentially useful ways to explain social and political phenomena.
Yet, because of their differences, important hurdles stand in the way of
combining the two models or using insights from one kind of model to
benefit the other. We suggest that a first step toward overcoming these
hurdles is appreciating what is distinctive about each.

### Two Causal Models

Standard causal models used in qualitative and quantitative research are
similar and different in nonobvious ways. To illustrate, consider the

following two models, which are common in the quantitative and qualitative paradigms, respectively:

$$Y = \beta_0 + \beta_1 X_1 + \gamma_1 C_1 + \gamma_2 C_2 + \cdots + \epsilon, \tag{4.1}$$

(A AND B AND not C) OR (A AND C AND D AND E) is sufficient for Y.

$$\tag{4.2}$$

Obvious incarnations of equation (4.1) include the most popular general linear models such as OLS regression as well as other models in vogue such as difference-in-differences regression. The basic form of the equation also encompasses log-linear models and polynomial regression. While logit models use a nonlinear function, they are linear in the exponent. Logit models are normally used because they can treat dichotomous dependent variables, not because the analyst believes causal patterns are nonlinear.[1] Looking at research in the best journals, some member of the family of equation (4.1) is the most commonly used approach to causal modeling in the quantitative tradition (see the appendix).

For our purposes, a key feature of equation (4.1) is that the researcher is interested in estimating the effect of $X_1$ on $Y$ (i.e., $\beta_1$). Beyond the variable linked to the core hypothesis (i.e., $X_1$), the model includes control or confounding variables (i.e., $C_i$). A significant bivariate effect, $\hat{\beta}_1$, between $X_1$ and $Y$ is rarely convincing; one has to respond to the concern that this relationship might disappear when controlling for variable $C_i$. A huge number of refinements to equation (4.1) exist in the methodological literature, but this basic additive, linear functional form remains the norm in the most highly regarded substantive research that uses quantitative methods.

If one moves to debates among quantitative methodologists about best practices, differences among subcultures become apparent. Most notably, the Neyman-Rubin-Holland model or "potential outcomes" framework proposes a different approach to statistical research than the general linear model, one much more clearly linked to the ideal of a randomized experiment (see Morgan and Winship 2007). The basic model of this framework is:

$$\text{Causal effect} = \overline{Y}_{(X=1)} - \overline{Y}_{(X=0)}. \tag{4.3}$$

---

[1] Statistical methods for estimating nonlinear models do exist, e.g., Bates and Watts (1988), but these often are not taught or used in political science and sociology.

The "causal effect" is a random variable like $Y$ in equation (4.1), and one is typically testing the hypothesis that the causal effect is significantly different from zero. The framework is clearer than the general linear model approach that the goal is to estimate the *average* causal effect of $X$. In this basic model, control variables are not needed because assignment to treatment is randomized across a large number of observations.

While the potential outcomes framework is quite influential among statistical methodologists, it has yet to become widespread in research practice (see the appendix).[2] A key reason why is that the approach becomes quite complex as one moves from dichotomous variables to continuous ones and introduces other nuances, such as interaction terms or mediator variables. Nevertheless, many methodologists would insist that the basic causal model for the quantitative paradigm should be equation (4.3), not equation (4.1), the latter which dominates research practice.

Bayesian approaches are another important subculture among contemporary statistical methodologists. Although Bayesian analysis has been around for decades, historically it has not been much used in social science research. Yet with recent advances in computational power and the rise of Markov Chain Monte Carlo methods, major barriers to applied analyses have been reduced. Within political science, a vibrant Bayesian subculture exists among quantitative methodologists (e.g., see Schrodt 2010 for an enthusiastic view). This subculture begins with a quite different set of assumptions and philosophy than equation (4.1) (see Jackman 2009 for a good discussion). Perhaps because it differs so substantially from frequentist approaches, the Bayesian subculture does not engage much the potential outcomes framework, at least directly.[3]

Among statistical methodologists, in short, there are a variety of important groups, and they have debates among themselves. Yet given that we are attempting to describe the dominant research practices that inform work that is regarded by the larger scholarly community as the best scholarship in the social sciences, the basic model of equation (4.1) is the most relevant one for our purposes.

Turning to the qualitative paradigm, we suggest that equation (4.2) underlies much research. This suggestion is not without controversy because qualitative researchers are often unsystematic and do not write out equations formally. Nevertheless, we find that their arguments often implicitly take a form similar to that of equation (4.2). Here set-theoretic ideas replace the algebra and statistics of the additive model.

---

[2] Pearl (2000) offers another influential probabilistic approach to causation that has not yet had a major impact on research practice.

[3] For example, Jackman's (2009) influential book does not have an index entry for "potential outcomes" and makes virtually no reference to the idea of a causal effect.

We have used words to express the model, but one can also use mathematical logic. In equation (4.4), the causal model identifies two combinations of factors that generate, i.e., are sufficient for, an outcome. The model uses logical notation and Boolean operators. The $\wedge$ symbol represents the logical AND, the $\vee$ symbol represents the logical OR, the $\neg$ symbol means logical negation, and the $\rightarrow$ symbol represents sufficiency:

$$(A \wedge B \wedge \neg C) \vee (A \wedge C \wedge D \wedge E) \rightarrow Y. \tag{4.4}$$

One can write the same equation using the notation of set theory, where $\cap$ means intersection, $\cup$ means union, $\overline{C}$ means complement of $C$, and $\subseteq$ means subset or equivalent set:

$$(A \cap B \cap \overline{C}) \cup (A \cap C \cap D \cap E) \subseteq Y. \tag{4.5}$$

As written in equations (4.4) and (4.5), these causal models look quite different from the quantitative model of equation (4.1). However, one can write the same equation in a way that makes it seem more like its quantitative counterpoint:

$$Y = (A * B * c) + (A * C * D * E). \tag{4.6}$$

When presented this way, a possible reaction to the set-theoretic/logic model is to say that it is a way of talking about interaction terms. But as with translations between languages, the analogy between the logical AND and multiplication in a statistical model is only partial. As we discussed in the "Mathematical Prelude," there are substantive differences that are not captured by the analogy.

Using equation (4.6), we can also translate the qualitative model into statistical terms:

$$Y = \beta_1 (A * B * c) + \beta_2 (A * C * D * E) + \epsilon. \tag{4.7}$$

Would one ever see such a model in a research article? The answer is no. There is nothing that prohibits statistical software from estimating such a model. However, standard statistical advice offers good reasons to reject such practices. For example, there is no intercept term. Estimating equation (4.7) assumes that the intercept is zero, which is something one should probably test for and not just assume. In contrast, the concept of an "intercept" makes little sense in the set-theoretic/logic paradigm.

## Set-Theoretic Models and Within-Case Analysis: An Illustration

Most social scientists learn the general linear model in one or more statistics classes. However, set-theoretic causal models are unfamiliar to many, including often the qualitative researchers who implicitly use them. Thus it is helpful to see how something like equation (4.5) looks in practice. To illustrate, we examine Brady's analysis (2010) of the effect of the early media call that proclaimed an Al Gore victory in Florida in the 2000 presidential elections. This example shows how a set-theoretic model is implicitly used in the within-case analysis of a specific outcome.

Brady's approach is to question the influential conclusion of Lott (2000), who asserts that at least 10,000 votes were lost for George W. Bush in the ten panhandle counties of Florida. These were the counties where the polls had not closed when the networks prematurely declared Gore the winner. Brady argues that Lott's use of a difference-in-differences regression model (see Angrist and Pischke 2009) is not appropriate and generates faulty inferences.

Instead of using a cross-case statistical methodology, Brady employs within-case analysis to estimate the number of votes lost. He considers the mechanisms that had to be in place for the premature media call to have cost Bush votes that he counterfactually would have received. In particular, Brady carries out a series of "hoop tests" (see the chapter "Within-Case versus Cross-Case Causal Analysis" for a discussion of this kind of test) in which he identifies conditions that are necessary for the early media call to have caused Bush to lose the vote of a Florida resident.

Brady's hoop tests propose that for Bush to have lost voter $i$, the voter must simultaneously have membership in three sets. First, the voter must be a member of the set of individuals who lived in the eastern panhandle counties of Florida; second, the voter must be a member of the set of eligible voters who had not already voted; and third, the voter must be a member of the set of individuals who heard the media call for Gore. In terms of logic, membership in each of these sets is *necessary* for the individual to be coded as a potential lost vote for Bush. Thus, he employs (implicitly) the following set-theoretic equation:

$$Y \subseteq L \cap E \cap H. \tag{4.8}$$

In this equation, $L$ stands for resident of eastern panhandle county; $E$ is eligible voter who did not vote before the media call; $H$ is heard media call for Gore; and $Y$ is maximum possible lost vote for Bush because of early media call. This equation says that the set of *possible* vote changes is the intersection of the three sets, $L$, $E$, and $H$. It presents a simple but useful way of calculating the maximum possible vote loss, which is the total number of individuals with membership in the intersection of the three sets.

In Brady's work, then, a key challenge is estimating the size of the population of those people who are members of all three of these sets. He makes these estimates through a within-case analysis that draws on previous voting patterns and media exposure in Florida as well as general knowledge of voting behavior. According to Brady's calculations, "The approximate upper bound for Bush's vote loss was 224 and ... the actual vote loss was probably closer to somewhere between 28 and 56 votes. Lott's figure of 10,000 makes no sense at all" (Brady 2010, 240).

This simple example illustrates three key differences between a set-theoretic causal model and the general linear statistical model:

1. No control variables. For example, in the difference-in-differences design, there are various control variables (aka fixed effects) for each Florida county.

2. Different dependent variable. Equation (4.8) gives an estimate of maximum possible vote loss. As we discussed in the "Mathematical Prelude," the maximum (or minimum) in set-theoretic models often play the role of the mean in statistical models.

3. Necessary and sufficient conditions. Brady's model posits a set of conditions that are individually necessary for a possible lost vote.

For our purposes here, the issue is not whether Lott's statistical model is better or worse than Brady's set-theoretic one. It is that they work quite differently, consider different dependent variables, and yield different kinds of results.


## Causal Complexity

Both quantitative and qualitative researchers assume that causal patterns in the real world are in certain ways quite complex. Likewise, they assume that modeling causation is itself a complex endeavor. However, the form of causal complexity varies across the quantitative and qualitative paradigms.

In the quantitative culture, causal complexity is seen through the fact that analysts assume that there are always many causes of a dependent variable. In equation (4.1), for example, there are several independent variables included. Moreover, the error term, i.e., $\epsilon$, is usually interpreted as in part composed of missing independent variables. In this tradition, one normally assumes that there are so many causes that it is impossible to identify all of them.

Although there are many causes of the dependent variable, the focus in quantitative research is often on one particular independent variable. In the causal model represented by equation (4.1), for example, the focus is on $X_1$; the other independent variables are treated as "controls" and are not of special interest themselves. The challenge raised by causal complexity is to develop a good estimate of the average effect of the variable of interest, given that there are many other influences. This challenge is vexing because some of these other causes affect the main independent variable of interest as well as the dependent variable (introducing potentially spurious relationships), and thus they need to be identified and included in the statistical model. More generally, one needs control variables to produce causally homogeneous groups.[4]

In the qualitative paradigm, by contrast, causal complexity is seen in the fact that researchers often model causal patterns in which attention is focused on *combinations* of causes (Ragin 1987). As illustrated in equation (4.2), qualitative researchers frequently are looking for causal packages or recipes that produce (i.e., are sufficient for) the outcome. We see this in equation (4.7), which rewrites the qualitative model in statistical terms: the $\beta$s relate to causal packages, not individual variables. We also see it in the Brady example in which the combination of three sets generates the maximum possible vote loss.

In the search for causal recipes, the role of individual variables is often downplayed, especially when the individual variables are not necessary conditions. The question, "What is the average effect of cause $C$?" may not make much sense if the role of $C$ varies across causal configurations. In equation (4.2), for example, $C$ sometimes has a positive effect and sometimes a negative effect, depending on the other causal factors with which it appears. Likewise, $B$ matters in the combined presence of $A$ and in the absence of $C$, but in other settings it has no effect on the outcome. Hence, adequately specifying the effect of $B$ requires saying something about the context (i.e., other causal factors) in which $B$ appears.

Now the same thing can occur with statistical interaction terms. In equation (4.1), we presented the most common statistical model, but interaction hypotheses and models are not uncommon (see the appendix):

$$Y = \beta_0 + \beta_1 X_1 + \beta_1 X_2 + \beta_3 X_1 * X_2 + \gamma_1 C_1 + \gamma_2 C_2 + \cdots + \epsilon. \qquad (4.9)$$

With this model, it is possible for the impact of $X_1$ to be positive in some range of $X_2$ and negative in another range of $X_2$. Both cultures agree that in the presence of interaction effects there is often little one can say about the individual impact of the constituent variables of the interaction term.

---

[4] This is a key point in the philosophical–statistical literature on causation (e.g., Cartwright 1989, 55–56).

However, a good statistician would almost never estimate a complex set-theoretic model like equation (4.6). To estimate this equation, statistical practice suggests that one should include all lower order terms such as $A$, $AB$, $AC$, and $AD$ in the model. Although there are very good statistical reasons for this practice, in set-theoretic models these reasons do not exist. It is hypothetically possible to develop statistical methods for modeling the kinds of causal configurations suggested in qualitative models. But these statistical models—for example, Boolean probit and Boolean logit (Braumoeller 2003)—fall well outside of the statistical mainstream.

In fact, the causal expressions of a set-theoretic model are really not interaction terms at all. They are particular causal combinations. In the formulation of equation (4.6), we do not have the generic $X_1 * X_2$, but rather a specific causal combination that refers to membership in $A$, $B$, and negated $C$ (i.e., $c$). It is membership in this specific configuration of $A$, $B$, and $c$ that is sufficient for $Y$. Thus, in the set-theoretic model, the logical operator AND joins causal factors together as "packages" or what might be called "sufficiency combinations" (to highlight the idea that the combination is sufficient for the outcome). It encourages one to think about the whole package as something greater than its individual components (Ragin 1987).

Causal arguments in qualitative fields such as comparative-historical analysis routinely involve these sufficiency combinations. Thus, Skocpol (1979) proposes that the combination of state breakdown and peasant revolt is sufficient for a social revolution in agrarian-bureaucratic societies; Downing (1992) argues that medieval constitutionalism and the absence of a military revolution were sufficient for early democracy; and Mahoney (2010) suggests the combination of a small indigenous population and high level of economic development was sufficient for a high level of social development in the context of late colonial Spanish America. In some cases, the individual factors in a causal combination are located at different points in time. For example, in Luebbert's argument (1991) about interwar regimes in Europe, the combination of weak liberals before World War I and a red-green alliance after World War I are both part of the causal package that generates social democracy.

## Equifinality

Another difference between the causal models used in the qualitative and quantitative paradigms revolves around the concept of "equifinality" (George and Bennett 2005) or what Ragin (1987) calls "multiple causation." Equifinality is the idea that there are multiple causal paths to the same outcome. In a set-theoretic causal model, equifinality is expressed using the logical OR. In equation (4.6), for example, there are two causal paths

$ABc$ OR $ACDE$; either one is sufficient to attain the outcome. It is worth noting that equifinality does not require causal combinations. For example, the following model expresses equifinality without causal conjunctions: $A \vee B \vee C \rightarrow Y$. The distinctive feature of equifinality is the presence of multiple conditions or combinations of conditions that generate the same outcome, not the presence of conjunctural causation as discussed previously.[5] In practice, qualitative causal models designed to accommodate more than a small number of cases often include both conjunctions of causal factors and equifinality (as in equation (4.6)).

The presence of equifinality is not unique to qualitative causal models. Implicit in statistical models such as equation (4.1) are potentially thousands of paths to a particular outcome. The right-hand side of the statistical equation essentially represents a weighted sum, and as long as that weighted sum is greater than the specified threshold—for example, in a logit analysis—then the outcome is predicted to occur. With this equifinality interpretation of equation (4.1), there are countless ways to reach a particular value on a dependent variable. One has equifinality in spades. Indeed, equifinality is so pervasive that it hardly makes sense to talk about it at all.

What makes equifinality a useful concept for qualitative work is the fact that, in this paradigm, *there are only a few causal paths* to a particular outcome. Each path is normally a specific conjunction of factors, but there are not very many of them. Within the typically more limited scope conditions of qualitative work (see the chapter "Scope"), the goal is to identify all the causal paths present in the population.

In qualitative research, in fact, analysts will normally try to assign all cases under study to specific causal paths. Since the overall research goal is to explain cases, one does so by identifying the causal path that each case follows. For example, Hicks et al. (1995) conclude that there are three separate paths to an early welfare state, and their analysis allows one to identify exactly which cases followed each of the three paths (see also Esping-Andersen 1990). In qualitative research, these causal paths can play a key organizing role for general theoretical knowledge. To cite another example, Moore's (1966) famous work identifies three different paths to the modern world, each defined by a particular combination of variables, and the specific countries that follow each path are clearly identified.

Within quantitative research, it does not seem useful to group cases according to common causal configurations on the independent variables. While one could do this, it is not a practice within this tradition. To

---

[5] We think that much of the discussion of equifinality inappropriately views its distinctive aspect as the representation of combinations of factors. If one focuses mainly on this aspect using a statistical perspective, as do King, Keohane, and Verba (1994, 87–89), one may believe (inappropriately) that equifinality is simply a way of talking about interaction terms.

understand why not, it is useful to consider how the statistical equation (4.1) seems when viewed through the lens of logic. In Boolean algebra, the "+" symbol stands for the logical OR and indicates different causes or combinations that are each sufficient for the outcome. Thus, from the view of logic, the statistical equation (4.1) could be read as indicating that each variable is itself sufficient for $Y$. Most researchers would regard this proposition as preposterous, since individual factors are almost never sufficient by themselves for outcomes; only combinations of factors are sufficient. Thus, just as equation (4.2) when translated into a statistical model makes little sense, so translating the algebraic–statistical model into logic is problematic.

In fact, each variable in the statistical equation (4.1) is just one of many potential causes influencing the outcome. The reality is that the overall model is *the path*. A nice illustration of this point comes from multimethod work that first tests a statistical model and then uses the results to select case studies for intensive analysis (e.g., Lieberman 2005). When selecting cases, one might choose observations on the line or off the line (or both), depending on one's research goals. But the line itself is the singular causal path for the whole population. The full causal model applies to all cases and stands as *the* explanation for all of them.

A key upshot about the use of equifinality in the statistical culture follows from this discussion. Although in one sense it is correct to see statistical models as assuming extensive equifinality, in another sense that is not true. With equifinality, as conventionally understood, one assigns each case to the particular causal recipe that generated its outcome. This practice does not exist in the quantitative tradition. Here it makes more sense to think about individual cases in terms of their residuals—i.e., how close they are to the line representing the causal model as a whole. There is no equifinality because the model as a whole is the explanation for the population.


## Conclusion

The standard causal models used in the two cultures are quite different and in many ways difficult to compare. But from the perspective of a dialogue between cultures, it is better to understand the differences than to fight over who is right or better. The logic and set theory that form the basis of the qualitative model of causation are not more or less rigorous than the probability theory and statistics that underlie the quantitative model. The qualitative approach emphasizes that causal factors are context dependent and operate together as overall packages. Equifinality is a useful concept for this approach, given that its typical causal model implies a few causal paths to an outcome. The quantitative approach sees causal complexity in the fact that there are a large number of causes for any outcome. Equifinality is not a useful concept for this approach, given that its causal model simultaneously suggests massive equifinality and just one general causal path.

## References and Suggested Readings

Versions of the statistical model presented in equation (4.1) can be found in countless statistics textbooks. This model is also at the core of King, Keohane, and Verba's (1994) argument. For writings on interaction terms in the statistical culture, see Allison (1977), Brambor, Clark, and Golder (2006), Franzese (2003), and Kam and Franzese (2007). Morgan and Winship (2007) offer an excellent introduction to the potential outcomes framework. Dunning (forthcoming) also provides an accessible treatment. Two prominent expositions of the Bayesian approach for the social sciences are Jackman (2009) and Gill (2007). In the philosophical literature, the set-theoretic/logic causal model goes back to at least Mackie (1980) and continues to be developed today (e.g., Baumgartner 2009). In the social sciences, this model was formalized by Ragin (1987; 2000). For discussions of the qualitative approach to causal complexity from a statistical standpoint, see Achen (2005), Braumoeller (2003; 2004), Clarke, Gilligan, and Golder (2006), Eliason and Stryker (2009), and Seawright (2005).

Achen, C. 2005. Two cheers for Charles Ragin. *Studies in Comparative International Development* 40:27–32.

Allison, P. 1977. Testing for interaction in multiple regression. *American Journal of Sociology* 83:144–53.

Angrist, J., and J.-S. Pischke. 2009. *Mostly harmless econometrics.* Princeton: Princeton University Press.

Bates, D., and D. Watts. 1988. *Nonlinear regression analysis and its applications.* New York: John Wiley & Sons.

Baumgartner, M. 2009. Inferring causal complexity. *Sociological Methods and Research* 38:71–101.

Brady, H. E. 2010. Data-set observations versus causal-process observations: the 2000 U.S. presidential election. In *Rethinking social inquiry: diverse tools, shared standards*, 2nd edition, edited by H. E. Brady and D. Collier. Lanham, MD: Rowman & Littlefield.

Brambor, T., W. Clark, and M. Golder. 2006. Understanding interaction models: improving empirical analyses. *Political Analysis* 14:63–82.

Braumoeller, B. 2003. Causal complexity and the study of politics. *Political Analysis* 11:209–33.

Braumoeller, B. 2004. Hypothesis testing and multiplicative interaction terms. *International Organization* 58:807–20.

Cartwright, N. 1989. *Nature's capacities and their measurement.* Oxford: Oxford University Press.

Clarke, W., M. Gilligan, and M. Golder. 2006. A simple multivariate test for asymmetric hypotheses. *Political Analysis* 14:311–31.

Downing, B. 1992. *The military revolution and political change: origins of democracy and autocracy in early modern Europe.* Princeton: Princeton University Press.

Dunning, T. Forthcoming. *Natural experiments in the social sciences.* Cambridge: Cambridge University Press.

Eliason, S., and R. Stryker. 2009. Goodness-of-fit tests and descriptive measures in fuzzy-set analysis. *Sociological Methods and Research* 38:102–46.

Esping-Andersen, G. 1990. *The three worlds of welfare capitalism.* Cambridge: Polity Press.

Franzese, Jr., R. J. 2003. Quantitative empirical methods and the context-conditionality of class and modern comparative politics. *CP: Newsletter of the Comparative Politics Organized Section of the American Political Science Association* 14:20–24.

George, A., and A. Bennett. 2005. Case studies and theory development in the social sciences. Cambridge: MIT Press.

Gill, J. 2007. *Bayesian methods: a social and behavioral sciences approach,* 2nd edition. London: Chapman and Hall.

Goertz, G. 2006. Assessing the trivialness, relevance, and relative importance of necessary or sufficient conditions in social science. *Studies in Comparative International Development* 41:88–109.

Hicks A., J. Misra, and T. Ng. 1995. The programmatic emergence of the social security state. *American Sociological Review* 60:329–50.

Jackman, S. 2009. *Bayesian analysis for the social sciences.* New York: Wiley.

Kam, C. D., and R. J. Franzese Jr. 2007. *Modeling and interpreting interactive hypotheses in regression analysis.* Ann Arbor: University of Michigan Press.

King, G., R. Keohane, and S. Verba. 1994. *Designing social inquiry: scientific inference in qualitative research.* Princeton: Princeton University Press.

Lieberman, E. S. 2005. Nested analysis as a mixed-method strategy for comparative research. *American Political Science Review* 99:435–52.

Lott, Jr., J. R. 2000. Gore might lose a second round: media suppressed the Bush vote. *Philadelphia Inquirer,* Tuesday, November 14, p. 23A.

Luebbert, G. 1991. *Liberalism, fascism, or social democracy: social classes and the political origins of regimes in interwar Europe.* New York: Oxford University Press.

Mackie, J. 1980. *The cement of the universe: a study of causation.* Oxford: Oxford University Press.

Mahoney, J. 2010. *Colonialism and postcolonial development: Spanish America in comparative perspective.* Cambridge: Cambridge University Press.

Moore, Jr., B. 1966. *Social origins of dictatorship and democracy: lord and peasant in the making of the modern world.* Boston: Beacan Press.

Morgan, S., and C. Winship. 2007. *Counterfactuals and causal inference: methods and principles for social research.* Cambridge: Cambridge University Press.

Pearl, J. 2000. *Causality: models, reasoning, and inference.* Cambridge: Cambridge University Press.

Ragin, C. 1987. *The comparative method: moving beyond qualitative and quantitative strategies.* Berkeley: University of California Press.

Ragin, C. 2000. *Fuzzy-set social science.* Chicago: University of Chicago Press.

Ragin, C. 2008. *Redesigning social inquiry: fuzzy sets and beyond.* Chicago: University of Chicago Press.

Schrodt, P. 2010. Seven deadly sins of contemporary quantitative political analysis. Paper presented at the annual meeting of the American Political Science Association.

Seawright, J. 2005. Qualitative comparative analysis vis-à-vis regression. *Studies in Comparative International Development* 40:3–26.

Skocpol, T. 1979. *States and social revolutions: a comparative analysis of France, Russia, and China.* Cambridge: Cambridge University Press.

# Chapter 5

## Asymmetry

The symmetric/asymmetric distinction is ... [a] fundamental
dimension to any relationship—despite the fact that most of us are
completely insensitive to it.
     *—Stanley Lieberson*

### Introduction

A core difference between the quantitative and qualitative cultures concerns
their tendencies to analyze either symmetric or asymmetric relationships.
Quantitative scholars naturally gravitate toward relationships that are symmetric, whereas qualitative scholars tend to analyze relationships that have
asymmetric qualities. Ultimately, whether a relationship is symmetric or
asymmetric is an empirical question. Nevertheless, the norms of the two
cultures lead them to look for one kind of relationship but not the other.

Causal models and explanations can be asymmetric in various ways. In
this chapter, we focus mainly (though not exclusively) on what might be
called "static causal asymmetry."[1] This expression means that the explanation of occurrence is not the mirror image of that of nonoccurrence. Causal
symmetry is present when the same model explains both occurrence and

---

[1] Dynamic causal asymmetry, which also comes up in this chapter, involves the idea that the
movement of a variable, say from presence to absence, does not have the same impact as moving
in the other direction. With a fully *symmetric* causal effect, $X$ will have the same effect on $Y$
regardless of the direction of change. One can view this kind of causal symmetry in terms of
a counterfactual: causal relationships are symmetric when they are counterfactually *reversible*.
The effect on $Y$ of a given change on $X$ would disappear if $X$ returned to its original value. For
a discussion, see Lieberson (1985, chapter 4).

nonoccurrence. For example, with logit models the explanation for success is the inverse of that of failure. Practically speaking, the coding of zero and one is arbitrary and nothing changes if they are flipped. One can use the same causal model equally well for all values of $Y$. By contrast, with causal asymmetry, the model that explains presence is not the same as the model that explains absence. One cannot use the same causal model for all values of $Y$.

## Symmetric versus Asymmetric Models

To start simple, consider a $2 \times 2$ table. As we saw in the "Mathematical Prelude," almost all measures of association for $2 \times 2$ tables are symmetric. Flipping rows or columns does not change the nature of the association. Within the statistical culture, this is a *positive* feature. It would be distressing if the, perhaps arbitrary, coding of dichotomous variables could overturn or alter one's findings. In fact, the very counterfactual definition of causality used in the statistical culture (see the next chapter "Hume's Two Definitions of Cause") implies symmetry: one is no more interested in moving from zero to one than vice versa.

As we move from $2 \times 2$ tables to continuous variables, the symmetry of the statistical culture is normally preserved (in research as actually practiced). For example, in OLS regression, one estimates a model under the assumption that causal effects are symmetric. A given unit change on $X$ is understood to have the same effect on $Y$ regardless of the starting point of $X$ and regardless of whether the value of $X$ increases or decreases. One can easily see this with a linear regression line. The line posits a completely symmetric effect. With logit models, a given increase on $X$ will have the same size of impact on the probability of $Y$ as an equivalent decrease. Similarly, the $Y_t - Y_c$ term in the potential outcomes framework is symmetric.

By contrast, set-theoretic models normally assume asymmetric relationships built around necessity and sufficiency. For example, consider a hypothesis about a necessary condition. When $X = 0$, the hypothesis has a precise prediction: the outcome should not occur. More formally, the absence of a necessary condition yields a point prediction: $P(Y = 1 | X = 0) = 0$. In stark contrast, when $X = 1$, the necessary condition model makes a vague claim: $P(Y = 1 | X = 1) > 0$. The presence of a necessary condition ($X = 1$) merely allows for the "possibility" of $Y = 1$. All this means is that the probability of $Y = 1$ is greater than zero.

We see the same basic asymmetry when we think in terms of $Y$ and its causes. The absence of a necessary cause is enough by itself to explain the $Y = 0$ cases. By contrast, the presence of a necessary cause is only a partial explanation for the $Y = 1$ cases. Work in cognitive psychology shows that people gravitate toward single-factor necessary condition explanations for $Y = 0$ cases but not for $Y = 1$ cases. Thus, when asked to explain failures or nonoccurrences, subjects are more likely to resort to one-variable necessary condition explanations. When asked to explain successes, they often have more complex, multivariate explanations that may not invoke any necessary conditions.

With sufficient conditions, the asymmetry works the other way: $X = 1$ generates a pinpoint prediction, whereas $X = 0$ makes a vague claim merely stating the outcome is possible.[2] Here the presence of a sufficient condition does a fine job explaining any $Y = 1$ case; by contrast, the absence of a sufficient condition says very little about a case's value on $Y$.

As one moves from dichotomous variables to continuously coded fuzzy-set variables, these same principles of asymmetry apply. With a necessary cause, for example, low values on $X$ make quite specific predictions about $Y$ values (i.e., $Y$ will be less than or equal to $X$). At the minimum, where $X = 0$, $Y$ must also be exactly zero. As values on $X$ become larger, the range of values that $Y$ can assume increases. At the maximum, where $X = 1$, $Y$ is free to assume any value and remain consistent with the hypothesis. The diagonal line that characterizes a necessary condition is built around this asymmetry: $Y$ is deeply constrained at low values of $X$ but not at high values.

## Examples of Asymmetric Explanations with Set-Theoretic Models

As Lieberson (1985, 63) points out, "most empirical studies operate with the assumption that social relations are symmetrical." This is certainly true for the quantitative culture, which constitutes a great deal of empirical research in the social sciences. Yet, in the qualitative culture, one finds many examples of asymmetric relationships.

Table 5.1 is a simple and understandable illustration (at least for academics) of an asymmetric relationship. The table contains actual data on admissions to a leading sociology department in 2009 (see Vaisey 2009). The set-theoretic interpretation is that scoring above the median (620) on the quantitative GREs is a virtual (only one exception) necessary condition for admission. This necessary condition formulation is an adequate explanation for the nonadmission of all students who scored below average. Students with low quantitative GRE scores can explain their rejection in terms of this

---

[2] In the social sciences, one rarely proposes a single factor that is sufficient all by itself for a positive outcome. Instead, one groups together multiple causes that are jointly sufficient for the outcome.

**Table 5.1**

Asymmetry in Two-Way Tables: Admissions to a Leading Sociology
Program, 2009

Quantitative GRE

| | < 620 | > 620 |
|---|---|---|
| Admit | 1 | 34 |
| No admit | 98 | 209 |

*Source:* Thanks to Stephen Vaisey for sharing these data. See also Vaisey (2009).

one variable. This is not the full story, of course, since most of these students would have (counterfactually) been rejected even if their scores had been higher. Most would have still lacked a set of conditions sufficient for admission. In this sense, their nonadmission was overdetermined. Nevertheless, their low GRE math scores were enough to virtually ensure their fate.

By comparing the students who were admitted with those who were not, we can see clearly that quantitative GRE scores are not a complete explanation of admission. Most students who score above average are still not admitted; additional factors play a role in separating the above average scorers into admissions and rejections.[3]

One might therefore ask about the various factors that cause admission. Assume that we have a simple—but pretty realistic—scenario: the factors that influence admission are (1) test scores, (2) GPA, (3) quality of undergraduate institution, and (4) letters of recommendation. A more realistic model would add a few additional factors (e.g., writing sample), but our points can be made with these four factors. A logit model of admission using these variables would be: $Y = \beta_0 + \beta_1 T + \beta_2 G + \beta_3 U + \beta_4 L + \epsilon$ ($T$—test scores, $G$—GPA, $U$—undergraduate institution, and $L$—letters of recommendation). A possible alternative set-theoretic model would be: $Y = T * G * (U + L)$. This model suggests the following explanation for failure: $\neg Y = \neg T + \neg G + (\neg U * \neg L)$. Thus, failure can be caused by low test scores or low grades or the combination of a low quality undergraduate institution and unimpressive letters.

With the logit model, notice how there is a single explanation of success and failure: the weighted sum of the causal factors is either high enough to cross some threshold of success or it is too low and leads to failure.[4]

---

[3] Of course, it is likely that variation in above average GRE quantitative scores contributed to the outcome as well.

[4] It is possible to construct a logit model with dichotomous variables where there are only a couple paths to success, and where the number paths to failure will be different from the paths to success (thanks to Thad Dunning for pointing this out). Obviously, the number of possible paths to success in a logit model will depend on the nature of the variables and the parameter

The whole model involves comparing zero cases with one cases. One cannot conceive writing separate logit models for the $Y = 1$ and $Y = 0$ cases.[5] By contrast, with the set-theoretic approach, the explanations of success and failure—while related and using the same factors—have different forms. There are two paths to success (i.e., $T * G * U$ and $T * G * L$), whereas there are three paths to failure (i.e., $\neg\, T$, $\neg\, G$, and $(\neg\, U * \neg\, L)$). At least three factors must be considered to achieve success, whereas one factor is often enough to generate a failure. This seems reasonably consistent with actual admissions procedures: committee members look for fatal flaws to quickly eliminate most applications, whereas they consider a range of factors and carefully read successful applications.

This simple example calls attention to an important feature of logic-based models:

> *Asymmetry of Explanation.* The explanation for failure is often different from the explanation for success.

The causes of a failure outcome are not necessarily equivalent to the absence or negation of the causes of the success outcome. In fact, in qualitative studies that use formal Boolean methods, such as Qualitative Comparative Analysis (QCA), researchers routinely arrive at quite different final models for the success and failure cases (Ragin 2000). The following three examples illustrate this point:

1. Wickham-Crowley (1992) explores the causes of successful revolutionary guerrilla movements in Latin America. His Boolean analysis shows that five conditions are individually necessary and jointly sufficient for successful social revolutions: (A) guerrilla attempt; (B) peasant support; (C) strong guerrilla military; (D) patrimonial praetorian regime; and (E) loss of U.S. support. Thus, his causal model for success is:

   Successful Social Revolution = $ABCDE$.

   By contrast, Wickham-Crowley's explanation of failed revolutionary guerrilla movements is quite different:

   Absence of Social Revolution = $ABd + bce + bcD$.

---

estimates. However, there will be many paths to success when continuous variables with non-extreme parameter estimates are used (as they commonly are).

[5] Statistical models that assume asymmetry do exist. For example, Markov transition matrices do not assume that the probability of transitioning to state $i$ from state $j$ is the same as the probability of moving in the opposite direction.

The asymmetry is obvious: there is one path with five factors to success, whereas there are three paths each containing three factors to failure. Notice that the causal effect of some of the individual factors depends heavily on context (i.e., the other factors with which they are combined). For example, causal factor B (peasant support for guerrillas) is necessary for social revolution, but also helps cause the absence of social revolution when a guerrilla attempt is led against a regime that is not patrimonial praetorian. One can also think about the asymmetry of these equations in the following way: whereas $ABd$ is enough to ensure the absence of social revolution, the reverse is not true. That is, negating these causes will not produce a social revolution.

2. Stokke (2007) considers the factors that lead targets to comply with international fishing regimes. He examines five causal factors: (A) Advice—explicit recommendations from the regime's scientific advisory body; (C) Commitment—the target's behavior explicitly violates a conservation measure; (S) Shadow of the future—perceived need of the target to strike new deals under the regime; (I) Inconvenience—the behavioral change is inconvenient for the target; and (R) Reverberation—the target risks being scandalized for not complying. Stokke's final model for success is the following:

$$Success = Ai + ARS.$$

Thus, there are two paths to success and clear scientific advice (A) is a necessary condition in general for successful compliance. One can run Stokke's data and generate a model of failure (i.e., not-Success):

$$Failure = sI + Ir.$$

Again, the equation of failure is not simply the negation of the equation for success; the equations are not symmetric. For example, the factor Advice is a necessary condition in the equation for success, but it does not appear at all in the equation for failure.

3. Mahoney (2010) argues that variations in Spanish colonialism can explain differences in long-run levels of economic development among the Latin American countries. At the most aggregate level, his explanation emphasizes three causal factors: (M) Mercantilist colonial core—country was heavily settled by Habsburg Spain (1500–1700); (L) Liberal colonial core—country was heavily settled by Bourbon Spain (1700–1821); and (W) Warfare—country experienced costly warfare

during postcolonial period. His aggregate findings can be summarized as follows:

Higher Economic Development = $mL + mlw$,

Intermediate Economic Development = $ML$,

Lower Economic Development = $Ml + mlW$.

Clearly, there is not a perfect symmetry across these explanations. There are two paths to a higher level of economic development: (1) a country can be a marginal territory during the Mercantilist Habsburg phase of colonialism and a core region during the Liberal Bourbon phase; or (2) a country can be marginal during both phases and then avoid costly Warfare during the postcolonial period. There is only one road to intermediate economic development, and it entails having been a colonial core during both the Mercantilist and Liberal phases. For this path, the occurrence of costly postcolonial warfare is irrelevant. Finally, there are two ways to achieve lower levels of development: (1) a country can be a core territory during the Mercantilist Habsburg phase of colonialism and a marginal region during the Liberal Bourbon phase; or (2) a country can be marginal during both phases and then experience costly Warfare during the postcolonial period.

Finally, to illustrate the potential value of looking for asymmetric relationships, let us consider the prize-winning article by Howard and Roessler (2006), "Liberalizing Electoral Outcomes in Competitive Authoritarian Regimes."[6] The dependent variable is the liberalization of the regime, not necessarily democratization, but rather movement in that direction. The key independent variable that we and they focus on is "opposition coalition." This means that groups and parties opposed to the government in power have formed a coalition in the forthcoming election (the unit of analysis is the election). Table 5.2 reproduces their statistical results.

The statistical findings in table 5.2 clearly show a strong effect for the opposition coalition variable. It is arguably the strongest relationship in the table, and rightly Howard and Roessler devote much of their attention to this variable. It is equally true that this variable explains both success and failure: absence goes with failure and presence with success. In the context of this chapter, we can ask whether the opposition coalition variable might work asymmetrically in explaining the outcome. In other words, is it possible that

---

[6] Thanks to Carsten Schneider for finding this example and letting us use it. See Schneider (2007) for an extensive reanalysis of these data.

**Table 5.2**

A Symmetric Statistical Model: Explaining Liberalizing Electoral Outcomes

| Independent variables | Parameter estimates |
| --- | --- |
| Opposition coalition | 7.8** (3.0) |
| Opposition mobilization | .91* (0.4) |
| Incumbent overthrow | 3.2* (1.5) |
| Economic growth | 0.3 (.2) |
| Foreign direct investment | −.1 (.3) |
| Foreign aid | .01 (.02) |
| Parliamentarism | −3.3 (2.2) |
| Regime openness | 1.0 (1.0) |
| Prior liberalizing change | −1.4 (1.7) |
| Constant | −1.3 (5.2) |
| N | 50 |

*Source:* Howard and Roessler 2006, 375.

*Note:* Standard errors in parentheses.

the effect of the presence of an opposition coalition is different than the effect of its absence?

Typically, all the reader knows is what is in the statistical results table, i.e., table 5.2. To explore whether there is causal asymmetry, one option would be to do a full-blown QCA analysis (see Schneider 2007). However, to keep things simple, we examine a 2×2 table (see table 5.3). As we saw in the "Mathematical Prelude," looking at data through set-theoretic eyes can result in interpretations that are different from statistical analyses.

On the one hand, it is easy to see why one might believe this table is an excellent example of causal symmetry: 73 percent (8/11) of the cases of opposition coalition result in liberalization, and 82 percent (32/39) of the cases of no opposition coalition result in no liberalization. Hence, the presence/absence of opposition coalition seems to predict presence/absence of liberalization in a quite symmetric way.

On the other hand, if we put on qualitative lenses, our attention is drawn to those cells that are almost empty. This way of viewing the data calls attention to potential asymmetries. Looking across the rows, we find that absence of an opposition coalition comes close to being a necessary condition for the absence of liberalization—i.e., 91 percent (32/35) of the no liberalization cases also lack an opposition coalition. This suggests that the absence of opposition is quite important in explaining failure.[7]

---

[7] A more extended analysis would explore the extent to which this is a trivial necessary condition or has low coverage (Goertz 2006; Ragin 2008).

**Table 5.3**

Statistical Analyses and Asymmetric Causation: Explaining Liberalizing
Electoral Outcomes

Opposition coalition

|  |  | 0 | 1 |
|---|---|---|---|
| LEO | 1 | 7 | 8 |
|  | 0 | 32 | 3 |

*Source:* Schneider 2007.

*Note:* LEO stands for liberalizing electoral outcome.

Of the cases that achieve liberalization, nearly 50 percent (7/15) manage
to achieve this success without an opposition coalition. Hence, the presence
of an opposition coalition is not at all necessary for success and is not
close to sufficient either. It would seem that there are paths to liberalization
that do not include the presence of an opposition coalition, but it seems
the path to failure almost always includes the absence of an opposition
coalition. Hence our little analysis of these data follows the same form as the
sociology admissions data. We have a variable which seems more important
for explaining failure than explaining success.

Obviously, this example is merely illustrative. We have not considered
the control variables and other factors that could lead to a different interpretation. Our key point is that those features of the data that stand out as
most important can vary a great deal depending on whether one is attuned to
symmetric patterns or asymmetric ones. Although the data themselves do not
change, the inference that one draws shifts depending on one's perspective.

## Conclusion

The basic causal models at the core of the two cultures differ on the issue
of symmetry. Set-theoretic models work with asymmetric relationships.
They assume that different values on $X$ may have different effects on $Y$.
Likewise, they routinely generate different explanations for different values
of $Y$ (e.g., success versus failure). By contrast, statistical models (as used in
real research) are usually symmetric. Linear regression models assume that
a given unit change on $X$ will have the same effect on $Y$ regardless of the
starting point of $X$. In a logit model, if the zeros are changed to ones for the
dependent variable, or vice versa, the same parameter estimate is generated
except with a sign flip. The explanation of nonoccurrence is the mirror image
of the explanation of occurrence.

We are not arguing that one approach is better than the other. Ultimately, the existence of symmetry versus asymmetry depends on the data and causal model being tested. However, we do believe that this difference is a critical reason why it is difficult to compare qualitative and quantitative causal models. It is hard to translate the fundamental symmetry of standard statistical models into the basic asymmetry of set-theoretic models. Analogously, it is hard to capture the asymmetry of set-theoretic models with the standard symmetric tools of statistics.

## References and Suggested Readings

The methodological literature generally does not call attention to the static causal symmetry of statistical models, though occasionally it is scrutinized (e.g., Abbott 2001, chapter 1). Standard discussions of Qualitative Comparative Analysis stress that, as a normal part of the methodology, one would separately estimate a model of success ($Y = 1$) and a model of failure ($Y = 0$) (for example, Ragin 2000, 2008 and Schneider and Wagemann forthcoming). The dynamic casual symmetry of statistical models is discussed and critiqued in Lieberson (1985, chapter 4). King, Keohane, and Verba (1994, 89–91) offer a brief reaction to Lieberson.

Abbott, A. 2001. *Time matters: on theory and method.* Chicago: University of Chicago Press.

Goertz, G. 2006. Assessing the trivialness, relevance and relative importance of necessary or sufficient conditions in social science. *Studies in Comparative International Development* 41:88-99.

Howard, M., and P. Roessler. 2006. Liberalizing electoral outcomes in competitive authoritarian regimes. *American Journal of Political Science* 50:365–81.

King, G., R. Keohane, and S. Verba. 1994. *Designing social inquiry: scientific inference in qualitative research.* Princeton: Princeton University Press.

Lieberson, S. 1985. *Making it count: the improvement of social research and theory.* Berkeley: University of California Press.

Mahoney, J. 2010. *Colonialism and postcolonial development: Spanish America in comparative perspective.* Cambridge: Cambridge University Press.

Ragin, C. 1987. *The comparative method: moving beyond qualitative and quantitative strategies.* Berkeley: University of California Press.

Ragin, C. 2000. *Fuzzy-set social science.* Chicago: University of Chicago Press.

Ragin, C. 2008. *Redesigning social inquiry: fuzzy sets and beyond.* Chicago: University of Chicago Press.

Schneider, C. 2007. Opposition in transition. does unity bring dictators down? A QCA re-analysis of Howard & Roessler's study of liberalizing electoral outcomes. Manuscript, Central European University.

Schneider, C., and C. Wagemann. Forthcoming. *Set-theoretic methods in the social sciences*. New York: Cambridge University Press.

Stokke, O. 2007. Qualitative comparative analysis, shaming, and international regime effectiveness. *Journal of Business Research* 60:501–11.

Vaisey, S. 2009. QCA 3.0: The "Ragin Revolution" continues. *Contemporary Sociology* 38:308–12.

Wickham-Crowley, T. 1992. *Guerrillas and revolution in Latin America: a comparative study of insurgents and regimes since 1956*. Princeton: Princeton University Press.

# Chapter 6

# Hume's Two Definitions of Cause

That and no other is to be called cause, at the presence of which
the effect always follows, and at whose removal the effect
disappears.
> —*Galileo*

Most causes are more accurately called INUS conditions.
> —*William R. Shadish, Thomas D. Cook, and*
> *Donald T. Campbell*

## Introduction

A famous quote from David Hume provides a useful way to discuss the
different approaches to causation in the quantitative and qualitative cultures:

> We may define a cause to be *an object followed by another, and where all
> the objects, similar to the first, are followed by objects similar to the second*
> [definition 1]. Or, in other words, *where, if the first object had not been, the second
> never would have existed* [definition 2]. (David Hume in *Enquiries Concerning
> Human Understanding, and Concerning the Principles of Morals*)

As many philosophers have suggested, Hume's phrase "in other words" is
problematic. The phrase makes it appear as if definition 1 and definition 2
are equivalent, when in fact they represent quite different approaches. Lewis
writes that "Hume's 'other words' ... are no mere restatement of his first
definition. They propose something altogether different: a counterfactual
analysis of causation" (Lewis 1986a, 160).

Following Lewis, we shall call Hume's definition 2 the "counterfactual definition." By contrast, we shall call definition 1 the "constant conjunction definition," to highlight Hume's idea that causes are always followed by their effects.[1] In this chapter, we consider how these two definitions are related to understandings of causation in the qualitative and quantitative research traditions.

It bears emphasizing that we are using Hume's ideas simply as a device for discussing the different ways in which the concept of "cause" is used in the quantitative and qualitative cultures. We are focusing on the implicit philosophical understandings of cause that help to animate the two paradigms. It is also worth noting that our interpretations should not be attributed to Hume himself. Hume's views on causation have been the source of enormous debate among philosophers, and we make no claim to resolving that debate.

## The Quantitative Tradition

Before the rise of the potential outcomes framework (see Morgan and Winship 2007), statistical discussions of causation focused on Hume's constant conjunction definition (definition 1) within a probabilistic framework. For example, Suppes, in an early and prominent analysis, wrote that "roughly speaking, the modification of Hume's analysis I propose is to say that one event is the cause of another if the appearance of the first event is followed with a high probability by the appearance of the second" (Suppes 1970, 10).[2] Under this probabilistic approach, it seems natural to understand the constant conjunction definition in terms of association: $X = 1$ is associated with $Y = 1$.

One can also develop a statistical interpretation of Hume's counterfactual definition (definition 2). Doing this requires some work, however, because Hume's counterfactual definition implies a single case. Unlike definition 1, which states "all objects [plural] are followed ...," definition 2 states "if the first object [singular] had ..." Interpreting definition 2 in a constant conjunction fashion, therefore, requires expanding Hume's idea to multiple cases.

---

[1] This view of causation underpins the covering law model formalized in mid-twentieth century social science. For example: "A [covering, scientific (Hempel 1965)] law has the form 'If conditions $C_1, C_2, \ldots, C_n$ obtain, then always $E$'" (Elster 1999, 5).

[2] Obviously, Suppes's account is more complex. Particularly when dealing with observational data, as opposed to experimental data, one must be concerned with spurious relationships and the like.

The quantitative tradition accomplishes this move by interpreting both definition 1 and definition 2 in terms of constant conjunction across many cases. A correlation of 1.00 means that there is a constant conjunction of $X = 1, Y = 1$ and of $X = 0, Y = 0$. Definitions 1 and 2 can thus be fused together into one statistical interpretation. Definition 1 holds that when the cause is present, the outcome will be present (probabilistically). Definition 2 holds that when the cause is absent, the outcome will be absent (probabilistically). Since it makes no statistical sense to just look at cases of $X = 1$ without cases of $X = 0$ (or vice versa), the two definitions become joined as one. Neither definition can stand alone and make statistical sense. But when fused together, they offer a coherent symmetric understanding of causation, one in which the emphasis is on what follows different values on the independent variable.

Currently, a leading view on causation among methodologists in political science and sociology is the potential outcomes framework. Perhaps its most important innovation within statistical circles was the emphasis on the counterfactual basis of causation. For example, Morgan and Winship's (2007) excellent overview is called *Counterfactuals and Causal Inference*. Earlier statistical and probabilistic accounts are understood to have ignored or underappreciated this crucial aspect of causation.

The Neyman-Rubin-Holland model at the core of this approach starts with the individual case and then builds a full-blown statistical model of causation. Using the basic experimental setup, an individual, $i$, is subject to a treatment. The counterfactual is then what *would have happened* if $i$ had received the control. Since the individual cannot receive both the treatment and control at the same time, one of the two possibilities must always remain a counterfactual. This reality leads to a fundamental problem:

*Fundamental Problem of Causal Inference.* It is impossible to *observe* the value of $Y_t(i)$ [$t$=treatment, $c$=control] and $Y_c(i)$ on the same unit and, therefore, it is impossible to *observe* the effect of $t$ on $i$. (Holland 1986, 947)

Since using statistics to estimate or evaluate causal effects requires relatively large amounts of actual data, the best the statistician can do is estimate the *average causal effect*, or, to use the more popular terminology, the average treatment effect (ATE) in the sample.

The important point is that the statistical solution replaces the impossible-to-observe causal effect of $t$ on a specific unit with the possible-to-estimate *average* causal effect of $t$ over a population of units. (Holland 1986, 947)

The arrival at ATE as the basis for a counterfactual theory of causation completes what we call the "causal inference circle" (in analogy to the hermeneutic circle) in the quantitative culture:

1. One starts with Hume's definition 2, which stresses the counterfactual for subject $i$.

2. One interprets the definition using algebra and statistics: the counterfactual is the *difference* between treatment and control, $Y_t(i) - Y_c(i)$ (Holland 1986, 947).

3. One applies definition 1 in its constant conjunction form for treatment and control separately, i.e., for $X = 1$ and $X = 0$.

4. One calculates the average difference between treatment and control in all the cases, i.e., ATE.

5. The ATE then provides the individual case counterfactual for subject $i$.

In this circle, Hume's constant conjunction definition 1 is doing the heavy lifting, even though the starting point is his counterfactual definition 2. The counterfactual starting point raises an impossible to resolve problem. As a result, the scholar must quickly turn to definition 1 and use notions of constant conjunction for both treatment and control to make any headway. The consequence is, however, that this framework follows earlier statistical approaches in reducing the counterfactual definition 2 to the constant conjunction definition 1 in the actual practice of estimating causal effects.

## The Qualitative Tradition

Looking at things from the perspective of the qualitative tradition, Hume's definitions can be understood in terms of logic. Philosophers and qualitative methodologists focus on the logical form of the constant conjunction definition: "If $X = 1$, then $Y = 1$." Reading the if–then clause as a statement of logic, definition 1 treats "cause" as a relationship of *sufficiency* between $X$ and $Y$. This sufficiency interpretation calls attention to the $X = 1$ cases (i.e., cases where the cause is present). The researcher starts with the cause being present, and then looks to see if there is a corresponding effect. In this sense, the qualitative interpretation of definition 1 is similar to the quantitative one.

At this point, however, the two traditions part company. A qualitative interpretation does not suggest the further inference that Hume's constant conjunction definition implies a correlation between $X = 0$ and $Y = 0$ cases. Rather, this view suggests that if the cause is *not* present, the outcome could be either present or absent. A qualitative interpretation treats definition 1 as a claim about sufficiency that can be investigated in its own right. Thus, unlike the statistical interpretation which fuses together definitions 1 and 2, the sufficiency interpretation of definition 1 stands completely on its own, and it can be valid independent of the conclusions reached when using definition 2.

Another key difference between the two traditions related to definition 1 concerns the fact that effects rarely always follow individual, single causes (at least in the social sciences). As we saw above, quantitative approaches have long addressed this issue with probabilistic assumptions. Although these assumptions are also sometimes incorporated into qualitative research, another standard solution is to link causal sufficiency with "multiple, conjunctural" causation (Ragin 1987). As discussed in the chapter "Causal models," qualitative researchers treat causation as combinatorial or "conjunctural" in the sense that several *different* causes must combine together, e.g., $X_1 * X_2 * X_3$, to generate an outcome. Individual causes, e.g., $X_1$, are not sufficient for the outcome by themselves.

At the same time, qualitative researchers treat causal sufficiency as potentially "multiple" in the sense that there are often "different combinations" of factors that are each sufficient for the same outcome. This is the general principle of equifinality: no single package of causes generates all $Y = 1$ outcomes. Different packages each lead to the same result. This idea is critical in the context of definition 1; the implication is that a value of zero on a given sufficiency package does not imply that $Y = 0$ because other causal packages might yield $Y = 1$.

This logic-based approach generates its own chain of reasoning for starting with Hume's definition 1 and arriving at the individual case:

1. One starts with Hume's definition 1, which stresses constant conjunction.

2. One interprets this definition to mean that $X = 1$ is sufficient for $Y = 1$.

3. One treats $X$ as consisting of a package of causal factors, e.g., $X_1 * X_2 * X_3$.

4. One establishes a generalization that all causal packages $X_1 * X_2 * X_3$ "are followed by" $Y = 1$.

5. If case $i$ has $X_1 * X_2 * X_3$, then this package is interpreted as the cause of $Y = 1$.[3]

---

[3] This final inference about $i$ assumes that the generalization in step 4 is valid. This is analogous to our previous assumption that there is a significant average treatment effect.

We thus end up with a causal claim about case $i$, just as we did for the statistical causal inference circle. Despite this similarity, the steps used in the process of reasoning are quite distinct, and the nature of the causal claim about $i$ at the end is clearly different. The statistical approach uses both definitions 1 and 2, while this version of the qualitative approach uses only definition 1.

Hume's counterfactual definition 2 can also be viewed from the lens of logic. Within philosophy, counterfactual aspects of causation have long received attention. Arguably the most influential account of causation within philosophy for decades was that of David Lewis. His book *Counterfactuals* was originally published in 1973, well in advance of the rediscovery of counterfactuals in statistics. Consistent with Hume's definition 2, Lewis develops his counterfactual definition in terms of the *individual* case:

> My analysis is meant to apply to causation in particular cases. It is not an analysis of causal generalizations. (Lewis 1986a, 161–62)

> Event $e$ depends causally on the distinct event $c$ iff, if $c$ had not occurred, $e$ would not have occurred. (Lewis 1986b, 242)

Other literatures outside of statistics also emphasize causation in individual cases, including Max Weber's famous analysis of counterfactuals (1949) and Hart and Honoré's (1985) analysis of causation in the law. When the focus is on individual events, the counterfactual account is the natural choice (including in the potential outcomes framework).

Much of the philosophical literature on counterfactuals remains at the single case level, but general explanations are often a central goal of social science, and hence it is of particular interest to social scientists to see how definition 2 can be reformulated in terms of causal regularities. The key move in the qualitative tradition is to interpret the counterfactual in terms of a necessary condition. Thus, using logic, one can restate definition 2 in the following way: if $\neg X_i$, then $\neg Y_i$. This seems completely natural since Hume says "if the first object had not been." Hypotheses about necessary causes bring us back to Hume's constant conjunction definition 1 in the sense that the focus returns to many cases and general patterns.

The process through which qualitative researchers generalize counterfactuals suggests another causal inference circle that begins with definition 2:

1. One starts with Hume's definition 2, which stresses the counterfactual.

2. One interprets this definition in terms of logic: if $X$ had not occurred, then $Y$ would not have occurred, i.e., if $\neg X_i$, then $\neg Y_i$.

3. One generalizes the individual case counterfactual to all cases, i.e., if $\neg X$ then $\neg Y$ for all $i$.[4]

4. One converts this counterfactual into a general statement, using definition 1, about a necessary cause; that is, $X$ is necessary for $Y$.

5. If $X$ is present in case $i$ then $X$ is a cause of $Y$.

In this circle, the key move is the conversion of the individual case counterfactual into a regularity statement about a necessary cause. In effect, the analyst stays with definition 2 throughout the circle, bringing in definition 1 to produce a generalization across cases. The retention of definition 2 is accomplished by assuming that the definition can be directly extended to many cases, thus allowing for the generalization.

## Conclusion

Hume's famous quotation contains two definitions of causation. Definition 1 suggests a constant conjunction between cause and effect, such that effects always follow causes. This definition assumes many cases and has affinities with quantitative views on causation. Definition 2 suggests a counterfactual view of causation, in which the absence of a cause leads to the absence of an outcome. This definition is built around a single case and has important linkages to qualitative views of causation.

Although it seems natural that quantitative scholars would gravitate more toward definition 1, in recent years, as attention has turned to counterfactuals, definition 2 has become the starting point for defining causation among statistical methodologists. Nevertheless, the quantitative approach quickly sets aside the counterfactual notion of causation as applied to individual cases out of a conviction that it is impossible to estimate this kind of causation. In the statistical culture, there are really not two different definitions, because each one individually would make no sense. The statistical approach fuses the definitions into one in moving from the impossible to estimate definition 2 to the possible to estimate ATE.

In the qualitative tradition, the two definitions remain separate. Definition 1 is understood to represent a claim about causal sufficiency, whereas definition 2 is understood to represent a claim about a necessary condition. As a result, different sets of scholars may gravitate toward one definition

---

[4] Of course, if $\neg X$ then $\neg Y$ is equivalent to if $Y = 1$ then $X = 1$. However, this formulation reverses the causal direction of the counterfactual version. The "if $Y = 1$ then $X = 1$" formulation nonetheless remains important for empirical testing, since often one uses this version for case selection (see the chapter "Case Selection and Hypothesis Testing").

rather than the other. Scholars who use methods such as Qualitative Comparative Analysis for testing causal sufficiency may gravitate more naturally toward definition 1 and the sufficiency approach (Ragin 1987). By contrast, qualitative scholars who explore hypotheses about necessary causes may more naturally embrace the counterfactual definition 2 (Goertz and Starr 2003). Nevertheless, these two definitions of causation easily coexist since they are rooted in the same tradition of logic and set theory.

Is there a right interpretation of Hume's two definitions? Although we are not historians of philosophy, we think that one's view of the most *useful* interpretation of Hume will be strongly influenced by one's methodological background and approach. Our own view, consistent with the two cultures argument, is that each interpretation makes good sense within the overall tradition within which it is embedded.

## References and Suggested Readings

Hume's discussion of cause figures prominently throughout the philosophical literature on causation. It is the point of departure for such influential works as Suppes's (1970) probabilistic theory of causation, Lewis's (1973) counterfactual definition of cause, Mackie's (1980) discussion of INUS causes, Salmon's (1998) "ontic" or mechanistic view of causality, and the more recent work of Baumgartner (2008; 2009). Famous works on logic (e.g., Copi 1982) and causation in the law (Hart and Honoré 1985) also centrally engage Hume. A classic treatment of Hume's views is Beauchamp and Rosenberg (1981). In the social sciences, methodologists have given less attention to Hume's writings on causality, though his work is discussed in Holland (1986), Goertz and Starr (2003), and especially Brady (2008). Along with Holland, the core works making up the Neyman-Holland-Rubin definition of causality (ATE) discussed in this chapter are Neyman (1923/1990) and Rubin (1974; 1978). See also King, Keohane, and Verba (1994) and Morgan and Winship (2007).

Baumgartner, M. 2008. Regularity theories reassessed. *Philosophia* 36:327–54.
Baumgartner, M. 2009. Inferring causal complexity. *Sociological Methods & Research* 38:71–101.
Beauchamp, T. L., and A. Rosenberg. 1981. *Hume and the problem of causation.* Oxford: Oxford University Press.
Brady, H. E. 2008. Causation and explanation in social science. In *The Oxford handbook of political methodology*, edited by J. M. Box-Steffensmeier, H. E. Brady, and D. Collier. Oxford: Oxford University Press.
Copi, I. M. 1982. *Introduction to logic,* 6th edition. New York: Macmillan.
Elster, J. 1999. *Strong feelings: emotion, addiction, and human behavior.* Cambridge: MIT Press.

Goertz, G. 2006. Assessing the trivialness, relevance, and relative importance of necessary or sufficient conditions in social science. *Studies in Comparative International Development* 41:88–109.

Goertz, G., and H. Starr, eds. 2003. *Necessary conditions: theory, methodology, and applications.* New York: Rowman & Littlefield.

Hart, H. L. A., and T. Honoré. 1985. *Causation in the law,* 2nd edition. Oxford: Oxford University Press.

Hempel, C. 1965. *Aspects of scientific explanation.* New York: Free Press.

Holland, P. 1986. Statistics and causal inference (with discussion). *Journal of the American Statistical Association* 81:945–60.

Hume, D. 1975 (1777). *Enquiries concerning human understanding, and concerning the principles of morals.* Oxford: Oxford University Press.

King, G., R. Keohane, and S. Verba. 1994. *Designing social inquiry: scientific inference in qualitative research.* Princeton: Princeton University Press.

Lewis, D. 1973. *Counterfactuals.* Cambridge: Harvard University Press.

Lewis, D. 1986a. Causation. Postscripts to "Causation." *Philosophical papers, vol. 2.* Oxford: Oxford University Press.

Lewis, D. 1986b. Causal explanation. *Philosophical papers, vol. 2.* Oxford: Oxford University Press.

Mackie, J. 1980. *The cement of the universe: a study of causation.* Oxford: Oxford University Press.

Morgan, S., and C. Winship. 2007. *Counterfactuals and causal inference: methods and principles for social research.* Cambridge: Cambridge University Press.

Neyman, J. 1923/1990. On the application of probability theory to agricultural experiments: essay on principles. *Statistical Science* 5:465–72.

Pearl, J. 2000. *Causality: models, reasoning, and inference.* Cambridge: Cambridge University Press.

Ragin, C. 1987. *The comparative method: moving beyond qualitative and quantitative strategies.* Berkeley: University of California Press.

Ragin, C. 2008. *Redesigning social inquiry: fuzzy sets and beyond.* Chicago: University of Chicago Press.

Rubin, D. B. 1974. Estimating causal effects of treatments in randomized and nonrandomized studies. *Journal of Educational Psychology* 66:688–701.

Rubin, D. B. 1978. Bayesian inference for causal effects: the role of randomization. *The Annals of Statistics* 6:34–58.

Rubin, D. B. 1990. Comment: Neyman (1923) and causal inference in experiments and observational studies. *Statistical Science* 5:472–80.

Salmon, W. C. 1998. *Causality and explanation.* Oxford: Oxford University Press.

Schneider, C., and C. Wagemann. Forthcoming. *Set-theoretic methods in the social sciences.* New York: Cambridge University Press.

Suppes, P. 1970. *A probabilistic theory of causality.* Amsterdam: North Holland.

Weber, M. 1949. *Max Weber on the methodology of the social sciences.* New York: Free Press.

# PART II

Within-Case Analysis

# Chapter 7

# Within-Case versus Cross-Case Causal Analysis

Within-case comparisons are critical to the viability of small-N analysis.
—*David Collier*

## Introduction

One of the most basic differences between the qualitative and quantitative traditions concerns the relative importance of within-case versus cross-case analysis for causal inference. In qualitative research, there is always a major focus on specific events and processes taking place within each individual case. Leading qualitative methodologies of hypothesis testing, such as process tracing and counterfactual analysis, are fundamentally methods of within-case analysis. To use these methods, qualitative analysts must locate key observations from within their individual cases.

Qualitative studies also often include a cross-case component. This is true for both small-N studies, which are relatively common in the social sciences, and medium-N qualitative studies, which are not common (see the appendix). While some leverage can be gained by increasing the N of qualitative studies, if the total number of cases remains small, the main basis for causal inference must derive from within-case analysis. Small-N comparison usually does not permit strong cross-case tests of hypotheses.[1] Only when the N of a qualitative study increases beyond a small number of cases does it become possible to engage in strong hypothesis testing with cross-case methods.

[1] Small-N comparison does allow for certain tests, such as tests designed to eliminate hypotheses positing potential necessary or sufficient causes.

By contrast, quantitative research traditionally involves exclusively cross-case comparison. Because they work with large-N datasets, quantitative scholars often know little about most of their cases. In survey research, for example, the scholar virtually by definition knows almost nothing about the individuals responding, beyond their answers to the specific questions asked. The same is true when scholars use large-N datasets for countries: they do not know very much or anything about many countries beyond the variables measured. Given human and resource limitations, it is unrealistic to expect large-N researchers to have expertise for most of their cases.

Nevertheless, because quantitative researchers systematically measure and compare cases across specified variables, they can and do derive inferences from cross-case tests. The large number of cases they analyze allows, in principle, for strong tests that reach findings that are not simply the product of chance or the result of confounding variables. Insofar as quantitative researchers are oriented toward combining their large-N cross-case analysis with in-depth case studies, they move toward a different research design—a mixed-method research design. When mixed-method research is pursued, quantitative analysts combine cross-case and within-case analysis in a single study.

In general, nevertheless, small-N qualitative inferences depend mainly on within-case analysis, whereas large-N quantitative inferences depend mainly on cross-case analysis. One can thus state the difference between the two paradigms that concerns us in this chapter quite sharply:

> In small-N qualitative research, the main leverage for causal inference derives from within-case analysis, with cross-case methodologies some-times playing a supporting role.

> In large-N statistical research, the main leverage for causal inference derives from cross-case analysis, with within-case methodologies some-times playing a supporting role.

The distinction between within-case and cross-case analysis runs through many of the contrasts discussed in this book. It is also central to the contrast between qualitative and quantitative research drawn out in leading works on qualitative and multi-method research, such as George and Bennett (2005) and Collier, Brady, and Seawright (2010).

## Within-Case Analysis in Case-Study/Small-N Research versus Experimental/Statistical Research

It is useful to briefly contrast the typical roles (or nonroles) of within-case and cross-case analysis in case studies versus experiments. First, consider an explanatory case study, where one seeks to explain why a particular case has a specific outcome. By definition, a case study focuses mainly on a single case, such that cross-case analysis is not the central mode of inference. Contrasts and comparisons, implicit and explicit, with other cases may well be made. In addition, when testing hypotheses with process tracing and counterfactual analysis, the researcher will draw on established generalizations and findings from other cases. However, a case study—by definition—is primarily a sustained analysis of a single case.

In the effort to formulate a good explanation, the case-study researcher will inevitably carry out an over-time, processual analysis of the case. Many different observations at different points in time will be considered. The analyst will normally identify historical junctures when key events directed the case toward certain outcomes and not others. She or he may well pause to consider how small changes during these junctures might have led the case to follow a different path. Consideration will also be given to the ways in which historical events are linked across time, one leading to another, yielding a sequence of causes that culminate in the outcome of interest. The overall explanation likely will be rich with details about specific events, conjunctures, and contingencies.

Now consider an experimental study, where one seeks to estimate the effect of some treatment of interest. The effort to formulate a valid answer will usually involve entirely cross-case analysis. The researcher will try to *isolate* the effect of the treatment of interest. Random assignment to treatment and control groups for large numbers of individuals (or other units) ideally serves to neutralize the prior effects of history and all other confounding causes. An experiment is precisely designed to tell us about causal effects net of everything else, including context and history. Experiments are, in this sense, fundamentally cross-case designs.

The differences in the use of within-case and cross-case analysis in a case study versus a randomized study are largely reproduced as one moves to small-N qualitative research and large-N statistical research as normally practiced in contemporary political science and sociology. Small-N qualitative researchers remain centrally concerned with tracing within-case processes in order to explain particular outcomes. While many qualitative studies employ cross-case analysis and often use simple methods of matching, such as Mill's method of difference, the narrative remains centered on within-case processes. Indeed, unless the N of the study is more than a handful of cases, it is unrealistic to believe that these small-N comparative methods—by themselves—offer a strong basis for most kinds of causal inference. Without any within-case analysis, the leverage gained for testing explanations when moving from one case to three or four cases is modest. The within-case analysis must do the heavy lifting for hypothesis testing.

The large-N quantitative culture, by contrast, retains much of the experimental focus of using cross-case analysis to estimate causal effects net of all other influences. To be sure, time-series statistical techniques—the natural quantitative analogue for process tracing—have been around for decades (e.g., Box and Jenkens 1976). However, pure time-series analyses are quite rare in political science and sociology. Interrupted time-series analysis also has a long history (e.g., Campbell and Stanley 1963), but it has received a new lease on life—and name—with the recent emphasis on regression discontinuity designs (e.g., Dunning 2012). In practice, statistical results often depend on a varying (and almost never analyzed) mix of time-series and cross-sectional variance. For any given study, one can ask how much of the variance is cross-sectional and how much is time-series. Yet even in areas where it seems like there is a strong time-series component—e.g., the comparison of 20 industrial states over a period of 30 years—most of the variation is cross-sectional. Thus, while many quantitative analyses examine processes over time within a case, the cross-sectional element overwhelmingly drives the results in published research.

## Causal-Process Observations versus Data-Set Observations

The relative importance of within-case versus cross-case analysis in the two cultures is highlighted in Collier, Brady, and Seawright's (2010) discussion of the main kind of observations used to gain leverage for causal inference in qualitative versus quantitative research. They link causal inference in qualitative research to the use of "causal-process observations" (CPOs), which imply and require within-case analysis. By contrast, the main observations used for causal inference in quantitative research are "data-set observations" (DSOs), which presuppose a cross-sectional research design.

A CPO is "an insight or piece of data that provides information about context or mechanism and contributes ... leverage in causal inference" (Collier, Brady, and Seawright 2010, 184). As the concept's label and definition suggest, causal-process observations are specific pieces of information gathered from within cases that allow researchers to assess whether a given causal factor exerts the causal role assigned to it by a hypothesis or theory.

Three examples serve to illustrate some uses of CPOs in qualitative within-case analysis:

1. Luebbert (1991, 308–9) uses CPOs from within Germany to refute Gerschenkron's (1943) and Moore's (1966) thesis that a fascist regime is caused by a landed elite that delivers mass peasant support in favor of fascism. He points to evidence showing that landed elites

in Germany could not deliver large numbers of rural votes. In fact, rural support for fascism was found mainly in areas where the family peasantry predominated, not where landed elites were located. These observations, though small in number and drawn from within a single case, strongly challenge the Gerschenkron-Moore thesis about the origins of fascism.

2. Walt (1996) hypothesizes that revolutions cause wars. To test this hypothesis, he develops a theory of the intervening mechanisms through which revolutions lead to wars. These mechanisms include changes in the preferences and capacities of the revolutionary state as well as changes in the revolutionary state's relationship with other states (e.g., creating new conflicts of interests and spirals of suspicion). The mechanisms suggest specific CPOs that should be present within cases if the theory is correct. Walt's empirical analysis focuses on seven case studies in which revolution is associated with war. The strength of the argument, however, is not the simple correlation between revolution and war across this small N. Rather the main empirical support for the argument stems from the fact that Walt is able to point to CPOs within each case that correspond to his predicted mechanisms.

3. Tannenwald (1999) argues that the existence of a "nuclear taboo"—a normative prohibition against nuclear weapons that "has stigmatized nuclear weapons as unacceptable weapons of mass destruction"— is a cause of the nonuse of nuclear weapons by the United States since World War II. Beck (2006) raises the concern that Tannenwald analyzes only four DSOs (i.e., four historical episodes) and thus has a tiny sample. By contrast, Brady, Collier, and Seawright (2006) argue that the main leverage for causal inference in Tannenwald's study comes from CPOs, not her four DSOs. In particular, Tannenwald calls attention to specific conversations among high level decision makers that suggest sustained discussion and even consideration of nuclear use was inhibited by prevailing norms. The strength of her study is not based mainly on the comparison of the four historical periods, but rather on her ability to find considerable within-case evidence of increasingly strong normative prohibitions in the debate about the use of nuclear weapons.

As these examples suggest, qualitative researchers identify CPOs in conjunction with the study of events and processes taking place within cases. The CPOs gathered in these studies are not variable scores to be assembled into a rectangular dataset. They are specific within-case observations that have bearing on the hypothesis being considered for that particular case. For instance, some of Tannenwald's key data are specific statements from foreign policy decision makers who appear constrained in their ability to bring up the possibility of using nuclear weapons. The force of her argument derives from the fact that these statements would not exist unless there was some normative prohibition stigmatizing the use of nuclear weapons in the United States—i.e., a nuclear taboo. Likewise, Luebbert's expertise on Germany provided him with specialized information that seriously challenged the idea that landed elites were responsible for the delivery of votes in favor of fascism. Scholars with only superficial knowledge of German history would not have been able to make this argument.

By contrast, the standard observation in quantitative research is a DSO, which is equivalent to a row in a rectangular data set—i.e., the scores for a given case on all measured variables. In mainstream statistical research, adding DSOs is a standard method for increasing degrees of freedom. Potentially isolated and noncomparable observations from within particular cases—i.e., CPOs—are not used in the quantitative paradigm. If information applies to only one or a small number of cases, it will often be discarded because it cannot be used in conjunction with statistical tests.

Collecting DSOs for statistical tests requires within-case data only in the sense that the analyst must measure specific variables across a large number of cases. The analyst need not have any specialized knowledge about any specific cases. The historical details and particularities of the individual cases are not relevant to the statistical test. One can, in principle, do a good job testing a causal model while knowing little about the features of individual cases beyond their scores on the measured variables.[2]

In sum, when qualitative and quantitative analysts "add new observations" to their studies, they often mean very different things. For qualitative researchers, this often means the discovery of new pieces of evidence or facts from within particular cases. It is similar to the discovery of new clues in detective work: novel facts are uncovered that allow one to make stronger inferences regarding hypotheses or theories that pertain to specific cases. By contrast, for quantitative researchers, adding new observations normally means adding new cases—i.e., adding new instances of the main unit of analysis. In the quantitative tradition, it is hard to think about adding observations without increasing the size of the N. But in qualitative research, the addition of CPOs normally does not affect the number of cases. In fact, in case-study research, one may work with a single case (i.e., one DSO) but have several telling CPOs that provide a strong basis for causal inference (Collier, Brady, and Seawright 2010).

---

[2] However, the task of correctly specifying the causal model to be tested statistically may require good qualitative knowledge of cases.

## Process-Tracing Tests versus Statistical Tests

The prolific use of process tracing in qualitative research also illustrates the importance of within-case analysis for this tradition. Although process tracing is not the only within-case mode of hypothesis testing available to qualitative researchers (e.g., see the chapter "Counterfactuals"), it is a central qualitative method, and it offers a sharp contrast to mainstream statistical methods of hypothesis testing, which are based on cross-case analysis.

Process tracing is used to evaluate hypotheses about the causes of a specific outcome in a particular case.[3] The method is built around two main kinds of tests: hoop tests and smoking gun tests (Van Evera 1997). As we shall see, there is an inherent connection between process tracing tests, generalizations about necessary and/or sufficient conditions, and the use of specific within-case observations (i.e., CPOs).

### *Hoop Tests*

A hoop test proposes that a given piece of evidence must be present within an individual case for a hypothesis about that case to be valid (Van Evera 1997). While passing a hoop test does not confirm a hypothesis, failing a hoop test eliminates the hypothesis. In this sense, the presence of the evidence posited by the hoop test is a *necessary condition* for the hypothesis to be valid (Bennett 2008).

Hoop tests can concern the independent variable, the dependent variable, or a mechanism (see Collier 2011; Mahoney 2010; forthcoming). When the test concerns the independent or dependent variable, the analyst uses CPOs to establish whether the cause and outcome occurred in the ways posited by the hypothesis under investigation. Often hoop tests challenge hypotheses by calling into question the descriptive facts of a case.

For example, as discussed in the chapter "Causal Models," Brady (2010) uses hoop tests in his analysis of the effect of the early media call that proclaimed an Al Gore victory in the 2000 presidential elections in Florida. He does so by identifying a series of conditions that are *necessary* for the early media call to have cost Bush the vote of the Florida resident *i*. These necessary conditions include the following four: (1) the resident lived in the eastern Panhandle counties of Florida; (2) the resident had not already voted when the media call was made; (3) the resident heard the media call; and (4) the resident favored Bush.

On the basis of these hoop tests, Brady eliminates nearly all Florida residents as possible lost votes for Bush. In fact, he estimates that only 280

---

[3] Process tracing can also be used for hypothesis and theory formulation.

residents can pass all four of the hoop tests. Of this 280, he reasons that most of them were not deterred from voting (e.g., people vote for reasons other than the fact that their single vote will determine the president). This brings his estimate down to 28 to 56 lost votes (he quadruples this estimate to reach an upper bound estimate of 224). But it is the hoop tests that do the heavy lifting in Brady's argument.

Analysts can also use hoop tests to explore whether there is, in fact, a causal connection between an independent variable and a dependent variable. These hoop tests direct attention to intervening mechanisms between the posited cause and outcome. For example, consider Luebbert's rejection of the Gerschenkron-Moore hypothesis mentioned previously (i.e., labor repressive landed elites were a key cause of fascism in Germany). A necessary condition for this hypothesis to be valid is that landed elites directly or indirectly control the peasantry such that peasants vote in favor of fascist candidates. Yet Luebbert shows, using within-case data from Germany, that this mechanism was not present. Landed elites in Germany either could not deliver peasant votes or, if they could, they were more concerned with maintaining patronage networks and actually supported liberal candidates. Hence, the hypothesis fails the hoop test and is cast away.

Failing a hoop test is a standard way of falsifying a hypothesis. But does passing a hoop test lend strong evidence in favor of a hypothesis? The answer is "it depends." Specifically, it depends on the relative difficulty of the hoop test. Passing a difficult hoop test does lend substantial positive support in favor of a hypothesis, but passing an easy hoop test does not. Just as some hoops are smaller than others, and thus more difficult to jump through, some hoop tests are more demanding and thus harder to pass (Mahoney forthcoming).

The relative difficulty of passing a hoop test is directly related to the frequency at which the condition necessary for the hypothesis to be valid appears in the data or real world. If the condition is almost always present, the hoop test is easy, since the hypothesis will almost automatically pass. By contrast, if the condition necessary for the hypothesis to be valid is quite rare or abnormal to a given context, the hoop test will be hard to pass (see Hart and Honoré 1985; Braumoeller and Goertz 2000; Goertz 2006; Ragin 2008).

## Smoking Gun Tests

Smoking gun tests propose that if certain specific pieces of evidence (i.e., specific CPOs) are present, then the hypothesis must be valid. Passing a smoking gun test lends decisive support in favor of a hypothesis, though failing a smoking gun test does not eliminate a hypothesis. In this sense, the presence of the CPOs identified in a smoking gun test are a *sufficient condition* for the validity of a hypothesis.[4]

As with hoop tests, smoking gun tests can concern an independent variable, the dependent variable, or a mechanism. In the Tannenwald study, for example, she uses smoking gun tests to establish that her main independent variable—the nuclear taboo—existed. She has several specific examples in which decision makers are normatively constrained in their ability to even raise the issue of using nuclear weapons in foreign policy discussions. Core smoking gun evidence is closed door discussions of decision makers. Their comments—smoke—would not make any sense if there were not a gun in the form of the nuclear taboo.

While passing a smoking gun test counts as strong evidence in favor of a hypothesis, the consequences of failing a smoking gun test can vary. Some smoking gun tests are easier to fail than others. Failing an easy smoking gun test provides evidence that a hypothesis is not valid. As an example, consider John Snow's (1855, 1965; see also Freedman 1991) famous work showing that cholera is an infectious disease rather than a product of noxious odors in the air (i.e., miasmas). A relatively easy smoking gun test in favor of the miasma theory would be to show that the disease sometimes spreads to new areas (e.g., islands) without being brought to these places by human carriers. Yet Snow discovered exactly the opposite: the disease always follows the paths of human travel. Although this evidence does not completely refute the miasma theory, it certainly counts heavily against it. By contrast, failing a hard smoking gun test does not provide much disconfirming evidence. If the smoking gun test is quite difficult to pass, one would not necessarily expect the hypothesis to pass it, even if it is valid. For example, the concrete identification of 10,000 specific individuals in the Florida panhandle who wanted to vote for Bush but chose not to after hearing the premature media call would be smoking gun evidence in favor of Lott's (2000) argument. Yet this is a very difficult smoking gun test, and the fact that it cannot be supported does not count heavily against Lott's argument. Instead, Brady (2010) works to refute the argument by carrying out hoop tests.

The relative difficulty of a smoking gun test is related to the more general commonality of the condition (i.e., the CPO) used in the test. All smoking gun tests make reference to a condition (or a combination of conditions) whose presence is sufficient for the validity of the hypothesis under investigation. However, the frequency at which this condition is present can vary. Hypotheses that fail a smoking gun test in which the condition is often present or "normal" in a given context are more likely to

---

[4] Sherlock Holmes is famous for saying that once you have eliminated all the impossible explanations (i.e., hoop tests), then the remaining one must be true. This suggests that one could possibly arrive at the correct explanation purely using hoop tests.

be wrong than hypotheses that fail a smoking gun test in which the condition is only rarely present.

We suspect that scholars are not often able to use strong smoking gun tests to confirm hypotheses in the social sciences. The typical evidence collected is more like shell casings than a smoking gun: its presence suggests a smoking gun, but the smoking gun itself is not observed. Normally, several key pieces of evidence need to be combined together to make a really convincing case. To continue with the metaphor, the presence of the shell casings in combination with the fact that the suspect had a gun matching those casings starts to look more like evidence sufficient to confirm the hypothesis. Or to return to the case of Snow's research on cholera: he used many different kinds of evidence to support the infectious disease theory (see the chapter "Causal Mechanisms and Process Tracing").

The fact that qualitative researchers often combine several pieces of evidence together to try to arrive at sufficiency accords nicely with the typical causal model used in this tradition—i.e., a conjunctural model in which *combinations of factors* are sufficient for outcomes. The upshot is that a convincing explanation of a case normally requires several bits of evidence that add up to a smoking gun explanation. A single observation is rarely enough to support a hypothesis. By contrast, individual pieces of evidence can easily mean the failure of a hoop test and thus the rejection of a hypothesis. This helps to explain why qualitative researchers often find that it is easier to use within-case analysis to eliminate a hypothesis than to convincingly support a hypothesis.

## Conclusion

Although cross-case and within-case analysis are, respectively, the central modes of causal inference in large-N and small-N analysis, there is certainly no reason why one cannot design a research project that draws on both types of analysis. In fact, best practices in both cultures often point toward research designs that combine the two.

On the quantitative side, as discussed further in the next chapter, it is increasingly common for statistical researchers to supplement their work with qualitative case studies. A causal variable from a regression analysis can be examined with case studies to determine whether it works in ways posited by the theory being tested. With this supplementary analysis, the researcher uses within-case analysis and searches for those CPOs that have probative value in assessing the causal impact of the variable. On the side of qualitative research, when a researcher develops a finding for one or a small number of cases, it is natural to ask if the finding applies more generally (see the chapter "Scope"). Consequently, the small-N finding might stimulate a broader cross-case test using a larger N (Lijphart 1971).

In short, while most research *as practiced* depends mainly on either cross-case analysis or within-case analysis, the two modes can and (according to many leading methodologists) often should be combined. The growing popularity of different kinds of multimethod research suggests that scholars increasingly are finding ways for achieving this synthesis.

## References and Suggested Readings

Discussions of within-case analysis—under various names—have a long history in the field of qualitative methodology. See Barton and Lazarsfeld's (1955) "process analysis," Smelser's (1968, 72–73; 1976, 217–18) "intra-unit" or "within-unit comparison," and Campbell's (1975, 181–82) "pattern matching." A classic work on process tracing is George and McKeown (1985); a major contemporary statement is George and Bennett (2005). See also Bennett (2006; 2008) for important updates. Hoop tests, smoking gun tests, and straw in the wind tests are discussed in Van Evera (1997), Collier (2011), and Mahoney (forthcoming). The distinction between causal-process observations and data-set observations is developed in Collier, Brady, and Seawright (2010). For different types of causal-process observations, see Mahoney (2010).

The literature on time-series analysis and time-series cross-sectional analysis is reviewed in Pevehouse and Brozek (2008) and Beck (2008). For sophisticated efforts to incorporate mediating processes within a potential outcomes statistical framework, see Glynn and Quinn (2011); and Imai, Keele, Tingley, and Yamamoto (2011). See also Pearl (2010) and Green, Shang, and Bullock (2010).

Barton, A. H., and P. F. Lazarfeld. 1955. Some functions of qualitative analysis in social research *Sociologica* 1:324–61.

Beck, N. 2006. Is causal-process observation an oxymoron? *Political Analysis* 14:347–52.

Beck, N. 2008. Time-series cross-sectional analysis. In *The Oxford handbook of political methodology*, edited by J. Box-Steffensmeier, H. Brady, and D. Collier. Oxford: Oxford University Press.

Bennett, A. 2006. Stirring the frequentist pot with a dash of Bayes. *Political Analysis* 3:339–44.

Bennett, A. 2008. Process tracing: a Bayesian perspective. In *The Oxford handbook of political methodology*, edited by J. Box-Steffensmeier, H. Brady, and D. Collier. Oxford: Oxford University Press.

Bennett, A., and C. Elman. 2006. Complex causal relations and case study methods: the example of path dependence. *Political Analysis* 14:250–67.

Blalock, Jr., H. M. 1964. *Causal inferences in nonexperimental research.* Chapel Hill: University of North Carolina Press.

Bollen, K. A. 1989. *Structural equations with latent variables.* New York: Wiley.

Box, G., and G. Jenkins. 1976. *Time series analysis: forecasting and control,* revised edition. San Francisco: Holden Day.

Brady, H. E. 2010. Data-set observations versus causal-process observations: the 2000 U.S. presidential election. In *Rethinking social inquiry: diverse tools, shared standards,* 2nd edition, edited by H. E. Brady and D. Collier. Lanham, MD: Rowman & Littlefield.

Brady, H. E., D. Collier, and J. Seawright. 2006. Toward a pluralistic vision of methodology. *Political Analysis* 14:353–68.

Braumoeller, B. F., and G. Goertz. 2000. The methodology of necessary conditions. *American Journal of Political Science* 44:844–58.

Campbell, D. T. 1975. "Degress of freedom" and the case study. *Comparative Political Studies* 8:178–93.

Campbell, D. T., and J. C. Stanley. 1963. *Experimental and quasi-experimental designs for research.* Boston: Houghton Mifflin Company.

Collier, D. 2011. Understanding process tracing. *PS: Political Science and Politics* 44:823–30.

Collier, D., H. Brady, and J. Seawright. 2010. Sources of leverage in causal inference: toward an alternative view of methodology. In *Rethinking social inquiry: diverse tools, shared standards,* 2nd edition, edited by H. E. Brady and D. Collier. Lanham, MD: Rowman & Littlefield.

Collier, R. B, and D. Collier. 1991. *Shaping the political arena: critical junctures, the labor movement, and regime dynamics in Latin America.* Princeton: Princeton University Press.

Dunning, T. 2012. *Natural experiments in the social sciences.* Cambridge: Cambridge University Press.

Freedman, D. 1991. Statistical models and shoe leather. In *Sociological Methodology,* edited by P. Marsden. San Francisco: Jossey-Bass.

George, A., and A. Bennett. 2005. *Case studies and theory development in the social sciences.* Cambridge, MIT Press.

George, A. L., and T. J. McKeown 1985. Case studies and theories of organizational decision making. In *Advances in information Processing in Organizations,* vol. 2, edited by R. F. Coulam and R. A. Smith. Greenwich, CT: JAI Press.

Gerschenkron, A. 1943. *Bread and democracy in Germany.* Berkeley: University of California Press.

Goertz, G. 2006. Assessing the trivialness, relevance, and relative importance of necessary or sufficient conditions in social science. *Studies in Comparative International Development* 41:88–109.

Glynn, A. N., and K. M., Quinn. 2011. Why process matters for causal inference. *Political Analysis* 19:273–86.

Green, D. P., E. H. Shang, and J. G. Bullock. 2010. Enough already about "black box" experiments: studying mediation is more difficult than most scholars suppose. *Annals of the American Academy of Political and Social Science* 628:200–8.

Hart, H. L. A., and T. Honoré 1985. *Causation in the law*, 2nd edition. Oxford: Oxford University Press.

Imai, K., L. Keele, D. Tingley, and T. Yamamoto. 2011. Unpacking the black box of causality: learning about causal mechanisms from experimental and observational studies. *American Political Science Review* 105:765–89.

Lijphart, A. 1971. Comparative politics and the comparative method. *American Political Science Review* 65:682–93.

Luebbert, G. M. 1991. *Liberalism, fascism, or social democracy: social classes and the political origins of regimes in interwar Europe.* Oxford: Oxford University Press.

Mahoney, J. 2010. After KKV: the new methodology of qualitative research. *World Politics* 62:120–47.

Mahoney, J. Forthcoming. The logic of process tracing in the social sciences. *Sociological Methods and Research.*

Moore, Jr., B. 1966. *Social origins of dictatorship and democracy: lord and peasant in the making of the modern world.* Boston: Beacon Press.

Pearl, J. 2000. *Causality: models, reasoning, and inference.* Cambridge: Cambridge University Press.

Pearl, J. 2010. The mediation formula: a guide to the assessment of causal pathways in non-linear models. Technical Report R-363.

Pevehouse, J. C., and J. D. Brozek. 2008. Time-series analysis. In *The Oxford handbook of political methodology,* edited by J. Box-Steffensmeier, H. Brady, and D. Collier. Oxford: Oxford University Press.

Ragin, C. 2008. *Redesigning social inquiry: fuzzy sets and beyond.* Chicago: University of Chicago Press.

Smelser, N. J. 1968. *Essays in sociological explanation.* Englewood Cliffs, NJ: Prentice-Hall.

Snow, J. 1855, 1965. *On the mode of communication of cholera,* 2nd edition. London: John Churchill.

Tannenwald, N. 1999. The nuclear taboo: the United States and the normative basis of nuclear non-use. *International Organization* 53:433-68.

Van Evera, S. 1997. *Guide to methods for students of political science.* Ithaca: Cornell University Press.

Walt, S. M. 1996. *Revolution and war.* Ithaca: Cornell University Press.

# Chapter 8

# Causal Mechanisms and Process Tracing

To explain by reference to causal mechanisms ... provides a
powerful source of causal inference when carried out through the
method of process tracing, which examines processes within
single cases in considerable detail.
                    —*Alexander L. George and Andrew Bennett*

## Introduction

Our intuitive understandings of causality include a generative process in
which a cause yields an effect by triggering the operation of certain
mechanisms and processes. When individuals are presented with data sug-
gesting an association between two variables, they routinely want additional
information related to mechanism before declaring the association to be
causal in nature (Ahn, Kalish, Medin, and Gelman 1995). Social scientists
are no different: they believe that causal effects are transmitted through
linking processes of one kind or another.

The large social science and philosophy of science literature that has
developed around the idea of a "causal mechanism" encompasses a heterogeneous set of arguments and definitions (see the suggested readings for this
chapter). For our purposes, we do not need to delve into the complexities of
this literature. Instead, we can understand causal mechanisms to mean the
intervening processes through which causes exert their effects. We propose
that any relatively well-developed theory will provide a discussion of causal
mechanisms. This is equally true for theories tested in the quantitative
and qualitative research traditions: they propose ideas about the causal
mechanisms that link independent variables to dependent variables.

The key issue we explore in this chapter is how the qualitative and quantitative traditions *empirically assess* theories about mechanisms when making causal inferences. In the qualitative culture, researchers carry out this assessment by attempting to *observe* mechanisms through process tracing and through the analysis of causal-process observations (Collier, Brady, and Seawright 2010a; 2010b; George and Bennett 2005). In the qualitative paradigm, the within-case analysis of specific cases and the effort to observe mechanisms go together quite naturally.

By contrast, statistical methods are not designed to observe mechanisms within particular cases. Inference using statistics—whether based on observational or experimental data—depends on the cross-case analysis of many observations. In this tradition, researchers may presume that a given mechanism is at work if a variable exerts its predicted effect in a statistical test. However, they do not normally try to empirically study mechanisms themselves. The reasons why variables exert causal effects are part of the theory, but not usually included in the statistical test (see the appendix).

## Mechanisms and Causal Inference

One learns early on that "correlation is not causation" through examples of spurious correlations, such as the association between the number of storks present in a region and the rate of fertility of a region. Students are taught in their first methods classes to try to think of third antecedent variables that might cause both variables and thus explain the correlation (e.g., a variable measuring urban versus rural location might explain both number of storks and rate of fertility). When students are first presented with these examples, however, the reason that they suspect the correlation may be spurious usually comes from the absence of intuitive causal mechanisms, not because they immediately realize there is a particular antecedent variable that explains away the correlation. One is skeptical of the stork–fertility correlation as a causal relationship because there is no plausible mechanism (Porpora 2008).

Within the social sciences, many statistical methodologists assume that causal inference with observational data is extremely difficult. Observational studies lack the random assignment of a controlled experiment, requiring control variables to deal with confounding factors. We have heard from, typically young, quantitative methodologists that regression is simply data description.[1] It is regarded as—at best—a blunt tool for causal inference (see also Collier, Brady, and Seawright 2010b).

[1] "Without an experiment, a natural experiment, a discontinuity, or some other strong design, no amount of econometric or statistical modeling can make the move from correlation to causation persuasive" (Sekhon 2009, 503).

Recognition of the challenges of making causal inferences with observational data has fostered growing interest in experiments. Social scientists are now engaged in experiments of all sorts, including survey experiments, laboratory experiments, and field experiments (experiments have always been used in psychology, of course). In political science, it is now common to see articles in the top journals employing experiments. Even when discussing regression designs, methodologists now often adopt the terminology of experiments, such as treatment and control. For some quantitative methodologists, in fact, the new slogan might be:

No strong causal inference without an experiment.

With a good experiment, one can assess the average effect of a given treatment without observing causal mechanisms. As Green and colleagues (2010, 206–7) put it, "One can learn a great deal of theoretical and practical value simply by manipulating variables and gauging their effects on outcomes, regardless of the causal pathways by which these effects are transmitted."[2] However, in the social sciences—as in all sciences—scholars still want to fill in the black box of experiments if at all possible. When researchers present experimental findings, they routinely have to answer questions concerning the mechanism linking treatment and effect. They try hard to answer, because a well-developed theory identifies the mechanism behind an observed effect.

In the qualitative culture, by contrast, researchers regard the identification of mechanisms as crucial to causal inference. They see mechanisms as a nonexperimental way of distinguishing causal relations from spurious correlations:

> Mechanisms help in causal inference in two ways. The knowledge that there is a mechanism through which $X$ influences $Y$ supports the inference that $X$ is a cause of $Y$. In addition, the absence of a plausible mechanism linking $X$ to $Y$ gives us a good reason to be suspicious of the relation being a causal one.... Although it may be too strong to say that the specification of mechanisms is always necessary for causal inference, a fully satisfactory social scientific explanation requires that the causal mechanisms be specified. (Hedström and Ylikoski 2010, 54; see also George and Bennett 2005)

---

[2] The enterprise of studying mediators using experiments faces many difficulties (see Bullock and Ha forthcoming). Likewise, statistical techniques to assess mediators with observational data require very strong assumptions and are hard to carry out in practice (e.g., Imai et al. 2011).

One might even say that a norm has developed in the qualitative culture that making a strong causal inference requires process tracing within individual cases to see if proposed causal mechanisms are present. Thus, for qualitative scholars the slogan might be:

No strong causal inference without process tracing.

The quantitative and qualitative research paradigms therefore have different ideas about strong causal inference. Unsurprisingly, they may view each other's standards with some skepticism. For instance, the idea that process tracing provides a strong basis for causal inference is not widely embraced in the quantitative culture. King, Keohane, and Verba suggest that process tracing is "unlikely to yield strong causal inference" and can only "promote descriptive generalizations and prepare the way for causal inference" (1994, 227–28). Other scholars stress that causal mechanisms are not "miracle makers" that resolve fundamental difficulties in causal analysis (e.g., Gerring 2010; Norkus 2004). From a statistical point of view, inferences about causal mechanisms must meet the requirements of good causal inference that apply to any potential treatment or variable. Causal mechanisms do not require a new understanding of causality (King, Keohane, and Verba 1994), though the econometric issues involved in estimating the effects of causal mechanisms are distinctive (e.g., MacKinnon 2008).

Process tracing can intersect with large-N analyses in various ways (Collier, Brady, Seawright 2006; 2010c). Sometimes the causal mechanism is worked out first in case studies and then large-N analyses are used to confirm the finding. For example, consider Snow's work showing that water—not miasma in the air—is the mechanism of transmission for cholera (Snow 1855; 1965, see also Freedman 1991).[3] Snow started his research as would a typical qualitative analyst: with the intensive examination of $Y = 1$ cases, i.e., people with cholera. He noted that the causal agent seemed to be something that attacked first the alimentary canal. This would make tainted water or food the likely mechanism of transmission. He made other key observations: sailors developed the disease only when they landed or took on supplies, the disease followed lines of commerce, and individuals living in buildings with a private water supply were often free from the disease. He carried out a method of difference design using two adjacent apartments, one of which had contaminated water. He did the same with selected individuals. He then convincingly tested the hypothesis with a quasi-experiment that drew on data from a large number of households that received water from

---

[3] This example is at the center of a debate between Collier, Brady, and Seawright (2006; 2010c) and Beck (2006; 2010).

different sources (Dunning 2008). The large-N natural experiment confirmed the causal mechanism that he had developed through qualitative research.

Sometimes one has a large-N statistical finding, usually with observational data, but the causal mechanism is disputed. In this setting, too, process tracing has been used to adjudicate among rival mechanisms. For example, a long line of cross-national quantitative studies have found a positive relationship between economic development (usually measured with GDP per capita) and democracy (see Robinson 2006 for a literature review). This relationship is in fact considered one of the most robust statistical findings in political science and political sociology (e.g., Geddes 1999). Yet, for nearly everyone, the finding seems incomplete because it leaves behind a black box and does not allow scholars to assess alternative theories of mechanisms. For qualitative researchers, this black box must be filled with a close analysis of the actual sequences that lead to democracy in particular cases. One must move from the statistical association to qualitative research aimed at identifying mechanisms before causation can be established.[4]

Rueschemeyer, Stephens, and Stephens's (1992) *Capitalist Development and Democracy* is a good example of the effort to observe causal mechanisms within individual cases using historical research. They propose that development fosters changes in the balance of power among different classes (especially landlords and workers), and that this changed balance of power is a critical mechanism for democracy. More specifically, they hypothesize that development fosters two necessary conditions for "full" democracy: (1) the absence of powerful landlords, and (2) the presence of strong, prodemocratic working classes.[5] Although these factors are nearly universal mechanisms, they are not sufficient conditions; democratization depended on other factors related to the state, political parties, and the international system.

Because process tracing is so central to causal inference in qualitative work, researchers in this tradition may be skeptical of studies that do not identify or test for causal mechanisms. For example, they may not be convinced that large-N findings that are not validated by supplementary

---

[4] As Rueschemeyer, Stephens, and Stephens (1992, 4) put it: "The repeated statistical finding [of a relationship between development and democracy] has a peculiar 'black box' character that can be overcome only by theoretically well grounded empirical analysis ... Comparative historical studies, we argue, carry the best promise of shedding light into the black box ... historical research gives *insight into sequences* and their relations to surrounding structural conditions, and that is indispensable for developing valid causal accounts. Causal analysis is inherently sequence analysis."

[5] "Democracy could only be established if (1) landlords were an insignificant force, or (2) they were not dependent on a large supply of cheap labor, or (3) they did not control the state" (Rueschemeyer, Stephens, and Stephens 1992, 270). "The organized working class appeared as a key actor in the development of fully democracy almost everywhere, the only exception being the few cases of agrarian democracy in some of the small-holding countries" (Rueschemeyer, Stephens, and Stephens 1992, 270).

process tracing are really causal. It is not hard to find examples where the intensive examination of individual cases leads to doubts about hypothesized causal mechanisms from statistical or formal analyses:

1. Cusack, Iverson, and Soskice (2007) argue that the economic preferences of business and labor are the key mechanisms linking coordinated labor markets to the creation of proportional representation electoral systems in Western Europe. These authors find a significant statistical relationship between labor market coordination and proportional representation systems. However, they do not examine the institutional preferences of business and labor that are hypothesized to drive this relationship. Kreuzer (2010) scrutinizes this argument by examining whether historical research provides any evidence that these actors cared about the form of electoral systems. After looking at each of Cusack, Iverson, and Soskice's 18 cases, he concludes that their proposed mechanism is not operating: "I was unable to find any evidence linking the institutional preferences of business organizations, union, parties, or their respective leaders to labor markets. As a matter of fact, I was unable to find any evidence that business or unions explicitly preferred one electoral system over another. There is plenty of discussion of parties' institutional preferences, but none of it points to economic factors" (2010, 376).[6]

2. Using cross-national statistical analysis, Collier and Hoeffler (2001) and Fearon and Laitin (2003) find that there is a strong negative relationship between GDP per capita and civil war. The two sets of authors disagree, however, about the causal mechanism: Collier and Hoeffler understand the mechanism in terms of the effects of poverty on economic opportunities, whereas Fearon and Laitin view the mechanism in terms of the capacity of the state to prevent civil war. Based on case-study evidence, Sambanis finds only marginal support for either mechanism. He proposes that GDP per capita likely exerts its effect in interaction with other variables: "the reason that countries have different proclivities to civil war might have more to do with the way other independent variables, such as ethnicity and democracy, behave at various levels of income" (2004, 266). Sambanis suggests that the lack of empirical support for the mechanisms proposed in the theories by Collier and Hoeffler and by Fearon and Laitin calls into question their practical utility. "If large-N studies make incorrect

[6] In their rebuttal, Cusack, Iverson, and Soskice (2010) argue that party leaders were identified with economic interests, and thus one would not expect labor and business leaders to actively push for a particular electoral system. Instead, they suggest that party preferences should be the focus of tests concerning the causal mechanism.

assumptions about causal paths, they will lack explanatory power . . . We know that by increasing GDP per capita, we will *somehow* reduce the risk of civil war, but a more targeted policy intervention might be both more effective and easier to implement" (2004, 273).

3. Acemoglu and Robinson (2006) show that military coups are more likely in countries with higher levels of economic inequality. Using game theory, they identify a mechanism to explain this relationship: the amount of redistribution under democracy will be higher in unequal societies, and thus elites have greater incentive to enlist the military to overthrow the democracy. Slater and Smith (2010), however, criticize this explanation by using case study evidence that shows "militaries are virtually never the agents and very rarely the allies of economic elites." Militaries normally carry out coups for reasons that have nothing to do with the specific economic interests of elite classes. Hence, they argue that the causal mechanism associated with Acemoglu and Robinson's game theoretic model is not present in the vast majority of military coups.

In short, qualitative researchers often view skeptically experimental and nonexperimental analyses that fail to identify mechanisms. In the qualitative culture, one cannot have a strong explanation if mechanisms are left as black boxes.

## Process Tracing in Multimethod vs. Qualitative Research

With the rise of multimethod work, process tracing is no longer the exclusive domain of qualitative research. Among quantitative researchers in some fields, it has become *de rigueur* to include individual case studies in the overall analysis. This trend is related to the downgrading of regression analysis that we discussed earlier. The intensive process tracing of selected cases is seen as a complement to large-N research in contexts where experiments are impossible. Statistical analyses provide some evidence that a postulated causal mechanism is at work in a large population of cases. Process tracing in selected individual cases is then used to explore whether the causal mechanism functions as advertised. This multimethod strategy is featured in prominent recent works that first present large-N statistical results and then follow them up with analyses of individual case studies (e.g., Fortna 2007; Lange 2009; Lieberman 2003; Pevehouse 2005).[7]

---

[7] Some scholars working in the tradition of game theory have also turned to process tracing as a means of testing the observable implications of their formal models, e.g., Bates et al. (1998).

Despite some convergence on process tracing as a useful tool of causal inference, scholars who supplement their statistical findings with process tracing do not appear to use the method in the same way as qualitative researchers. The use of process tracing to supplement statistical findings is complicated by the fact that, with statistical analysis, causal processes are not necessarily stable as one moves from the population to the individual case. For instance, imagine that in a statistical study the impact of $X_1$ is strongly positive in the population. Does this mean that $X_1$ cannot have a strongly negative impact for a particular subset of cases? The answer, of course, is "no." The impact of $X_1$ as one moves from a superset to subsets to particular cases is always contingent in statistical models; there is no mathematical reason why $X_1$ could not be negatively related to the outcome in particular subsets. Thus, when carrying out process tracing, one cannot be certain that causal mechanisms will operate as expected in randomly selected particular cases.[8]

In order to supplement statistical findings with process tracing, analysts generally try to select one or more cases where the main independent variable of interest should play the role that the theory assigns to it (see the chapter "Case Selection and Hypothesis Testing"). Perhaps because of the instability of findings when moving from the population to a subset of cases, however, analysts virtually never make a direct link between the data set value for the individual case, the parameter estimate in the statistical model, and the observations from the individual case study. When statistical researchers carry out process tracing in particular cases, their specific regression results tend to drop out of the picture.

Process-tracing researchers who begin with a statistical model often treat the independent variable of interest informally as a kind of contributing causal factor when conducting case studies. In the additive model that is usually used for the whole population, there are multiple causes, and the main variable of interest is just one of many. The effect of this variable is understood roughly as a causal weight for the dependent variable. Consequently, when conducting process tracing on that variable in a single case, the researcher explores how it "contributed to" or "added weight" in favor of the outcome. However, the analyst does not ordinarily view the individual variable as *necessary* for the outcome. Process tracing when used to supplement statistical research is not built around counterfactuals in the same way that is true of process tracing in qualitative research.

Another distinctive feature of process tracing when used as a supplement to statistical analysis concerns the role of variables other than the main

[8] One response by methodologists has been to think carefully about how to best select cases for process tracing in light of preliminary regression results (see the chapter "Case Selection and Hypothesis Testing").

one of interest (i.e., the control variables in the statistical model). Since these control variables are not of special interest, they are not ordinarily emphasized in the process tracing analysis. The effects of the control variables must be acknowledged, but the attention is directed at the main variable of concern.

On the qualitative side, researchers do not necessarily begin with a cross-case finding that is then validated with process tracing. Instead, they may begin with process tracing and use this method as the central basis for causal inference. However, for the purposes of comparison, let us assume that the qualitative researcher begins with a set-theoretic model that applies to a population of cases. This scholar will retain a set-theoretic approach to causation when conducting process tracing within cases. This is true because, with set-theoretic causes, particular cases within a population follow the same causal pattern that applies to the population as a whole. When carrying out process tracing, one treats the cause in the individual case as having the same effect as for the whole population.

This stability in causal effects when moving from the population to the cases is most easily seen with necessary conditions. If $A$ is a necessary condition for $Y$ within a population, then it must be a necessary condition for any individual case (or subset of cases) from that population. For a substantive example, consider the hypothesis that an authoritarian regime is necessary for genocide. If valid, this hypothesis will remain true for any case of genocide. One can carry out process tracing under the assumption that the hypothesis should consistently work across all genocides.

Stability from the population to the cases also applies to sufficiency in a set-theoretic causal model, such as the following one: $Y = ABc + DE$. If a case has either combination (i.e., either $A * B * c$ or $D * E$), then it will have the outcome of interest. Process tracing to investigate mechanisms would choose a case where either $ABc$ or $DE$ is present, but not both (see the chapter "Case Selection and Hypothesis Testing"). The analyst would then explore how, say, $A$, $B$, and $c$ *combine* to produce the outcome. When conducting process tracing, he or she would work to identify the specific processes through which this causal combination generated the outcome of interest.

When a qualitative analyst conducts process tracing on a causal combination in a particular case (assuming that the case exhibits only one combination that generates the outcome), he or she can treat each of the individual variables in that combination as necessary for the case to experience the outcome. That is, if the case of $Y = 1$ exhibits only one causal combination, then each of the individual causal factors of the combination are essential for the outcome to have occurred in that one case. If a case with the combination $D * E$ lacked either $D$ or $E$, then it would not have experienced the outcome if the model is correct. Hence, one can normally conduct process tracing for the individual variables of a causal combination in the same way as necessary conditions.

Given this, analyses that start with a set-theoretic model usually must treat each variable in the causal combination possessed by the individual case as necessary when conducting process tracing for that particular case. Yet analysts usually do not focus on only one variable of special interest because all of the variables in the combination are essential for the outcome in the case. By contrast, when process tracing is combined with statistical research, the focus is centered on the main variable of interest. The only time process tracing when used as a supplement to statistical research might focus on packages of causes is if the main effect of interest was an interaction term. However, we do not know of examples of research in which the analyst uses process tracing to validate the posited mechanisms behind an interaction term from a statistical model.

In sum, each culture tends to remain true to its causal model when conducing process tracing in individual cases. Qualitative researchers apply a set-theoretic model based on necessary conditions and packages of conditions that are jointly sufficient for outcomes. As a general rule, one can identify a qualitative approach to process tracing by asking whether the analyst treats individual causes as necessary conditions and/or asks about the mechanism linking the combinations of conditions when discussing sufficiency. By contrast, multimethod researchers who begin with a statistical model normally adopt an additive approach to causality when conducting process tracing within particular cases. They explore through process tracing whether the individual factor of interest contributed to or added weight in favor of a specific outcome in a particular case. Because so many other causes are assumed to matter, they do not make the assumption that the factor of interest was necessary for the outcome.

## Conclusion

In the qualitative culture, it is standard and natural to study causal mechanisms and to use process tracing for case studies. One draws the inference that $X$ is a cause of $Y$ in part by tracing the process that leads from $X$ to $Y$ within one or more specific cases. Process tracing is facilitated by the fact that scholars in this research tradition employ within-case analysis. This mode of analysis lends itself to the effort to identify the mechanisms through which a specific causal factor exerts its effect on a particular outcome.

In the quantitative culture, growing concerns about the ability of regression analysis to generate strong causal inference has pushed the methodological agenda in two directions. On the one hand, experiments of various kinds are increasingly prestigious (though still a small minority of all research).

With an experiment, one can do a good job of estimating the average effect of a treatment without testing for mechanisms. Yet, since nearly all social science theories propose ideas about mechanisms, the black box left behind by experimental research can be viewed as problematic.

On the other hand, multimethod research in which quantitative analysts combine regression with case study analysis is increasingly considered to be a best practice. A variable that exerts a significant effect in a regression analysis is further examined with case studies to determine whether it works in ways posited by the theory being tested. Unlike in the qualitative tradition, however, process tracing in multimethod research sees causes in light of an additive model. The researcher does not use process tracing to test whether $X$ was necessary for $Y$. Rather, the main goal is to explore whether $X$ made a contribution toward $Y$'s level or occurrence.

## References and Suggested Readings

The literature on causal mechanisms embodies many different understandings and definitions of causal mechanism. For various views, see Bunge (1997); Elster (1989); Falleti and Lynch (2009); Gerring (2008); Hedström and Swedberg (1998); Mahoney (2001); Mayntz (2004); McAdam, Tarrow, and Tilly (2001); Norkus (2004); Sekhon (2004); Stinchcombe (1991); and Waldner (2012). On the method of process tracing, see George and Bennett (2005); Bennett (2006; 2008); Hall (2003); Roberts (1996); Van Evera (1997); Collier (2011); and Mahoney (forthcoming). The concept of a causal-process observation is developed by Collier, Brady, and Seawright (2006; 2010a). On multimethod research, see Gerring (2011) and Lieberman (2005). On the ways in which process tracing can supplement set-theoretic work, see Schneider and Rohlfing (2011). On the use of experiments and statistical methods to study mechanisms, see Bullock and Ha (forthcoming); Glynn and Quinn (2011); Green, Ha, and Bullock (2010); Holland (1988); Imai et al. (2011); and MacKinnon (2008). While experiments solve some problems of observational research, they have their own problems. Good discussions of the promises and pitfalls of experiments are found in Druckman, Green, Kuklinski, and Lupia (2011) and Morton and Williams (2010).

Acemoglu, D., and J. A. Robinson. 2006. *Economic origins of dictatorship and democracy*. New York: Cambridge University Press.

Ahn, W., C. W. Kalish, D. L. Medin, and S. A. Gelman. 1995. The role of covariation versus mechanism in causal attribution. *Cognition* 54:299–352.

Bates, R., A. Greif, M. Levi, J.-L. Rosenthal, and B. Weingast. 1998. *Analytic narratives*. Princeton: Princeton University Press.

Beck, N. 2006. Is causal-process observation an oxymoron? *Political Analysis* 14:347–52.

Beck, N. 2010. Causal process "observation": oxymoron or (fine) old wine. *Political Analysis* 18:499–505.

Bennett, A. 2006. Stirring the frequentist pot with a dash of Bayes. *Political Analysis* 3:339–44.

Bennett, A. 2008. Process tracing: a Bayesian perspective. In *The Oxford handbook of political methodology*, edited by J. Box-Steffensmeier, H. Brady, and D. Collier. Oxford: Oxford University Press.

Brady, H. E. 2010. Data-set observations versus causal-process observations: the 2000 presidential election. In *Rethinking social inquiry: diverse tools, shared standards*, 2nd edition, edited by H. E. Brady and D. Collier. Lanham, MD: Rowman Littlefield.

Bullock, J. G., and S. E. Ha. Forthcoming. Mediation analysis is harder than it looks. In *Cambridge handbook of experimental political science*, edited by J. Druckman, D. Green, J. Kuklinski, and A. Lupia. New York: Cambridge University Press.

Bunge, M. 1997. Mechanism and explanation. *Philosophy of the Social Sciences* 27:410–65.

Collier, D. 2011. Understanding process tracing. *PS: Political Science and Politics* 44:823–30.

Collier, D., H. E. Brady, and J. Seawright. 2006. Toward a pluralistic vision of methodology. *Political Analysis* 14:353–68.

Collier, D., H. E. Brady, and J. Seawright. 2010a. Sources of leverage in causal inference: toward an alternative view of methodology. In *Rethinking social inquiry: diverse tools, shared standards*, 2nd edition, edited by H. E. Brady and D. Collier. Lanham, MD: Rowman & Littlefield.

Collier, D., H. E. Brady, and J. Seawright. 2010b. Introduction to the second edition: a sea change in political methodology. In *Rethinking social inquiry: diverse tools, shared standards*, 2nd edition, edited by H. E. Brady and D. Collier. Lanham, MD: Rowman & Littlefield.

Collier, D., H. E. Brady, and J. Seawright. 2010c. Outdated views of qualitative methods: time to move on. *Political Analysis* 18:506–13.

Collier, P., and A. Hoeffler. 2001. Greed and grievance in civil war. World Bank Research Working Paper, No. 2355.

Cusack, T., T. Iverson, and D. Soskice. 2007. Economic interests and the origins of electoral systems. *American Political Science Review* 101:373–91.

Cusack, T., T. Iverson, and D. Soskice. 2010. Coevolution and political representation: the choice of electoral systems. *American Political Science Review* 104:393–403.

Druckman, J. N., D. P. Green, J. H. Kuklinski, and A. Lupia, eds. 2011. *Cambridge handbook of experimental political science*. New York: Cambridge University Press.

Dunning, T. 2008. Improving causal inference: strengths and limitations of natural experiments. *Political Research Quarterly* 61:282–93.

Elster, 1989. *Nuts and bolts for the social sciences*. Cambridge: Cambridge University Press.

Falleti, T. G., and J. F. Lynch. 2009. Context and causal mechanisms in political analysis. *Comparative Political Studies* 42:1143–66.

Fearon, J. D., and D. D. Laitin. 2003. Ethnicity, insurgency, and civil war. *American Political Science Review* 97:75–90.

Fortna, V. 2007. *Peacekeeping and the peacekept: maintaining peace after civil war.* Princeton: Princeton University Press.

Freedman, D. A. 1991. Statistical models and shoe leather. *Sociological Methodology* 21:291–313.

Geddes, B. 1999. What do we know about democratization after twenty years? *Annual Review of Political Science* 2:115–44.

George, A., and A. Bennett. 2005. *Case studies and theory development in the social sciences*. Cambridge: MIT Press.

Gerring, J. 2008. The mechanistic worldview: thinking inside the box. *British Journal of Political Science* 38:161–79.

Gerring, J. 2010. Causal mechanisms, yes, but . . . . *Comparative Political Studies* 43:1499–526.

Gerring, J. 2011. *Social science methodology: a criterial framework*, 2nd edition. Cambridge: Cambridge University Press.

Gerring, J., and J. Seawright. 2008. Case-selection techniques in case study research: a menu of qualitative and quantitative options. *Political Research Quarterly* 61:294–308.

Glynn, A. N., and Quinn, K. M. 2011. Why process matters for causal inference. *Political Analysis* 19:273–86.

Green, D. P., S. E. Ha, and J. G. Bullock. 2010. Enough already about "black box" experiments: studying mediators is more difficult than most suppose. *The Annals of the American Academy of Political and Social Science* 628:200–208.

Hall, P. A. 2003. Aligning ontology and methodology in comparative research. In *Comparative historical analysis in the social sciences*, edited by J. Mahoney and D. Rueschemeyer. Cambridge: Cambridge University Press.

Hedström, P., and R. Swedberg, eds. 1998. *Social mechanisms: an analytical approach to social theory*. Cambridge: Cambridge University Press.

Hedström, P., and P. Ylikoski. 2010. Causal mechanisms in the socila sciences. *Annual Review of Sociology* 36:49–67.

Holland, P. W. 1988. Causal inference, path analysis, and recursive structural equation models. *Sociological Methodology* 18:449–84.

Imai, K., L. Keele, D. Tingley, and T. Yamamoto. 2011. Unpacking the black box of causality: learning about causal mechanisms from experimental and observational studies. *American Political Science Review* 105:765–89.

King, G., R. Keohane, and S. Verba. 1994. *Designing social inquiry: scientific inference in qualitative research.* Princeton: Princeton University Press.

Kreuzer, M. 2010. Historical knowledge and quantitative analysis: the case of the origins of proportional representation. *American Political Science Review* 104:369–92.

Lange, M. 2009. *Lineages of despotism and development: British colonialism and state power.* Chicago: University of Chicago Press.

Lieberman, E. S. 2003. *Race and regionalism in the politics of taxation in Brazil and South Africa.* Cambridge: Cambridge University Press.

Lieberman, E. S. 2005. Nested analysis as a mixed-method strategy for comparative research. *American Political Science Review* 99:435–52.

MacKinnon, D. P. 2008. *Introduction to statistical mediation analysis.* New York: Taylor and Francis.

Mahoney, J. 2001. Beyond correlational analysis: recent innovations in theory and method. *Sociological Forum* 16:575–93.

Mahoney, J. Forthcoming. The logic of process tracing in the social sciences. *Sociological Methods and Research.*

Mayntz, R. 2004. Mechanisms in the analysis of social macro-phenomena. *Philosophy of the Social Sciences* 34:237–54.

McAdam, D., S. Tarrow, and C. Tilly. 2001. *Dynamics of contention.* Cambridge: Cambridge University Press.

Morton, R., and K. Williams. 2010. *From nature to the lab: experimental political science and the study of causality.* New York: Cambridge University Press.

Norkus, Z. 2004. Mechanisms as miracle makers? The rise and inconsistencies of the mechanistic approach in social science and history. *History and Theory* 44:348–72.

Pevehouse, J. 2005. *Democracy from above: regional organizations and democratization.* Cambridge: Cambridge University Press.

Porpora, D. V. 2008. Sociology's causal confusion. In *Revitalizing causality: realism about causality in philosophy and social science,* edited by R. Groff. London: Routledge.

Roberts, C. 1996. *The logic of historical explanation.* University Park: Pennsylvania State University Press.

Robinson, J. A. 2006. Economic development and democracy. *Annual Review of Political Science* 9:503–27.

Rohlfing, I. 2008. What you see and what you get: pitfalls and principles of nested analysis in comparative research. *Comparative Political Studies* 41:1492–514.

Rueschemeyer, D., J. D. Stephens, and E. H. Stephens. 1992. *Capitalist development and democracy.* Chicago: University of Chicago Press.

Sambanis, N. 2004. Using case studies to expand economic models of civil war. *Perspectives on Politics* 2:259–79.

Schneider, C. Q., and I. Rohlfing. 2011. Combining QCA and process tracing in set-theoretic multi-method research. Manuscript.

Sekhon, J. 2004. Quality meets quantity: case studies, conditional probability, and counterfactuals. *Perspectives on Politics* 2:281–93.

Sekhon, J. 2009. Opiates for the matches: matching methods for causal inference. *Annual Review of Political Science* 12:487–508.

Slater, D., and B. Smith. 2010. Economic origins of democratic breakdown? Contrary evidence from Southeast Asia and beyond. Manuscript.

Snow, J. 1855/1965. *On the mode of communicaiton of cholera*, 2nd edition. London: John Churchill.

Stinchcombe, A. L. 1991. The conditions of fruitfulness of theorizing about mechanisms in social science. *Philosophy of the Social Sciences* 21:367–88.

Van Evera, S. 1997. *Guide to methods for students of political science*. Ithaca: Cornell University Press.

Waldner, D. 2011. Process tracing and causal mechanisms. In *The Oxford handbook of the philosophy of social science*, edited by H. Kincaid. Oxford: Oxford University Press.

# Chapter 9

## Counterfactuals

We would be prepared to sustain the counterfactual claim that given the material distribution of power of the 1980s, a rapidly declining Soviet Union would have most likely sued for peace in the Cold War even if led by old thinkers.
　　—*Randall Schweller and William Wohlforth*

It is nearly impossible to imagine any of Gorbachev's competitors for the general secretaryship even undertaking, much less carrying through, his bold domestic and foreign reforms.
　　—*Robert English*

### Introduction

Counterfactuals are central to several different issues in social science methodology. In this chapter, we focus on the role of counterfactual analysis for making causal inferences in the qualitative and quantitative cultures. In an earlier chapter, we considered how counterfactuals are used to define causality itself (see "Hume's Two Definitions of Cause").[1]

Following our two cultures theme, we suggest that counterfactual analyses are an important mode of causal inference within the qualitative tradition, but not commonly used within the quantitative tradition. This difference lies in the fact that a counterfactual statement entails a claim *counter to what*

---

[1] In the quantitative culture, the Neyman-Rubin-Holland model is called by some the "counterfactual approach" because it begins with a counterfactual for the individual case *i*. In philosophy, a counterfactual definition of causation has a long and distinguished history (e.g., Lewis 1973; Collins et al. 2004). In qualitative methodology, necessary conditions and counterfactuals are viewed as inherently linked (e.g., Goertz and Starr 2003).

*actually happened.* Such claims are typically made about a specific cause and outcome in an individual case, not about what would have happened on average for a population of cases. For example, the epigraphs for this chapter offer classic counterfactual arguments about the causes of a specific event. In this case, the counterfactual claim about what would have happened if new thinkers like Gorbachev had not come to power turns out to be of great importance in the overall dispute about the role of ideas versus the distribution of material power as causes of the end of the Cold War.

To assess a counterfactual claim about a particular case, one normally needs to carry out a within-case analysis of that case. Since qualitative scholars are interested in explaining individual cases, the use of within-case analysis for assessing counterfactual claims comes quite naturally to them. They formulate counterfactuals that are "conceivable," in the sense that imagining that a cause had not occurred (or occurred differently) does not require fundamentally rewriting history (Weber 1949; Fearon 1991). The counterfactual analysis itself is carried out by explicitly considering a "possible world" (Lewis 1973) in which the causal antecedent is absent or different.

By contrast, since quantitative researchers are not typically interested in any specific case, it is less conventional for them to carry out counterfactual analyses for particular cases. When counterfactuals are used, their purpose is mainly to illustrate a general causal model. For example, quantitative scholars sometimes use counterfactuals to say something general about the average magnitude of the effect of $X$ on $Y$. The counterfactuals of this tradition typically involve hypothesizing extraordinary changes in a cause— e.g., estimating what would happen to a case if its value on $X$ changed from a very low score to a very high score (see King and Zeng (2006; 2007) for examples and a critique).

## Fundamental Problem of Causal Inference: Different Responses

With some exceptions (e.g., Pearl 2000), current views on causal inference within statistics start with a counterfactual for an individual case. Because it is impossible to actually observe the counterfactual for the individual case, scholars confront the Fundamental Problem of Causal Inference:

> *Fundamental Problem of Causal Inference.* It is impossible to *observe* the value of $Y_t(i)$ and $Y_c(i)$ on the same unit and, therefore, it is impossible to *observe* the effect of $t$ on $i$. (Holland 1986, 947)

The Fundamental Problem of Causal Inference is the problem of a counterfactual. For any given case, it is impossible to rerun history such that the case has a different value on $X$.

The big difference between the qualitative and quantitative traditions lies in their response to this problem. Quantitative scholars solve the problem by moving to a large-N solution focused on average effects. Thus, while counterfactuals are central to the very definition of causality in the quantitative tradition, the use of counterfactual analysis for causal inference drops out as option. The Neyman-Rubin-Holland counterfactual view of causation does not lend itself to the explicit counterfactual analysis of individual cases.

Once the average effect of $t$ is computed using statistical methods, the researcher can use this parameter estimate to carry out a counterfactual analysis for any particular unit in the population. Our key point in this chapter, though, is that the individual counterfactual does not play any role in the process of making the causal inference (i.e., estimating the average causal effect). One arrives at an estimated average causal effect without the aid of counterfactual analysis. The statistical results precede rather than follow any counterfactual analysis.

By contrast, the qualitative response to the Fundamental Problem of Causal Inference is to use general knowledge and within-case analysis to analyze counterfactually what would have happened if $X$ had assumed a different value in a particular case. Qualitative analysts believe it is possible to use existing generalizations and detailed knowledge of a particular case to test hypotheses about whether particular factors were causes of outcomes in specific cases. Counterfactual analysis is part of the effort to generate valid causal inferences about specific cases.

In short, both qualitative and quantitative scholars believe it is possible to carry out counterfactual analysis for individual cases. However, in the quantitative paradigm, this kind of analysis is not part of the process of making a causal inference. Instead, any counterfactual analysis *follows* the estimation of an average causal effect, and it is used to discuss the causal inference already made. By contrast, qualitative scholars focus on the individual case and use existing generalizations and within-case analysis to reason about counterfactuals for that case. In this paradigm, counterfactual analysis is often part of the process of causal inference itself.

## Constructing Counterfactuals

### Statistical Procedures and Extreme Counterfactuals

To illustrate the statistical approach to counterfactuals, it is useful to consider a standard practice in the evaluation of a given parameter estimate in a logit or probit analysis. With these models, there is often no immediately transparent way of conceptualizing the size of causal effects. One solution for analysts is to use counterfactuals to provide a sense of the magnitude of the effect of $X$ on $Y$. The standard procedure is basically the following:

1. Set all control variables (i.e., all variables except the counterfactual $X$ variable in question) to the mean or median—with the mean probably being the most common option. For dichotomous variables, use the mode.

2. Set the counterfactual antecedent $X$ to the minimum; a more conservative procedure would be the 25th percentile or perhaps one or two standard deviations below the mean.

3. Change $X$ from the minimum to the maximum (a more conservative procedure would be to use the 75th percentile or one or two standard deviations above the mean). This is the counterfactual.

4. Use the statistical model and estimated parameters to evaluate the counterfactual in terms of the change in the probability of $Y$.

5. The change in the probability of $Y$ in the counterfactual is used as an interpretation of the magnitude of the causal effect of $X$ on $Y$.

Countless articles and presenters have used this procedure, though often the analyst will not explicitly link the practice to counterfactual reasoning.

Under this procedure, $X$ is moved from a very low value to a very high value. One can thus say that the analyst follows a "maximum rewrite practice" or an "extreme counterfactual approach": the counterfactual involves maximal or extreme changes in $X$. This practice allows the researcher to illustrate dramatically the potential impact of a change in $X$ for $Y$.

When quantitative scholars pursue this kind of counterfactual reasoning, they do not normally link their counterfactual to any specific historical case. Likewise, they rarely ask about the *historical plausibility* of the given change on $X$ that is being proposed. As Fearon notes, whether the change is realistic is not relevant, because it is used simply for the purpose of model analysis:

> In regression analysis and other statistical means of testing causal hypotheses, one assumes that if any particular case in the sample had taken a different value on one of the independent variables, the dependent variable could have differed by a systematic component that is the same across cases plus a random component. One never even contemplates whether it would have been actually, historically possible for any particular case to have assumed different values on the independent variables. (Fearon 1996, 61)

In the quantitative tradition, then, the question of whether the counterfactual is plausible for the individual case does not arise. King and Zeng (2006; 2007) have forcefully argued that a plausible counterfactual is defined in terms of the data. Counterfactuals that stay within the data are plausible; those that extrapolate beyond the data are suspect. The data have to provide real world examples with which to conduct the counterfactual. Said differently, a counterfactual change on an independent variable in a single case that seems implausible to a historical expert of that case is not especially troubling as long as the data provides good comparison cases— basically matching cases—for estimating the effect of the change. In fact, in the quantitative culture, one could say that the plausibility of any given counterfactual is determined by how far the counterfactual is from the observed data.

## Qualitative Procedures and the Minimum Rewrite Rule

In the qualitative culture, the prototypical counterfactual is a claim about a particular—usually historically important—case. One asks what *would have happened* for a given outcome, $Y$, if some cause, $X$, had assumed a different value in a particular case of substantive interest. The researcher imagines that the causal event did not occur (or occurred in a different way) and explores whether the outcome would still have taken place (or taken place in the same way).[2] In the counterfactual hypothesis, the outcome is often specified as the absence or negation of an outcome rather than as a pinpoint prediction about a specific positive outcome (see Fearon 1996). In many instances, though certainly not all, the cause $X$ is a minor event that is believed to have had large subsequent consequences.

There is a natural connection between qualitative research and the analysis of specific counterfactual cases. If one proposes that $X$ is a cause of $Y$ in a particular case, one naturally asks what would have happened if $X$ had been different. If $X$ is believed to be a necessary condition for $Y$, in fact, the counterfactual absence of $X$ *must* generate the absence of $Y$ for the hypothesis to be valid. Likewise, at the individual case level, the absence of an INUS cause will normally lead to the absence of the outcome.[3]

Unsurprisingly, qualitative methodologists have led the discussion about how to maximize leverage for causal inference when carrying out counterfactual analyses. Going back to at least Weber (1949), scholars have proposed a "minimum rewrite" rule that holds that counterfactuals should

---

[2] Occasionally the researcher will examine a non-event (e.g., the absence of war), such that the counterfactual refers to a positive event (e.g., war).

[3] The exception is a case in which the outcome is overdetermined by the presence of multiple sufficient condition configurations.

require changing as little of the known historical record as possible (Stalnaker 1968, 104; Elster 1978; Tetlock and Belkin 1996b, 23–25; Reiss 2009). The counterfactual antecedent must be *conceivable* and ideally *plausible* given the character of the individual case. Plausibility is assessed on the basis of knowledge of the particular case and broader theory as well as generalized findings from other domains of research. "Miracle" counterfactual antecedents should be avoided. Often the most plausible counterfactual antecedents involve "small" changes (e.g., proposing that a leader had not been assassinated), which is one reason why qualitative researchers frequently look at small events when conducting counterfactual analyses (Fearon 1991, 193). Likewise, the counterfactual outcome normally must occur in a "possible world" that is not completely different from the actual world (see Lewis 1973). As Fearon puts it, "When we try to explain why some event *B* occurred, we implicitly imagine a contrast space in which *B* is absent *and the rest of the world is similar to the world in which B is present*" (1996, 57; see also Garfinkel 1990).

Good counterfactuals help direct qualitative researchers to specific pieces of evidence that they can use with process tracing when explaining specific outcomes (see the chapter "Causal Mechanisms and Process Tracing"). For example, one might counterfactually hypothesize that if Gore had won the 2000 presidential election, instead of Bush, the United States would not have initiated the Iraq War (see Harvey 2012). This counterfactual is historically plausible, and it calls attention to the role of individual leadership in driving foreign policy. It invites the researcher to look closely at differences between Bush and Gore, and to identify the distinctive beliefs and choices of Bush that led to decisions culminating in the war. It also encourages the analyst to consider alternative arguments, such as the idea that systematic pressures would have led the United States to attack Iraq even if Gore were in office. By contrast, the following hypothesis is not very useful: if Mother Teresa had won the 2000 presidential election, instead of Bush, the United States would not have initiated the Iraq War. It is impossible to imagine this occurrence without fundamentally changing the whole world, and the analysis provides few good pointers for identifying exactly what it was about Bush's presidential leadership that may have been crucial for the occurrence of the war.

Thus, we arrive at a fundamental difference in the typical counterfactual proposed in qualitative versus quantitative research. The former tradition proposes counterfactuals that follow the minimal rewrite rule and are historically plausible for the individual cases being analyzed. This standard follows directly from the fact that qualitative researchers are attempting to use counterfactual analysis to make a causal inference about a specific historical case. By contrast, scholars in the quantitative tradition propose extreme counterfactuals that involve maximal rewrites. They do so because the counterfactual is used for model analysis and illustrative purposes, not causal inference.

## What Is a Plausible Counterfactual? Cross-Case versus Within-Case Answers

In an important article, King and Zeng (2007) suggest that a plausible counterfactual in quantitative research is one where there are cases in the dataset that are similar to the counterfactual being proposed. Instead of talking about closest "possible worlds" (like some philosophers), they focus on closest *actual worlds* as found in data (see also Mikkelson 1996). They are critical of counterfactuals when the data cannot sustain them. One of their examples concerns state failure (dependent variable) in Canada:

> Our first extreme counterfactual is to suppose that Canada in 1996 had become an autocracy, but its values on other variables remained at their actual values. We find, as we would expect, that this extreme counterfactual is outside the convex hull of the observed data [on the control variables] and therefore requires extrapolation. In other words, we can ask what would have happened if Canada had become autocratic in 1996, but we cannot use history as our guide, as the world (and therefore our data) includes no examples of autocracies that are similar enough to Canada on other measured characteristics. (King and Zeng 2007, 192)

King and Zeng define a plausible counterfactual in *cross-case* terms. A counterfactual is reasonable if there are other cases similar to the counterfactual.

By contrast, the minimum rewrite rule used in qualitative research is a *within-case* notion: is the counterfactual proposal plausible for the individual case? For example, the counterfactual of Canada having an autocracy in 1996 is not plausible because it violates the minimal rewrite rule. One would have to fundamentally change Canada's history to arrive at this counterfactual antecedent. Certainly, one might use some cross-case evidence in evaluating the within-case counterfactual, but the judgment about reasonableness is ultimately a within-case decision that depends heavily on the analyst's knowledge of the case and its history.

To explore this idea further, we can examine how likely it would be to find cases where full authoritarianism becomes full democracy. With the Polity data, for example, how likely would it be for a country to move from –10 (authoritarian) to 10 (democracy) in a relatively short period of time? The statistical approach to answering is cross-sectional: are there any cases with a Polity value of 10 and Polity value of −10 but otherwise similar to one another on other variables?[4] The qualitative approach involves within-case analysis: how plausible is this kind of change for a particular case? The qualitative researcher does not rely exclusively on whether similar *actual* cases can be found (though this information usually plays some role). A counterfactual that is deemed implausible on the basis of the cross-sectional data could be regarded as plausible by a qualitative researcher working on a specific case. It is also possible that a qualitative researcher will regard a counterfactual as implausible on the basis of within-case knowledge even though the counterfactual cannot be ruled out by looking at cross-sectional statistical data.[5]

## Conclusion

In qualitative research, counterfactual analysis is central to within-case causal analysis. For individual case studies, counterfactual analysis is a major tool that researchers use in conjunction with process tracing when evaluating hypotheses. They rerun the history of a case under a counterfactual assumption in order to decide if a given factor played its hypothesized causal role. The results of these counterfactual experiments can strongly influence the findings generated by the cross-case analysis.

Although counterfactuals inform leading definitions of causality in the statistical culture (see the chapter "Hume's Two Definitions of Cause"), researchers in this culture do not normally engage in the counterfactual analysis of historical cases. They choose (potentially hypothetical) representative cases of the population, not real individual observations of special interest. They do not use theory and established findings to rerun history and thereby make judgments about what would have happened if a case had a different value on a causal variable. Instead, in this culture, a counterfactual is presented to interpret the results of the statistical estimation and to make general claims about causal effects.

---

[4] In fact, this kind of maximal rewrite is not supported by the data. The Polity data suggest that countries may move 10 to 15 points in a relatively short period of time, but not the full 20 points.

[5] A qualitative researcher might believe that a change in one direction, e.g., from full democracy to full authoritarianism, is plausible for the case, whereas a change in the opposite direction is not realistic. This point is worth making because it suggests the connection between counterfactuals and asymmetric notions of causality in qualitative research (see the chapter "Asymmetry").

## References and Suggested Readings

Undoubtedly, the most common point of departure for work on counterfactuals in the social sciences is Weber (1949). More recent key writings on counterfactual analysis include Fearon (1991; 1996) and Tetlock and Belkin (1996a). For qualitative examples of counterfactual analysis in the social sciences, see Tetlock and Belkin (1996b); Goertz and Levy (2007); and Lebow (2010). For work on counterfactuals by historians, see Fischer (1970, 15–21); McClelland (1975); and Ferguson (1999). Philosophical treatments can be found in Lewis (1973); Salmon (1994); and Woodward (2003). On counterfactuals in law, see the classic work by Hart and Honoré (1985).

Less has been said about using counterfactual analysis in conjunction with cross-case analysis. The key work from a set-theoretic perspective is Ragin (2008, chapters 8–9). From the perspective of statistical analysis, King and Zeng (2006; 2007) and Dawid (2000) offer good discussions of the kinds of counterfactuals that can and cannot be assessed. See also Pearl (2000).

Collins, J., N. Hall, and L. A. Paul, eds. 2004. *Causation and counterfactuals*. Cambridge: MIT Press.

Dawid, P. 2000. Causal inference without counterfactuals (with discussion). *Journal of the American Statistical Association* 95:407–50.

Elster, J. 1978. *Logic and society: contradictions and possible worlds*. Chichester: Wiley.

Fearon, J. 1991. Counterfactuals and hypothesis testing in political science. *World Politics* 43:169–95.

Fearon, J. 1996. Causes and counterfactuals in social science: exploring an analogy between cellular automata and historical processes. In *Counterfactual analysis in world politics*, edited by P. Tetlock and A. Belkin. Princeton: Princeton University Press.

Ferguson, N., ed. 1999. *Virtual history: alternatives and counterfactuals*. New York: Basic Books.

Fischer, D. H. 1970. *Historians' fallacies: toward a logic of historical thought*. New York: Harper & Row.

Garfinkel, A. 1990. *Forms of explanation: rethinking the questions in social theory*. New Haven: Yale University Press.

Goertz, G., and J. Levy, eds. 2007. *Explaining war and peace: case studies and necessary condition counterfactuals*. New York: Routledge.

Goertz, G., and H. Starr, eds. 2003. *Necessary conditions: theory, methodology, and applications*. New York: Rowman & Littlefield.

Hart, H. L. A., and T. Honoré. 1985. *Causation in the law*, 2nd edition. Oxford: Oxford University Press.

Harvey, F. 2012. *Explaining the Iraq war: counterfactual theory, logic and evidence*. Cambridge: Cambridge University Press.

Holland, P. W. 1986. Statistics and causal inference. *Journal of the American Statistical Association* 81:945–60.

Khong, Y. F. 1996. Confronting Hitler and its consequences. In *Counterfactual analysis in world politics: logical, methodological, and psychological perspectives*, edited by P. E. Tetlock and A. Belkin. Princeton: Princeton University Press.

King, G., and L. Zeng. 2006. The dangers of extreme counterfactuals. *Political Analysis* 14:131–59.

King, G., and L. Zeng. 2007. When can history be our guide? The pitfalls of counterfactual inference. *International Studies Quarterly* 51:183–210.

Lebow, R. N. 2010. *Forbidden fruit: counterfactuals and international relations.* Princeton: Princeton University Press.

Lewis, D. 1973. *Counterfactuals.* Cambridge: Harvard University Press.

McClelland, P. D. 1975. *Causal explanation and model building in history, economics, and the new economic history.* Ithaca: Cornell University Press.

Mikkelson, G. 1996. Stretched lines, averted leaps, and excluded competition: a theory of scientific counterfactuals. *Political Studies* 63:S194–S201.

Pearl, J. 2000. *Causality: models, reasoning, and inference.* Cambridge: Cambridge University Press.

Ragin, C. 2008. *Redesigning social inquiry: fuzzy sets and beyond.* Chicago: University of Chicago Press.

Reiss, J. 2009. Counterfactuals, thought experiments, and singular causal analysis in history. *Philosophy of Science* 76:712–23.

Rubin, D. B. 1974. Estimating causal effects of treatments in randomized and nonrandomized studies. *Journal of Educational Psychology* 66:688–701.

Rubin, D. B. 1990. Comment: Neyman (1923) and causal inference in experiments and observational studies. *Statistical Science* 5:472–80.

Salmon, W. C. 1994. Causality without counterfactuals. *Philosophy of Science* 61:297–312.

Stalnaker, R. C. 1968. A theory of conditionals. In *Studies in logical theory: essays*, edited by N. Rescher. Oxford: Blackwell.

Tetlock, P. E., and A. Belkin, eds. 1996a. *Counterfactual thought experiments in world politics: logical, methodological, and psychological perspectives.* Princeton: Princeton University Press.

Tetlock, P. E., and A. Belkin. 1996b. Counterfactual thought experiments in world politics: logical, methodological, and psychological perspectives. In *Counterfactual thought experiments in world politics: logical, methodological, and psychological perspectives*, edited by P. E. Tetlock and A. Belkin. Princeton: Princeton University Press.

Weber, M. 1949. Objective possibility and adequate causation in historical explanation. In *The methodology of the social sciences*, edited by M. Weber. New York: Free Press.

Woodward, J. 2003. *Making things happen: a theory of causal explanation.* Oxford: Oxford University Press.

# PART III

Concepts and Measurement

# Chapter 10

# Concepts: Definitions, Indicators, and Error

The essence of a thing ... is that without which the thing could neither be, nor be conceived to be.
> —*J. S. Mill*

In sum, measurement is valid when the scores, derived from a given indicator, can be meaningfully interpreted in terms of the systematized concept that the indicator seeks to operationalize.
> —*Robert Adcock and David Collier*

## Introduction

Scholars working in the two cultures employ different approaches to issues of conceptualization and measurement. Some of these differences are not particularly surprising. Qualitative scholars have long, involved, "wordy" discussions about the meaning of concepts. In this respect, they resemble (political) philosophers, who also spend much time on concept analysis. By contrast, quantitative scholars need data for their statistical models. Accordingly, they focus attention on the nature and quality of quantitative measures. They spend less time on the concept and more time on operationalization, measurement, and the resulting datasets.

This chapter focuses on two important differences between the quantitative and qualitative approaches to conceptualization and measurement. The first concerns the relative importance assigned to issues of concept definition versus issues of concept measurement. Qualitative researchers are centrally concerned with definitional issues and the meaning of their concepts. They normally adopt a semantic approach and work hard to identify the intrinsic defining attributes that make up the essence of a concept. By contrast, quantitative scholars focus their attention primarily on the quantitative measurement of latent variables. They seek to identify good indicators that are correlated with the latent variable under study.

The second big difference concerns error and the coding of cases. Qualitative scholars feel most certain about their estimates when working with cases that have extreme values, such as cases that approximate ideal types. They are least certain for cases with values in the middle of the full range of values. By contrast, quantitative scholars feel the least certain about cases with extreme values and most certain for cases with values near the mean. These differences are related to the relative emphasis placed on definitions versus indicators in the two cultures. Qualitative scholars match data to definitions, and thus feel most confident about instances where the definition definitely is or definitely is not met. By contrast, quantitative scholars use indicators and feel least confident about cases that exhibit values far removed from what is typical for the population as a whole.

## Defining Characteristics versus Indicators

In the qualitative culture, discussions and debates about concepts concern semantics—i.e., they concern the meaning of concepts. It is completely standard to ask questions and have discussions about the *definition* of concepts. For example, one might ask, "What is your definition of the welfare state?" A typical qualitative answer involves presenting a list of attributes or characteristics that constitute the concept. There is nothing too mysterious about this practice, because it is basically what dictionaries do. Dictionaries and the qualitative culture try to specify the characteristics that make an entity what it is. To use a common example from philosophy, a good definition of "copper" identifies the chemical characteristics that describe its nature, including any causal powers.

Within the quantitative culture, discussions and debates about concepts focus on issues of data and measurement, and less on semantics and meaning. While some discussion of the definition of a concept is normally necessary for gathering data about that concept, it is not the focus of attention. In the case of quantitative measurement articles, a concept section may not exist at all. Instead, researchers focus on the operationalization and measurement of the concept. Operationalization typically involves finding *indicators* comprised of numerical data that are correlated with the unmeasured, latent variable. Once such indicators are found, more or less involved measurement procedures can be applied for purposes of coding cases. These measurement procedures range from simple addition to complex Bayesian, latent variable models. The aggregation procedures or measurement model generate the scores for cases vis-à-vis the concept (variable) of interest.

As an example of this quantitative approach, consider the GTD terrorism dataset (CETIS 2007), which is now often used in statistical work on terrorism. Terrorism is a notoriously problematic concept (see Schmid and Jongman (1988) who discuss dozens of definitions). If one reads the GTD codebook, the problematic nature of the concept is clearly acknowledged in the introduction, but almost all of the codebook is about the data. Once it is acknowledged that the concept is hard to define, the definitional issue drops out of consideration. Discussions of the data proceed without reference to definitional issues. In fact, to identify the actual GTD definition of terrorism, one must read an appendix.

Not needing numerical data for large numbers of cases, qualitative scholars are freer to debate about concepts and their defining attributes. One hazard of this freedom lies in increasing the complexity of the concept. Qualitative definitions can be long, complicated, even Byzantine in character. One of our favorite examples is the influential definition of corporatism developed by Schmitter:

> Corporatism can be defined as a system of interest representation in which the constituent units are organized into a limited number of singular, compulsory, noncompetitive, hierarchically ordered and functionally differentiated categories, recognized or licensed (if not created) by the state and granted a deliberate representational monopoly within their respective categories in exchange for observing certain controls on their selection of leaders and articulation of demands and supports. (Schmitter 1974, 93–94)

This definition has many different attributes, some of which are contained within others. If one were to try to unpack Schmitter's definition into individual characteristics, there might be 10 or more features. Moreover, different people might come up with different lists.

In the quantitative culture, the process of coding data on corporatism involves the use of indicators. These indicators may not be explicitly mentioned in the definition of the concept. For example, labor centralization has been used as a quantitative indictor of corporatism (see Kenworthy (2003) for a discussion of other quantitative indicators). It is a matter of interpretation how this indicator fits with the abstract language of Schmitter's definition. In general, the move from concept to concrete data will almost always involve significant simplification. Often this simplification entails redefining a concept to include a more limited number of defining dimensions.

For qualitative researchers, the failure of indicators to represent well all defining attributes of a concept raises concerns. For these researchers, the attributes of a concept are obligatory features that literally are the concept. Each must therefore be measured. Qualitative researchers resist extreme modes of simplification. They believe that concepts must be defined independently of data considerations. The definition of a concept should not be driven by the data that are available to measure that concept.

Unlike the attributes that constitute a concept, quantitative indicators are optional, substitutable, and not necessarily definitional. Different indicators are *all* measures of the *same* conceptual entity. Treier and Jackman's (2008) discussion of the Polity measure of democracy illustrates nicely the difference between defining attributes and indicators. Polity defines democracy in terms of five attributes, and it suggests that each of these attributes is an inherent feature of democracy. For Treier and Jackman, however, these attributes are simply indicators for the latent democracy concept. Two of the five indicators do not meet the statistical requirements of their methodology and are thus discarded. Their final measure of democracy consequently uses only three of the five Polity dimensions.

Thus, what to the qualitative researcher is a defining feature may be an indicator for the quantitative researcher. For another example, consider Bollen and Grandjean's (1981) use of fairness of elections as an indicator of political democracy. To the qualitative scholar, fair elections are often viewed as a defining and obligatory attribute of democracy. It is not optional; this attribute is necessary for democracy (Bowman et al. 2005; Mainwaring et al. 2001).

In the qualitative literature on concepts, the language of indicators is often replaced by language such as minimal *requirements* for a democracy. A good example is Collier and Levitsky's influential notion of a diminished subtype: "For example, 'limited-suffrage democracy' and 'tutelary democracy' are understood as less than complete instances of democracy because they lack one or more of its defining attributes" (Collier and Levitsky 1997, 436–37). The very idea of a diminished subtype makes little sense if the attributes of the root concept are optional features that are not necessary for conceptual membership in that root concept.

A related difference concerns attributes/concepts in qualitative research versus indicators/variables in quantitative research. In the qualitative culture, the relationship between attributes and a concept is a semantic, definitional one. In the quantitative culture, the relationship between indicators and a latent variable is a *causal* one: in the standard view, the latent variable causes the indicators (Bollen 1989).[1]

---

[1] It is possible to model the causal arrow going the other direction (e.g., Bollen and Ting 2000), but that is rare.

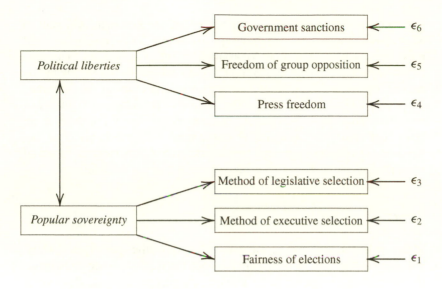

*Source:* Bollen and Grandjean 1981.

**Figure 10.1.** Latent variable models of political liberties and popular sovereignty

Figure 10.1 illustrates a typical latent variable model. The causal arrows in the figure run from the latent variables to the indicators. This helps to make sense of the idea that indicators are substitutable factors. The latent variable might be the cause of many different things, and the scholar is just choosing some of them. As noted above, cross-cultural tension arises when researchers treat these indicators as defining attributes. In the qualitative culture, defining attributes cannot be causally related to the concept of interest; they cannot even be temporally separated from the concept. They *are* the concept.

The idea that measurement should be based on causal theories has a long and distinguished history. Hempel (1952) made this connection using the natural sciences as his focus. For example, the usefulness of a thermometer to measure temperature depends on a causal theory of heat expansion. In the social sciences, the same idea underpins the large literature on latent variables and measurement (Bollen 1989). Our purpose is not to call into question the view that indicators and latent variables should be causally related. Within the quantitative tradition, and for many phenomena, this view makes perfect sense. It seems reasonable to believe that one's intelligence—latent variable—might affect one's performance on tests of intelligence. Likewise, it seems reasonable that one's political ideology might affect one's answers on a questionnaire about politics.

From a qualitative standpoint, nevertheless, the key issue will remain addressing the meaning of the concept of interest. These researchers will press the quantitative scholar by asking, "What exactly is the definition of intelligence (or political ideology)?" They will be dissatisfied with any answer that suggests the concept can be defined in terms of the indicators that are used to measure it.[2] From the qualitative perspective, the quality of indicators must always be assessed in light of the meaning of the concept being measured. Many quantitative researchers will agree in principle, but the concerns of this culture lead the discussion to center more on issues of measurement and indicators than on issues of meaning and definition.

## Error

When coding cases, the qualitative and quantitative paradigms exhibit important differences in their beliefs about the quality of our knowledge. Cases that are considered to be good candidates for accurate description and coding in one culture are often considered to be poor candidates in the other. The kind of case that the quantitative researcher assumes is subject to higher levels of measurement error is often precisely the kind of case that the qualitative researcher assumes is subject to the least amount of measurement error and vice versa.

To explore this difference, we can begin by clearing up the relationship between "error," which is central to all statistics, and "fuzziness," which is an important idea in qualitative research. These two concepts might, at first glance, seem quite similar. When quantitative scholars hear the word "fuzzy," they might initially believe that it suggests a lack of clarity, which in turn implies "uncertainty" or "error." Yet, in fact, the analogy between error and fuzziness is quite misleading. This analogy is an instance of the translation problem between statistics and fuzzy logic.

In statistics, error estimates concern the quality of our knowledge. Indeed, what distinguishes statistics from other ways of making numeric estimates about the world is precisely the inclusion of a stochastic element to allow us to say something about the accuracy of our estimates. By contrast, fuzzy-set membership values are statements about features of the world. For instance, if one asserts that a case has a fuzzy-set membership value of 0.75, one is making a claim about the empirical nature of that case—i.e., the case is mostly but not entirely within a given conceptual set. One is not making any assumptions or statements about error or the quality of knowledge. Nor is the claim probabilistic in any sense.

---

[2] The doctrine of operationalism holds that the meaning of concepts is found in the indicators and methods used to measure them. Most philosophers and social scientists reject this doctrine.

A better analogy is that a fuzzy-set membership score for a case is similar to a value on a given variable for a particular observation in a quantitative dataset. Although fuzzy-set membership values and variable values cannot be mechanically translated from one to the other (see the chapter "Semantics, Statistics, and Data Transformations"), there is a parallel between the two. A big difference is then that fuzzy-set membership values usually have no error or uncertainty estimates associated with them. In fuzzy logic mathematics, the idea of "second order" fuzziness does exist: how fuzzy is our fuzzy membership value (e.g., Klir and Yuan 1997; Arfi 2010)? This second-order fuzziness is a good qualitative analogy for an error estimate. However, while such a mathematical option exists in the fuzzy logic literature, it is not a natural thing to do in the qualitative culture and is rarely applied in practice in the social sciences.

Although they do not present explicit estimates of error, qualitative researchers do routinely discuss the difficulty of accurately coding particular cases. They may include elaborate discussions of their reasoning behind certain codes for individual cases. They may ground their decision in the existing expert literature or their own specialized knowledge. From a quantitative perspective, it might seem strange that these researchers would worry so much about the specific codings for a few individual observations. Within the quantitative culture, it is usually not a good investment of time and resources to focus so closely on a small number of problematic observations.

These qualitative coding decisions often are made by assessing the extent to which a case corresponds to an "ideal type," or a pure and complete example of a given concept. The ideal type serves as a standard against which all empirical cases can be evaluated; scholars "calibrate" (Ragin 2008) their case codes in light of this standard. In terms of a scale of fuzzy-set membership scores, the ideal type is at one extreme of the scale: ideal-typical cases have a membership value of 1.00. These cases unambiguously have all of the defining characteristics of the concept in question.

With this qualitative approach, the general intuition is that cases closer to the ideal type are easier to code, and thus that the error associated with these codings is lower (Eliason and Styker 2009; Ragin 2008). Likewise, cases with scores of 0.00 are usually easier to code, since it is often clear when something is not at all a member of the concept. By contrast, cases with fuzzy-set membership scores of .50 exhibit maximal fuzziness and can be especially difficult to code. Thus, as one moves from ideal types, with fuzzy-set membership scores of 1.00 toward maximal fuzziness of .50, it becomes more difficult to code accurately and error is more likely. As one moves down from .50 scores and approaches the 0.00 pole, coding again becomes easier and error less prevalent. Thus, in practice, there is often a roughly curvilinear relationship between level of fuzziness and level of error. This relationship

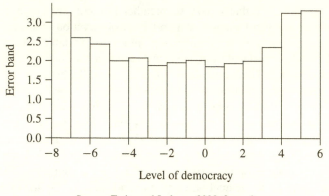

Level of democracy

*Source:* Treier and Jackman 2008, figure 2.
*Note:* The democracy scale is arbitrary.

**Figure 10.2.** Illustration of error in statistical measurement: level of democracy

is contingent and depends on the particular phenomenon being measured, but we think it is probably pretty common, at least in social science settings.

In the statistical tradition, the relationship between variable values and error follows the opposite pattern. If one asks where the largest error estimates will occur for a continuously coded variable, the statistical answer is among the cases with extreme (i.e., high or low) values. Error is greatest at the upper and lower bounds of a variable and lowest in the middle. This relationship is something that students learn early in their statistical training when they see a confidence band around a regression line. The estimated error is at its minimum at the mean of $X$ and the mean of $Y$. It gets progressively larger the further one moves from that middle point.

A good illustration of the relationship between variable values and error in the statistical tradition is Treier and Jackman's (2008) measurement model of democracy. Normally, the codes for democracy in a quantitative dataset (e.g., Polity or Freedom House) do not include any explicit error estimate. For example, one case may have a democracy value of 3 and another case a value of 6, but the error associated with those values is not estimated. Treier and Jackman's model provides a basis for making these estimates. Figure 10.2 presents Treier and Jackman's estimates of error for democracy measurement with Polity data. One sees the classic shape of a confidence band: it is narrowest in the middle and widest at the extremes.

From a qualitative perspective, these estimates of error for democracy seem counterintuitive. It is usually easy to code cases that are fully democratic or definitely not democratic; the ones that are hard to code are in the

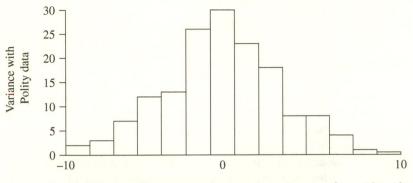

Level of Freedom House democracy (transformed to range from −10 to 10)

**Figure 10.3.** Variance for Freedom House and Polity scales of democracy

middle. Everyone agrees that Sweden is fully democratic and that North Korea is definitely not democratic. But how should we code borderline cases like contemporary Guatemala, Venezuela, and Honduras?

One way to explore this issue is to ask about the level of agreement between different datasets on democracy. Presumably, these datasets will tend to agree on the easy-to-code cases and be more likely to disagree on the hard-to-code cases. In figure 10.3, we report the variance for Polity and Freedom House codes using the country-years where the two datasets overlap (see Goertz 2008 for details). When both datasets completely agree, the variance between them is zero. As their disagreement grows, the variance between them increases. In the figure, we see clearly that the variance is lowest at the extremes of autocracy and democracy (i.e., −10 and 10); that is, there is little disagreement when Polity and Freedom House code an extreme autocracy (a score of −10) or full democracy (a score of +10). As we move toward the gray zone in the middle (a score of 0), we see that the variation in how they code a given country-year increases significantly. In fact, as we move down from a score of 10 to a score of 0, the variance increases by nearly 1000-fold (from .025 to 22.6). A large shift also happens as we move up from extreme autocracy (−10) to a score of 0, though the increase is "only" by a factor of 10.[3]

Contrasting figures 10.2 and 10.3 vividly illustrates the two cultures and their different views about the location of measurement error. Figure 10.2 is

---

[3] We leave it as an exercise to reevaluate Przeworski et al.'s (2000, 58–59) argument that their dichotomous coding of democracy produces less error than a continuous measure if error follows the variance as illustrated in figure 10.2 and the cut point between democracy and autocracy is zero.

what a quantitative researcher normally expects to find; figure 10.3 is what a qualitative scholar thinks will happen.

## Conclusion

This chapter has discussed the different approaches to concepts and measurement that animate the qualitative and quantitative traditions. In the qualitative tradition, in general, concepts are constructed through a semantic process, one in which the researcher specifies the meaning of a concept by identifying the attributes that constitute it. With this approach, qualitative scholars often feel most confident about the measurement of cases that have extreme values in relationship to the concept of interest. Thus, they find measurement to be easiest when looking at cases that definitely are or definitely are not instances of the concept of interest. Error becomes more likely as cases become ambiguous instances of the concept being measured.

In the quantitative tradition, in general, concepts are constructed through the identification of indicators that are caused by the concept of interest. For various well-known statistical reasons, error estimates are smaller at the mean than at the extremes; as such, quantitative scholars feel the least certain about cases with extreme values and most certain for cases that have values near the mean.

The distinctive orientations of each culture are reasonable, with long-standing histories and good methodological justifications behind them. They are closely related to the case-oriented versus population-oriented nature of the traditions. Nevertheless, such deep-seated differences make it hard (though not impossible) to go back and forth between them to arrive at a synthetic approach to concepts and measurement (Adcock and Collier 2001). This helps to explain why the qualitative literature on concepts and the quantitative literature on measurement have not had more to say to one another.

## References and Suggested Readings

It is of interest to compare qualitative and quantitative work on any given concept or variable in terms of the relative weight they give to conceptualization, measurement, and final data. Almost by definition, a "conceptual" article does not provide a measurement model (though it in principle could), and typically it does not systematically code cases. Individual cases are of course used as examples, but there is no systematic analysis. For example, the qualitative literature on the "quality" of democracy (e.g., Diamond and Morlino 2005) focuses on conceptual issues and spends less time on operationalization and systematic data coding. "Data articles" (e.g., see the *Journal of Peace Research*, which has regular "data feature" articles) may begin with a discussion of concepts, but this is often brief compared to the treatment of operationalization, indicators, measurement, and the resulting dataset. Measurement articles that use existing data focus almost entirely on the measurement issue (e.g., Bollen and Grandjean 1981; Treier and Jackman 2008).

It is also interesting to track concepts, measurement models, and resulting data as they change over time. For example, while the Polity measure of democracy has been around for decades (Gurr 1974; Gurr et al. 1990; Jaggers and Gurr 1995), Polity's concept and measure have not remained constant. It would be an interesting exercise to see which country-years have remained constant across the various versions of the dataset and which have not.

Adcock, R., and D. Collier. 2001. Measurement validity: a shared standard for qualitative and quantitative research. *American Political Science Review* 95:529–46.

Arfi, B. 2010. *Linguistic fuzzy logic methods in social sciences*. Berlin: Springer-Verlag.

Bollen, K. 1989. *Structural equations with latent variables*. New York: John Wiley & Sons.

Bollen, K., and B. Grandjean. 1981. The dimension(s) of democracy: further issues in the measurement and effects of political democracy. *American Sociological Review* 46:651–59.

Bollen, K., and K. Ting. 2000. A tetrad test for causal indicators. *Psychological Methods* 5:3–22.

Bowman, K., F. Lehoucq, and J. Mahoney. 2005. Measuring political democracy: case expertise, data adequacy, and Central America. *Comparative Political Studies* 38:939–70.

CETIS. 2007. GTD2 (1998–2004): global terrorism database, draft 1.0. Manuscript, University of Maryland.

Collier, D., and S. Levitsky. 1997. Democracy with adjectives: conceptual innovation in comparative research. *World Politics* 49:430–51.

Diamond, L., and L. Morlino, eds. 2005. *Assessing the quality of democracy*. Baltimore: Johns Hopkins University Press.

Eliason, S., and R. Stryker. 2009. Goodness-of-fit tests and descriptive measures in fuzzy-set analysis. *Sociological Methods & Research* 38:102–46.

Goertz, G. 2005. *Social science concepts: a user's guide*. Princeton: Princeton University Press.

Goertz, G. 2008. A checklist for constructing, evaluating, and using concepts or quantitative measures. In *The Oxford handbook of political methodology*, edited by J. Box-Steffensmier, H. Brady, and D. Collier. Oxford: Oxford University Press.

Gurr, T. 1974. Persistence and change in political systems, 1800–1971. *American Political Science Review* 68:1482–1504.

Gurr, T., K. Jaggers, and W. Moore. 1990. The transformation of the Western state: the growth of democracy, autocracy, and state power since 1800. *Studies in Comparative International Development* 25:73–108.

Hall, P. 2003. Aligning ontology and methodology in comparative research. In *Comparative historical analysis in the social sciences*, edited by J. Mahoney and D. Rueschemeyer. Cambridge: Cambridge University Press.

Hempel, C. 1952. Fundamentals of concept formation in empirical science. In *International encyclopedia of unified science,* vol. 2, no. 7. Chicago: University of Chicago Press.

Jaggers, K., and T. Gurr. 1995. Tracking democracy's third wave with the Polity III data. *Journal of Peace Research* 32:469–82.

Kenworthy, L. 2003. Quantitative indicators of corporatism. *International Journal of Sociology* 33:10–44.

Klir, G., and B. Yuan. 1997. *Fuzzy set theory: foundations and applications.* Englewood Cliffs: Prentice-Hall.

Mainwaring, S., D. Brinks, and A. Pérez-Liñán. 2001. Classifying political regimes in Latin America, 1945–1999. *Studies in Comparative International Development* 36:37–65.

Przeworski, A., M. E. Alvarez, J. A. Cheibub, and F. Limongi. 2000. *Democracy and development: political institutions and well-being in the world, 1950–1990.* Cambridge: Cambridge university Press.

Ragin, C. 2008. *Redesigning social inquiry: fuzzy sets and beyond.* Chicago: University of Chicago Press.

Schmid, A., and A. Jongman. 1988. *Political terrorism: a new guide to actors, authors, concepts, data bases, and literature.* New York: North Holland.

Schmitter, P. 1974. Still the century of corporatism? *Review of Politics* 36:85–131.

Treier, S., and S. Jackman. 2008. Democracy as a latent variable. *American Journal of Political Science* 52:201–17.

# Chapter 11

# Meaning and Measurement

In this messy controversy about quantification and its bearing on
standard logical rules we simply tend to forget that concept
formation stands prior to quantification.
  —*Giovanni Sartori*

## Introduction

Different academic cultures normally have distinct methodological vocab-
ularies. Although scholars from one culture may assume that they can
understand the concepts from another culture using their existing vocabulary,
in fact problems of translation often arise. With translations between natural
languages, a given word or idea sometimes cannot be fully expressed in
another language. Likewise, when the same term is used across different
methodological cultures in the social sciences, it may take on different
meanings or have different levels of importance. It is quite possible that a
concept that is central in one culture will have only low prominence in the
other.

Here we explore how these translation problems are manifested across
the qualitative and quantitative cultures for issues related to concepts and
measurement. In the quantitative culture, one speaks of *variables* and
*indicators*. $X$ and $Y$ are normally latent, unobserved variables for which
one needs (quantitative) indicators. To choose an example, consider the
variable "economic development." Although this variable cannot be directly
observed, it can be measured empirically with an indicator such as GDP per
capita. In practice, scholars in the quantitative culture might fuse the variable
and the indicator into one entity. For example, they may use economic

development and GDP per capita interchangeably. However, for the purposes of this chapter, we shall keep variables and their indicators quite separate. When we say "variable," we mean a latent construct of theoretical interest; when we say "indicator," we refer to numeric data for measuring the latent construct.

Qualitative scholars lack a unified way of talking about these issues. As a matter of convenience, or because of statistics courses and reining vocabulary, they too often use the variable-indicator language. Yet we believe that this language raises a translation problem and does not capture research practices in the qualitative culture. Instead of speaking in terms of variables and indicators, we need to distinguish between *concepts* and *data* to grasp the qualitative culture. By "concept," we mean a category (or set) in which cases can membership, including often different degrees of membership. For example, a standard qualitative concept is "economically developed country." By "data" we mean diverse qualitative and quantitative information that can be used to assess whether or the extent to which cases are members of concepts. There is an obvious analogy between "variable" and "concept," on the one hand, and "indicator" and "data," on the other. Concepts and variables are words and associated ideas that we use to formulate theories, while data and indicators are empirical information that we use to measure concepts and variables.

While variable-indicator and concept-data may seem like two ways of talking about basically the same thing, in fact they refer to different relationships. These differences are summarized in the title of this chapter, "Meaning and Measurement." For qualitative scholars, the relationship between a concept and data is one of *semantics*, i.e., meaning. These scholars explore how data can be used to express the meaning of a concept. For quantitative scholars, by contrast, the relationship between variable and indicator concerns the *measurement* of the variable. These scholars focus on how to use indicators to best measure a latent construct.

As an example, consider again how GDP per capita data might be used to analyze economic development. In the quantitative culture, a standard move is to say that a country's GDP per capita is a good indicator of its level of economic development. GDP per capita data then become the actual measure of level of economic development that is used in the statistical model. Qualitative researchers might also use GDP per capita data when analyzing economic development. However, they would normally ask how these data relate to what they "mean" by a specific category, such as economically developed country. Before being used in analysis, the data would normally have to undergo what we call a "semantic transformation" (cf. Ragin 2008 on "calibration"), such that they better fit the researcher's core concept of economically developed country. Quantitative researchers might also transform GDP per capita data (e.g., using the logged value of the data) before analyzing it in a statistical model,[1] but these transformations would be done for statistical reasons (e.g., because of skewed data), not to achieve a better fit with conceptual meaning.

When the final numeric measures of the variable "level of economic development" and the category "economically developed country" are compared across countries, they will often yield different specific values for particular countries. Thus, differences in the two cultures have direct, concrete implications for how scholars code and understand particular cases.

We argue that fuzzy-set analysis is a useful device for formally specifying the way in which qualitative researchers think about the concept-data relationship. After all, fuzzy logic at its origins was a mathematical theory of semantics (see Kosko (1993) and McNeill and Freiberger (1994) for accessible introductions). It was designed to solve problems related to modeling natural language terms. Classic examples are concepts like "tall person" and "rich person." For these concepts, we might have data on the height and wealth of individuals. Fuzzy-set analysis provides a set of tools for using this data to state the extent to which individuals are members of the categories tall person and rich person.

In the quantitative culture, if one wishes to assess a hypothesis about tall people or rich people, one might use data on height or income in the statistical analysis. Although the variable and the indicator need not be fused at the conceptual level, in practice the two are treated as the same thing for the purpose of statistical hypothesis testing. Qualitative scholars could also fuse the concept with the data in practice, but that is an unnatural procedure to follow. These researchers tend to perform a nonlinear semantic transformation to arrive at the final understanding of the extent to which individuals fall within the categories tall person and rich person.

Another way to think about this issue is that quantitative scholars typically assume a linear relationship between variable and indicator. There is a direct match between the indicator and the variable. Obviously, any one indicator may not be a perfect measure of the latent variable, which is why multiple indicators are often encouraged. However, there is no need to assume a nonlinear relationship between the indicator and variable. With fuzzy logic, by contrast, semantic transformations are virtually never linear. While a large array of transformations are used in fuzzy logic, linear is not popular at all.

The frequent use of linearity in the quantitative culture can be seen by considering contrasting pairs of variables, such as level of development versus level of underdevelopment. These two variables are normally treated as the exact inverse of each other: each unit increase for level of

---

[1] We discuss some common transformations, such as logging, in the chapter "Concepts, Semantics, and Data Transformations."

development entails an equal unit decrease for level of underdevelopment. This symmetry is reinforced by the fact that development and underdevelopment are measured with the same data (e.g., GDP per capita data). By contrast, fuzzy logic may well invoke one semantic transformation for economic development and a different (if related) one for economic underdevelopment. As a result, the final numeric measure for a case's membership in the set of developed countries will be negatively correlated with its membership in the set of underdeveloped countries, but the relationship may not be perfectly symmetric. One could not necessarily predict a country's fuzzy-set score for development on the basis of its score of underdevelopment. This assumption of the nonidentity of opposing pairs is the standard fuzzy logic position and is very common among qualitative researchers, e.g., peace is not the same as not-war (see the chapter "Conceptual Opposites and Typologies").

## Semantic Transformations and Set-Membership Functions

Differences in terminology often signal important contrasts in methodological practice. Core to the fuzzy-set approach to concepts is the notion of a "membership function." To illustrate, consider the concept of "tall" as applied to men. In fuzzy-set analysis, one asks about a given man's membership in the "set of tall man." In quantitative analysis, by contrast, one might ask about a man's score on the variable "level of tallness." To code cases, both qualitative and quantitative researchers might turn to data on height. But this data would be used in different ways.

By convention, fuzzy-set variables range from zero to one, i.e., [0,1]. From a strictly mathematical point of view, the restriction to [0,1] is arbitrary because anything in the $-\infty$ to $+\infty$ range can be rescaled into [0,1]. In practice, one could rescale data into [0,1] by simple transformations. The most obvious way to transform a continuous dataset into a [0,1] scale is to subtract the minimum value in the dataset and then divide the data by the range of the dataset. This makes the largest value in the dataset one and the smallest value zero. Statistically this is a linear transformation and in general makes no difference for the statistical results. So in many situations it is pointless from a statistical perspective to do this.[2]

One theoretical and methodological feature of the fuzzy-set membership approach is that one is *forced* to transform all data into [0,1]. While variable transformations are common in quantitative research (see the

---

[2] In some social sciences and during some time periods, there was a preference for standardized variables. Although standardizing variables does not change the substantive results, it does allow for comparison across variables because they all have the same units, i.e., standard deviations.

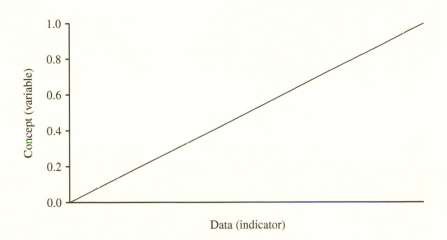

**Figure 11.1.** Semantic transformations: linear

chapter "Semantics, Statistics, and Data Transformations"), they are often completely optional. In fuzzy-set analysis, they usually cannot be avoided.

Figure 11.1 depicts a way for diagramming the relationship between data and concept. We have "data" on the X-axis and "concept" on the Y-axis. This figure is appropriate for illustrating fuzzy-set analysis because the researcher wants to know how the data on the X-axis relates to the semantic meaning of a concept as represented on the Y-axis. In contrast, these kinds of figures are not used for summarizing the relationship between an indicator and a concept in statistical analysis. In figure 11.1, the relationship is assumed to be perfectly linear. This is the fuzzy logic interpretation of what quantitative scholars are doing when they do not transform data from the original scales. In fuzzy-set analysis, however, this kind of linear transformation from data to concept is almost never done.

Instead, the semantic, fuzzy-set approach considers the meaning of the concept when transforming data into membership values. For example, the researcher would consider the meaning of "tall" when applied to men (Zadeh 1965). One simple way to explore the semantics of "tall man" is to ask if a 6-foot, 3-inch (1.9 meters) man is tall. One might respond, "yes, he definitely is tall." Translated into fuzzy-set terms, that man has 1.0 membership in the set of tall men. The same question can be asked about a man who is 5-foot, 7-inches (1.7 meters). The response might be that he is definitely "not tall," which means he has 0.0 membership in the set of tall men. What about someone who is 6-foot (1.83 meters)? Such a man is "sort-of" tall. This person might have a .50 membership in the set of tall men. These "half-empty, half-full" points are critical in semantic transformations.

The .50 membership level is roughly analogous to the median or mean since it represents a middle point. However, in practice, the .50 membership level works in radically different ways from a statistical average. In fuzzy-set logic, the .50 membership value is a "cross-over" point: it is where cases move from more in to more out of the set (and vice versa). It is also the zone where small changes in the data can mean large conceptual differences (see below). The .50 membership value has nothing to do with the distribution of the data. In general, one would almost never use the mean of the data as the .50 level in fuzzy-set analysis. For instance, while a 6-foot man might have a membership value of .50 for the set of tall men, this man has above average height.

## The Principle of Unimportant Variation

Figure 11.1 presented a linear semantic transformation. This kind of linear transformation is, in effect, the default move for relating an indicator to a variable implicit in many statistical analyses. In this section, we consider common nonlinear semantic transformations for connecting data to a concept in qualitative research.

The way we constructed the membership function for "tall man" offers an example. We said that a 6′3″ (1.9 meters) man had full membership in the set of tall men. So what about someone who is 7-feet tall (2.1 meters)? This man too would clearly be considered a full member of the set. In fact, anyone over 6′3″ is a full member. Of course, the same thing applies to men shorter than 5′7″ (1.7 meters): they have zero membership in the set of tall men. What this means is that variation in height above 6′3″ or below 5′7″ has no semantic meaning or importance vis-à-vis the concept of tall men.

We can now state a fundamental principle of semantic transformations in the qualitative culture:

> *Principle of Unimportant Variation*: There are regions in the data that have the same semantic meaning.

Variation in the data does not always translate into differences in the extent to which cases have membership in semantic categories. Two men with different heights could both be equally full members of the category tall man.

Figure 11.2 provides an example using the concept of economically developed country and data on GDP per capita (see Ragin 2000 for a similar example). Differences in GDP per capita between, say, Switzerland and

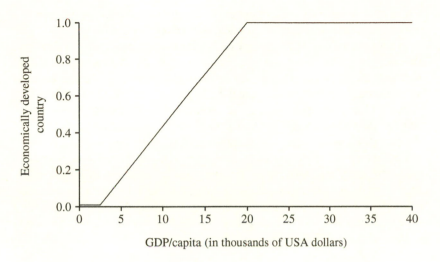

**Figure 11.2.** Semantic transformations: the Principle of Unimportant Variation

Sweden, do not manifest themselves in differences in their membership in the set of economically developed countries; they are both 1.00 members. Similarly, differences among most poor countries do not change their membership of zero in the set of economically developed countries.

One might well ask about the points in figure 11.2 where membership scores start to increase and decline. Are these cutoff points not "arbitrary"? A reasonable answer would be that researchers, statesmen, and prominent IGOs like the United Nations and the World Bank must mean something when they refer to economically developed countries. If they do mean something, then in principle one could work to decipher this meaning and use it to ground a decision about where the data begin to reflect important semantic variations. Thus, the choice about these kinds of cutoff points need not be arbitrary. In addition, the exact point where the membership functions start to decline may not be that critical as long as the slope of the line is modest (though often the slope is relatively steep).

The key point is quite intuitive: a difference of 4000–5000 dollars at the top does not matter much at all, but that same difference in the middle can be hugely important. This leads to the corollary of the Principle of Unimportant Variation, which could be called the principle of small differences but big impacts. Just as there are ranges where differences in GDP per capita do not matter for membership in the set of economically developed countries, there are other ranges where these differences are magnified. The magnified differences occur for membership values less than one and more than zero.

Here small differences in GDP per capita are translated into big differences in membership in the set of economically developed countries.

Although in figure 11.2 the slope of the line is constant for all membership values greater than zero and less than one on the Y-axis, it need not be transformed in exactly this way with fuzzy-set analysis. If the default semantic transformation is linear in the quantitative culture, the most popular option in fuzzy-set analysis is some variant of the S-curve (again, see the chapter "Semantics, Statistics, and Data Transformations"). Depending on the exact S-curve, the region of magnified effects could be found in different places, though it would normally be centered around the .50 membership value. In short, the Principle of Unimportant Variation usually applies to the top and bottom ends of the data scale, where memberships are zero or one. By contrast, the effects of variation are magnified around the .50 membership level, where small changes on the data scale often correspond to large semantic differences.

## Membership Functions and Scale Types

One learns, hopefully, in some methodology class the classic hierarchy of scale types. These go in order: nominal, ordinal, interval, and ratio. The differences between these are normally described in part based on the amount of information they contain for comparing cases. For example, nominal scales have little information because they allow for only categorical comparisons, whereas interval and ratio scales are the highest because they allow for measurement of size. Since Stevens's classic articles (1946; 1968), these scale types have become part of any basic statistical training.

So how do these scale types match up, or not, with membership functions in fuzzy-set analysis? A good place to start is with the zero point. Interval scales differ from ratio scales in that the latter have a true zero while the former do not. For example, the money in your bank account is on a ratio scale because reaching the zero point exhausts the account and being in debt is quite different than having a positive balance.

The zero membership value in fuzzy-set analysis does not play the same role. In fuzzy-set analysis, the zero value indicates the complete lack of *membership in a set*. For example, a country with a nonzero GDP per capita of 500 dollars would doubtless receive a 0.0 membership score for the category "rich country." In this sense, the zero value in fuzzy-set analysis is closer to the idea of the minimum point on a continuous scale, though there are differences here as well.

A similar point can be made for the 1.00 membership value in a fuzzy-set scale. The one value indicates full membership in a set. It plays a role somewhat similar to the maximum point on a continuous scale. Yet, in the

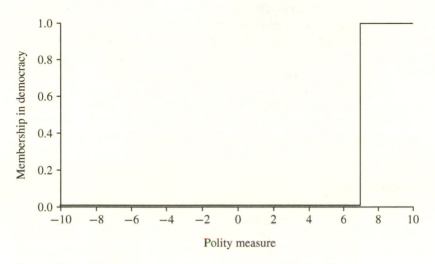

**Figure 11.3.** Dichotomous variables and membership functions

classic scaling schemes, there is no notion of a true maximum. For example, what would it mean to say that an individual has a maximum level of wealth? The individual could always have one dollar more.

In classical measurement theory, dichotomous variables are seen as occupying the bottom of the hierarchy of scales. If one has continuously coded data, it is almost always considered a bad move to dichotomize the data, since this involves throwing away information. Fuzzy-set analysis offers a quite different view of dichotomization. We can illustrate this difference by considering the Polity data (Marshall, Gurr, and Jaggers 2010), which is often used to measure democracy.

Figure 11.3 uses a common dichotomization scheme that scholars apply to the Polity data, where 7 is the cutoff point for democracy on the scale −10 to 10. From a statistical standpoint, one loses a tremendous amount of information by dichotomizing the Polity data: we go from a 21-point scale to a 2-point scale (see figure 11.3). By contrast, from a fuzzy-set point of view, dichotomization is just another semantic transformation function. The fuzzy-set objection to dichotomization of this sort is not the loss of information. Rather, the objection is that the slope of the curve, i.e., the vertical line at 7, is far too steep (the derivative is infinity). Here is a case where the cutoff point really would matter: the slightest change in data could lead to a complete shift in semantic meaning.

However, if one adjusts the slope so that it is not so extreme, then the dichotomous move will seem reasonable to a qualitative scholar as an approach for assessing membership in the set of democratic countries. Now the fuzzy-set membership value of cases would gradually decline from 1.0 as Polity scores decline below the cutoff point of 7. This can be seen by comparing the transformations (indicated by the lines) in figures 11.2 and 11.3. Although figure 11.3 is dichotomous, its basic form is really not that different from figure 11.2. The difference is merely the extent of the slope of the line connecting the maximum (i.e., 1.0) and the minimum (i.e., 0.0) membership values. To a fuzzy-set analyst, the dichotomous membership function, while problematic, may well seem more appropriate than the default linear assumption implicit in the use of the 21-point Polity scale.

## Conclusion

In this chapter, we have suggested that a fuzzy-set approach describes well the way in which qualitative researchers think about the relationship between data and membership in a concept. With this approach, a critical question involves asking about the appropriate semantic transformation to turn data into membership values. The researcher is concerned with matching the data to concept meaning, and thus the meaning of the concept is assumed to dictate the appropriate transformation. In this sense, with fuzzy-set analysis, conceptual meaning is in the driver's seat.

On the quantitative side, the kinds of nonlinear transformations used in fuzzy-set analysis are not commonly employed for linking data with a variable. Instead, because data are used as the indicators of a variable, it is normal and appropriate to view the data as standing in a linear relationship to the variable. A good indicator of a statistical variable ordinarily will not require transformation. Rather the values of the indicator will match closely the values of the variable. In this sense, with statistical analysis, one seeks indicators that do not require transformation to be used in measurement.

## References and Suggested Readings

The qualitative literature on concepts is a good point of entry for the semantic approach described in this chapter. See Collier and Gerring (2009); Collier and Levitsky (1997); Goertz (2005; 2008); and Sartori (1970; 1984). On the variable-indicator approach common in statistical research, see Blalock (1982) and Bollen (1989). With only a few exceptions, e.g., Adcock and Collier (2001) and Goertz (2005), these two literatures have not communicated with one another. The link between the fuzzy-set approach and semantics goes back to Zadeh (1965) and is emphasized in the excellent introductory works by Kosko (1993) and McNeill and Freiberger (1994). The notion of unimportant variation is discussed by Ragin (2000) using GDP per capita as one of his examples.

Adcock, R., and D. Collier. 2001. Measurement validity: a shared standard for qualitative and quantitative research. *American Political Science Review* 95:529–46.

Blalock, H. 1982. *Conceptualization and measurement in the social sciences.* Beverly Hills: Sage Publications.

Bollen, K. 1989. *Structural equations with latent variables.* New York: John Wiley & Sons.

Boyd, L., and G. Iverson. 1979. *Contextual analysis: concepts and statistical techniques.* Belmont: Wadsworth.

Collier, D., and J. Gerring, eds. 2009. *Concepts and methods in the social sciences: the tradition of Giovanni Sartori.* London: Routledge.

Collier, D., and S. Levitsky. 1997. Democracy with adjectives: conceptual innovation in comparative research. *World Politics* 49:430–51.

Gates, S., H. Hegre, M. Jones, and H. Strand. 2006. Institutional inconsistency and political instability: polity duration, 1800–2000. *American Journal of Political Science* 50:893–908.

Goertz, G. 2005. *Social science concepts: a user's guide.* Princeton: Princeton University Press.

Goertz, G. 2008. A checklist for constructing, evaluating, and using concepts or quantitative measures. In *The Oxford handbook of political methodology*, edited by J. Box-Steffensmier, H. Brady, and D. Collier. Oxford: Oxford University Press.

King, G., R. Keohane, and S. Verba. 1994. *Designing social inquiry: scientific inference in qualitative research.* Princeton: Princeton University Press.

Kosko, B. 1993. *Fuzzy thinking: the new science of fuzzy logic.* New York: Hyperion.

Marshall, M. G., T. R. Gurr, and K. Jaggers. 2010. *Polity IV project: political regime characteristics and transitions, 1800–2009.* Center for Systemic Peace, www.systemicpeace.org/polity/polity4.htm.

McNeill, D., and P. Freiberger. 1994. *Fuzzy logic.* New York: Simon and Schuster.

Ragin, C. 2000. *Fuzzy-set social science.* Chicago: University of Chicago Press.

Ragin, C. 2008. *Redesigning social inquiry: fuzzy sets and beyond.* Chicago: University of Chicago Press.

Sartori, G. 1970. Concept misformation in comparative politics. *American Political Science Review* 64:1033–53.

Sartori, G. 1984. Guidelines for concept analysis. In *Social science concepts: a systematic analysis*, edited by G. Sartori. Beverly Hills: Sage Publications.

Stevens, S. 1946. On the theory of scales of measurement. *Science* 103:677–80.

Stevens, S. 1968. Measurement, statistics and the schemapiric view. *Science* 161:849–56.

Zadeh, L. 1965. Fuzzy sets. *Information and Control* 8:338–53.

# Chapter 12

## Semantics, Statistics, and Data Transformations

Power [e.g., log] transformations can make a skewed distribution more symmetric. But why should we bother?

(1) Highly skewed distributions are difficult to examine because most of the observations are confined to a small part of the range of data.

(2) Apparently outlying values in the direction of the skew are brought in toward the main body of the data when the distribution is made more symmetric.

(3) Some of the common statistical methods summarize distributions using means. The mean of a skewed distribution is, however, not a good summary of its center.
                    —*John Fox*

### Introduction

Within the statistical culture, there are well-established norms about transforming variables that make practices such as standardization and logging data quite common and noncontroversial. These practices make good methodological sense given the research goals of this culture. However, when viewed from a qualitative perspective with its emphasis on making sense of individual cases, the same practices appear quite problematic. Variable transformations in the quantitative culture respond to the imperatives of statistics; qualitative scholars work under a different set of norms and values that emphasize the importance of semantics and the meaning embodied in concepts. This culture provides an alternative interpretation of what it means to, for instance, use logged GDP per capita or to standardize the Polity measure of democracy.

In this chapter, we introduce the Fundamental Principle of Variable Transformation as a way of describing the qualitative view of variable transformation. This principle holds that all transformations of variables must be meaning preserving or increasing. Thus, the principle requires that if one uses logged values for GDP per capita, the resulting data should better represent what the scholar means by the concept of interest, such as economic development or wealth, than the untransformed data. Within the qualitative culture, transformations that do not conform to this principle are viewed as suspect.

## Standardization versus Meaning Retention

A popular transformation is to standardize a variable. In statistical analysis, standardization often does not change the results, because most parameter estimates retain their properties—such as unbiasedness—when the variable is subject to a linear transformation.[1] To recall, the formula when standardizing variables is $(x_i - \overline{x})/s$, where $\overline{x}$ is the mean and $s$ is the standard deviation. For example, the raw data of the Polity scale of democracy codes cases from $-10$ to $10$ (Marshall, Gurr, and Jaggers 2010). Standardization converts these numbers into a new scale of standard deviations from the mean.

The results of standardization obviously depend on the underlying data, not on anything related to the definition of the concept being measured. The statistical mean, as well as the standard deviation, will change as the underlying data change. In fact, with standardization, the score for any one case can easily change if the scores for the other cases are altered. A case might not experience any real world change, yet its coding shifts because the codes for other cases are changing. From a qualitative perspective, this can seem odd: why should the score for a case depend on how the other cases happen to be coded?

To make this more concrete, let us consider the Polity dataset on level of democracy. A qualitative researcher might develop the rule that "full democracy" characterizes those cases beyond some threshold, such as all cases with values from 7 to 10. Under this rule, any proportion of the cases, including all or none of them, could be full democracies, depending on

---

[1] However, if the variable is further subject to transformation or analysis this may no longer be the case—e.g., if the transformed variable is used in interaction terms.

whether they meet the threshold. If the data are presented as standardized values, however, one must use a different rule, such as full democracy characterizes those cases that are at least two standard deviations above the mean. This rule ensures that only a small proportion of the cases will be coded as full democracies. A given case can slip in and out of the category of full democracy depending on how the other cases are coded. From a qualitative perspective, this is problematic. Whether a case is a full democracy or not depends on the definition of that concept and the features of the case, not on the distribution of levels of democracy within the population as a whole.

The use of standardized values can also have other consequences for research. For example, consider the advice that one should standardize variables in order to select case studies based on their "extreme" values (Gerring and Seawright 2008). There are good reasons why one would want to look at extreme cases. Given this, standardizing values is an obvious choice because we have some idea about what extreme means in terms of standard deviations: an observation that is 2–3 standard deviations from the mean is extreme. Thus, from within the statistical culture, this approach makes very good sense.

Within the qualitative culture, however, the approach is troubling. The standardization approach defines extreme values in terms of their relationship to the sample mean, which is treated as the "middle point." But for a qualitative researcher, the sample mean may, or may not, represent the middle point of a concept. The middle point corresponds to the *conceptual* middle value. For instance, with the Polity scale, which ranges from –10 to 10, the conceptual middle point might be zero.[2] By contrast, the sample mean for Polity is about +3.

With the Polity data, one consequence of standardization is that the most extreme cases are always authoritarian regimes. Because the sample mean is about +3, the authoritarian cases of –10 always have larger absolute standardized values than do the complete democracy cases with a value of +10. Within the statistical culture, this is not necessarily problematic: the most authoritarian cases are more extreme in terms of their deviation from the mean. From the qualitative perspective, however, standardization is seen as counterproductive. From this perspective, the extreme values are "obviously" the –10 and the +10 cases. These cases have the most possible extreme values in relationship to the conceptual middle point of the scale.

---

[2] Given that the Polity measure of regime type is democracy minus authoritarian, where both democracy and authoritarian range from zero to 10, there is much in the Polity procedure that would imply that zero is the conceptual middle point.

This leads us to what we call the Fundamental Principle of Variable Transformation in the qualitative culture:

*Fundamental Principle of Variable Transformation.* All data transformations should tighten the relationship between the data and the meaning of the concept.

In the previous chapter, we used the example of the concept of "tall man" and data on height. Qualitative researchers may transform the height data, but their motivation is to achieve a better fit with the concept of interest. By contrast, standardization, e.g., standardized height data, is usually not motivated by better fit with any concept, and hence it violates the Fundamental Principle of Variable Transformation.

In short, the qualitative, semantic approach will generally see standardization as a step backwards. It introduces irrelevant considerations, i.e., the potentially changing distribution of the data, into what is a semantic relationship. Standardizing data typically violates the Fundamental Principle of Variable Transformation. It brings in aspects of the real world distribution of data that are unhelpful and potentially misleading.[3]

## Logging versus Fuzzy-Set Transformations

Logging a variable (i.e., using the natural log of the variable) is very common and often recommended in statistical research. To take a classic example, the decision to log GDP per capita is rarely controversial. Although not all scholars carry out this transformation, one can find countless examples of research of all kinds where they do.

On the qualitative side, fuzzy-set analysis provides one set of tools for specifying the relationship between GDP per capita and the concept of wealthy or economically developed country. Fuzzy logic is concerned with how the data indicate the extent to which cases have membership in the set of wealthy or economically developed countries. Following standard conventions (see the previous chapter), a score of zero means that a country has no membership in the set of wealthy or economically developed countries, while a score of one means full membership—i.e., the case is a wealthy or economically developed country. Cases can also have any membership score between one and zero.

---

[3] Freedman (2009, 87–88) gives a nice illustration using Hooke's Law (see the chapter "Scope," where we consider Hooke's law as an example) for why standardization is often not a good idea.

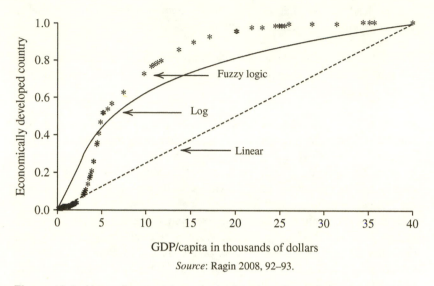

GDP/capita in thousands of dollars

*Source*: Ragin 2008, 92–93.

**Figure 12.1.** Linear, log, and fuzzy logic data transformations

It is useful to consider differences in the way in which the two cultures typically use GDP per capita to assess the extent to which countries are wealthy or economically developed. Often, the quantitative culture assumes a linear relationship between level of GDP per capita and the extent to which a country is economically developed, as illustrated in figure 12.1 by the dashed line. The usually unstated assumption is that economic development increases linearly with GDP per capita. If logged values are used, however, we arrive at the solid line in figure 12.1. One potential interpretation of this line (see below for another) is that there is a decreasing returns relationship between GDP per capita and economic development. In other words, the slope of the log curve in figure 12.1 decreases as GDP per capita gets larger.

In fuzzy-set analysis, the relationship between continuous quantitative data and membership scores often assumes an S-shaped curve. In figure 12.1, GDP per capita and economically developed country follow this pattern as illustrated by the starred line (see Ragin 2008, chapter 5). With this fuzzy-set transformation, cases with a range of low GDP per capita values all receive the same code of zero; from a semantic perspective, these cases all have no membership within the concept of interest (economically developed country). This is the Principle of Unimportant Variation discussed in the chapter "Meaning and Measurement." These cases are at the very low end of GDP per capita near the origin in figure 12.1. Once cases start to have membership in the concept, small differences yield large impacts in the extent to which they are members of the set of economically developed countries. The fuzzy-set line then becomes similar to the line for the log values, though the slope of the fuzzy-set line is even steeper for the range of values between $2,500 and $5,000 GDP per capita. On the other side of the fuzzy-set curve, cases that have a range of high levels are all coded as one, since they are all full members of the concept. As a result, the right-hand side of the fuzzy-set line flattens out quite dramatically.

With logged values, the variation at the upper end of GDP per capita also becomes relatively less important (though the slope does not become completely flat). Variation at the very low end (e.g., among cases with less than $2,500 GDP per capita) is extremely important. Here is a fundamental difference with the semantic, qualitative approach. From a semantic perspective focused on membership in "economically developed country," differences at the very low end are not important because all of these countries are clearly not economically developed countries. For example, the difference in GDP per capita between Chad and Mali is irrelevant; they both have zero membership in the category economically developed country. But for the scholar who logs GDP per capita, these same small differences at the lower end are accentuated by the log transformation (as indicated by the steep slope beginning at the origin for the log line in figure 12.1). From this perspective, the GDP per capita difference between Chad and Mali is quite important for their level of economic development. Small increases in GDP per capita mean large advances in economic development for poor countries; a similar change for a rich country is of little consequence.

This difference is related to the contrasting norms of the two cultures. In the qualitative culture, one must always ask about the meaning of the specific concept being measured, which is understood as a set in which cases can have membership. Transforming data so that GDP per capita match better what one means by wealthy or developed country is what researchers should be doing. In the quantitative culture, by contrast, logging it is motivated by the skewness of the data or increasing the fit of the statistical model. From a qualitative point of view these kinds of considerations seem inappropriate; from a statistical standpoint they often make very good sense, as suggested in the epigraph for this chapter.

## Rationales for Data Transformations

In order to understand the rationale behind these alternative data transformations, it is useful to look at the distribution of cases across different levels of GDP per capita. As figure 12.2 shows, the big majority of cases are toward the very low end. From a fuzzy-set perspective, the conclusion that one draws is that most countries simply have no membership in the

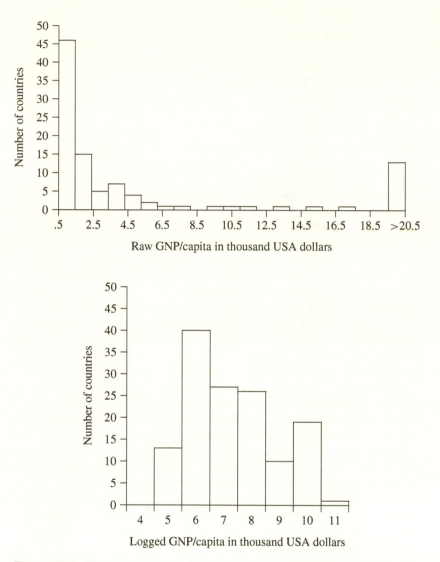

Figure 12.2. Distribution of countries by levels of raw and logged GDP per capita

category economically developed country. The histogram in figure 12.2 also makes it clear that there are a fair number of countries that are quite rich (i.e., cases with a GDP per capita of more than $20,000). These are the countries that are coded as having full membership in the set of economically developed countries. The number of cases that are in the middle (with fuzzy-set membership values between 0 and 1) is relatively small. Most cases are either fully in or fully out of the set of economically developed countries.

With a fuzzy-set transformation, what is the relationship between the raw data and the cutoff points? In particular, how does one decide where to draw the cutoff point for cases with full membership, no membership, and particular degrees of partial membership? In the case of figure 12.1, the data and coding decisions are from Ragin (2008). His discussion provides a good example of how one can use expert knowledge to draw cutoff points. Crucial to his coding decision was determining the threshold for full membership ($20,000 GDP per capita), the threshold for no membership ($2,500 GDP per capita), and the crossover point at which cases are as much members as not members of the category ($5,000 GDP per capita), which is designated by the 0.5 code in fuzzy-set analysis. He arrived at these cutoff points in part by exploring how scholars and important institutions like the World Bank determine if countries are rich or poor. He used their semantic practices when designing the shape of the S-curve in figure 12.1. Because the real world language of scholars and major institutions informs the transformation, the final set-membership scores for cases should be meaningful to this community. That is, the membership values of countries should resonate with the way in which these experts conceptualize and talk about wealth and economic development.

Thus, in the qualitative approach, one carries out data transformations in ways that aim to satisfy the Fundamental Principle of Variable Transformation. One transforms raw data so that they match better what the analyst or relevant community means by the concept. Since this is partly an interpretive process, the analyst ideally will state clear standards when making transformations. These standards may reflect ordinary language and common cultural conventions, expert knowledge and usage, and/or the substantive knowledge of the researcher about the phenomenon under study. It is possible to preserve or enhance the meaning of a given concept with a linear, log, or standardization transformation. But this cannot be assumed a priori; it needs to be demonstrated through an explicit appraisal of the match between the codes for cases and the meaning of the concept.

Turning now to log transformation in the statistical culture, the lower panel of figure 12.2 makes clear the radical changes that are produced in the distribution of cases when the logged value is used. The data now approach a normal distribution. This distribution was created by making large distinctions among the many countries that have very low levels of raw GDP per capita. Thus, the countries with less than $2,500 GDP per capita make up much of the variation on the left-hand side of the histogram in the lower part of figure 12.2. The low-end variation in GDP per capita that was irrelevant in the semantic, fuzzy-set approach is decisively important in the logged dataset.

When qualitative researchers see the changed distribution of cases after logging in an example such as figure 12.2, they are likely to view the practice as suspect. In this example, the new data imply that most countries have intermediate levels of economic development, which the qualitative researcher may feel is simply not true. He or she is likely to be concerned that the transformation distorts the underlying empirical reality.

Yet, from within the quantitative culture, quite sensible justifications exist for using logged values. Sometimes logging arises for theoretical reasons. For example, Jones et al. (2009) argue, and empirically show, that almost all government budgets follow a power law distribution. This distribution, $y \sim ax^b$, means that the obvious empirical test is to log both sides of the equation. This transformation is a reasonable thing to do.

Another common reason for logging is that the data are skewed. Logging is effective at removing this skewness, as illustrated in figure 12.2. The rationale behind this transformation calls attention to problems in the real world distribution of the data. If your research goal involves making valid inferences with statistical methods, then skewness of the data can be a serious problem that needs to be corrected.

Finally, another rationale sometimes offered for logging is that the resulting data provide a better fit in the statistical analysis, where better means stronger substantive impact or higher significance levels. This sort of rationale falls under the rubric of specification searches (e.g., Leamer 1978), which have been extensively debated by statisticians over the decades. One could imagine doing all sorts of variable transformations and then picking the one that gives the strongest results. Occasionally, one will find quantitative scholars debating whether improved fit justifies a particular kind of variable transformation.[4] From the qualitative, semantic perspective, however, the issue of model fit should be kept completely separate from the issue of how best to transform raw data. Transforming variables for the exclusive purpose of improving statistical fit runs a serious risk of violating the Fundamental Principle of Variable Transformation.

---

[4] For example, Kurtz and Schrank (2007) argue that governance is not related to economic growth. The World Bank economists in their response say, "In the next panel we show the effect of two minor departures from the original Kurtz and Schrank specification. Instead of entering per capita GDP in levels as they do, we enter it in log-levels. This is a very standard practice in cross-country empirics and statistically is more appropriate since the relationship between the dependent variable and log per capita GDP is much closer to being linear, and we are using a linear regression model" (Kaufman et al. 2007, 59).

## Conclusion

Both the quantitative and qualitative traditions transform raw data. Yet the norms they follow when carrying out these transformations vary a great deal. Quantitative researchers follow practices such as standardization and using logged values that assist in their efforts to carry out good statistical tests. Qualitative researchers almost never standardize or log raw data. Instead, they "calibrate" (Ragin 2008) the data to correspond to the meaning of a concept as defined by the analyst and/or the relevant expert community.

Once more, we are not arguing that one approach is inherently better than the other. In fact, we believe that both approaches usually make good sense within the context of their overall cultures. Thus, we have seen how, within the statistical culture, there are often very good reasons to standardize raw data or transform it using logged values. Likewise, within the qualitative culture, it makes sense to ignore some of the variation when assigning membership values to cases for a concept. What may be an inappropriate practice in one culture is quite appropriate in the other.

## References and Suggested Readings

Introductory statistics textbooks discuss calculating standardized values and making log transformations to remove skewness. On transforming raw quantitative data with fuzzy-set analysis, see especially Ragin (2008). For specific examples of quantitative and qualitative transformations, see the following annotated references.

Brown, J., J. Earle, and S. Gehlbach. 2009. Helping hand or grabbing hand? State bureaucracy and privatization effectiveness. *American Political Science Review* 103:264–83. Here is an example where most of the variables are logged.

Busse, M., and C. Hefeker. 2007. Political risk, institutions and foreign direct investment. *European Journal of Political Econony* 23:397–415. They want to log the foreign direct investment variable, but that can lead to negative values, so they transform the data using $y = \log(x + (x^2 + 1)^{.5})$.

Carment, D., S. Yiagadeesen, and S. Prest. 2009. State fragility and implications for aid allocation: an empirical analysis. *Conflict Management and Peace Science* 25:349–73. See how logged and standardized infant mortality is used as an indicator for standard of living.

Fearon, J. 2003. Ethnic and cultural diversity by country. *Journal of Economic Growth* 8: 195–222. He argues that one measure of ethnic diversity is better than another because the distribution of cases is not skewed.

Fischer, C., M. Hout, M. Jankowski, S. Lucas, A. Swindler, and K. Voss. 1996. *Inequality by design: cracking the bell curve myth.* Princeton: Princeton University Press. The authors critique the normalization of the *Bell Curve* data.

Freedman, D. 2009. *Statistical models: theory and practice*, revised edition. Cambridge: Cambridge University Press.

Gerring, J., and J. Seawright. 2008. Case-selection techniques in case study research: a menu of qualitative and quantitative options. *Political Research Quarterly* 61:294–308.

Goertz, G., and J. Mahoney. 2005. Two-level theories and fuzzy-set analysis. *Sociological Methods and Research* 33:497–538. The authors reconstruct Skocpol's qualitative data from her *States and social revolutions* as fuzzy sets.

Herrnstein, R., and C. Murray. 1994. *Bell curve.* New York: Free Press. The intelligence test scores they use are not normally distributed, so they transform the scores to make them normally distributed; see Fischer et al. (1996) for a critique.

Jaggers, K., and T. Gurr. 1995. Tracking democracy's third wave with the Polity III data. *Journal of Peace Research* 32:469–82.

Jones, B., F. Baumgartner, C. Breunig, et al. 2009. A general empirical law of public budgets: a comparative analysis. *American Journal of Political Science* 53:855–73.

Kaufmann, D., A. Kraay, and M. Mastruzzi. 2007. Growth and governance: a reply. *Journal of Politics* 69:555–62.

Kurtz, M., and A. Schrank. 2007. Growth and governance: models, measures, and mechanisms. *Journal of Politics* 69:538–54.

Leamer, L. 1978. *Specification searches: ad hoc inferences with nonexperimental data.* New York: John Wiley & Sons.

Londregan, J., and K. Poole. 1996. Does high income promote democracy? *World Politics* 49:1–31. To be able to use their preferred statistical methods, the authors transform the Polity scale using the following formula, where $S$ is the Polity democracy score: $T(S) = \log(S + 10.5) - \log(10.5 - S)$.

Mahoney, J. 2010. *Colonialism and postcolonial development: Spanish America in comparative perspective.* New York: Cambridge. The author uses qualitative historical data to construct fuzzy-set membership values for cases.

Marshall, M. G., T. R. Gurr, and K. Jaggers. 2010. *Polity IV project: political regime characteristics and transitions, 1800–2009.* Center for Systemic Peace, www.systemicpeace.org/polity/polity4.htm.

Ragin, C. 2000. *Fuzzy-set social science.* Chicago: University of Chicago Press.

Ragin, C. 2008. *Redesigning social inquiry: fuzzy sets and beyond.* Chicago: University of Chicago Press. See chapter 5 for an extensive discussion of fuzzy logic variable transformations and calibrations.

Zadeh, L. 1965. Fuzzy sets. *Information and Control* 8:338–53.

# Chapter 13

# Conceptual Opposites and Typologies

Bivalent logic is not the right logic for serving as a foundation for human sciences. What is needed for this purpose is fuzzy logic. Essentially, fuzzy logic is the logic of classes with unsharp boundaries.

—*Lotfi A. Zadeh*

## Introduction

A curious aspect of concepts is the terminology used to designate the opposite of a given concept. Often concepts come in opposing pairs such as democratic–authoritarian, war–peace, or wealthy–poor. A central issue with important theoretical and methodological implications concerns whether one concept in such a pair is equivalent to the negation of the other concept. For example, is wealthy = not-poor and war = not-peace? One can pose the question more generally:

Is the negated concept the same as the opposite concept?

To take our ongoing example of democracy, is not-democracy the same as authoritarianism?

We suggest that typically scholars in the qualitative tradition will answer this question "no." Qualitative scholars adopt an asymmetric approach, in which not-democratic is a different concept from authoritarianism. By contrast, researchers in the quantitative tradition typically answer the same question "yes" (at least in methodological practice). The quantitative tradition adopts a symmetric view of a concept and its negation when measuring and using them in statistical models. For example, the extent to which a regime is democratic is understood to be the exact inverse of the extent to which it is authoritarian.

A related question concerns the boundaries among concepts in typologies. A traditional view holds that typologies should be based on *mutually exclusive* categories. Every observation can only belong to one category.[1] A country cannot be coded as authoritarian and democratic at the same time. Yet, in practice, this approach to typologies is often at odds with what we see in the world. The ethnic categories used in government censuses are an obvious example. We might say that Barack Obama has nonzero membership in three categories: (1) African American, (2) White, and (3) African. Yet if we allow President Obama to have some degree of membership in all three categories, then we violate the mutually exclusive typology rule.[2]

In the qualitative tradition, scholars often reject the mutual exclusivity assumption of typologies (in actual research practice). Within this semantically oriented tradition, it makes good sense to say that President Obama has at least partial membership in two or three different ethnic categories. In this topic, we show how fuzzy-set analysis is the natural mathematical approach for analyzing typologies under this non-mutually exclusive assumption.

## Symmetric versus Asymmetric Approaches to Conceptual Opposites

To illustrate the different approaches to conceptual opposites, let us consider the concepts of democracy and authoritarianism. To keep things simple for now, imagine that one measures the concept of democracy dichotomously using Polity data (Marshall, Jaggers, and Gurr 2010). The Polity scale ranges from −10 to 10, and a possible move is to treat cases with a score of 7–10 as cases of democracy. The key issue then would be what does one call the cases with scores from −10 to 6? Should one call these instances of "authoritarianism" or instances of "non-democracy"?

In the quantitative culture, if one uses a dichotomous category (usually not the first choice), non-democracy and authoritarianism are measured the same. All cases with scores from −10 to 6 are both non-democracy and authoritarian. These cases are completely separate from the democracy cases with scores of 7 or higher. To illustrate the exclusivity of dichotomous

---

[1] In addition, a typology normally should be collectively exhaustive, i.e., all observations should be categorized.

[2] In August 2010, Goertz received an email from the university stating that new federal rules allow individuals to choose more than one ethnic group on federal forms.

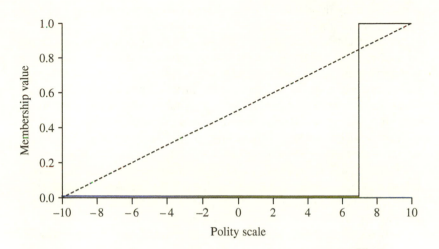

**Figure 13.1.** Illustration of symmetric membership functions in the quantitative culture

categories in this approach, figure 13.1 shows the relationship between Polity scores and the degree to which a case is a member of the set of democracies. The X-axis is a measure of level of democracy, while the Y-axis is membership in the set of democracies. As the figure suggests, the +7 cutoff point is understood in all or nothing terms: at or above this point, a case is completely in the set of democracies; below this point, it is completely out of the set of democracies.

The symmetry assumption for conceptual opposites also applies when continuous variables are used in the quantitative tradition (in general, continuous variables are strongly preferred in this tradition). It is normal and appropriate to employ the same continuous variable for hypotheses about authoritarianism as well as democracy. The extent to which a case is democratic is simply the inverse of the extent to which it is authoritarian. In figure 13.1, the dashed line illustrates the standard linear understanding of the relationship between the continuously measured Polity scores and continuously measured membership in the set of democracies (see the chapter "Meaning and Measurement"). In the quantitative tradition, the same linear relationship would apply to authoritarianism, except that it would now be an inverse relationship (i.e., Polity scores stand in a negative linear relationship to membership in authoritarianism). This symmetric pattern applies to many concepts. For instance, both economic development and economic underdevelopment can be measured using the same GDP per capita data. If one has a good measure of the extent to which a case is economically developed, one simultaneously has a good measure of the extent to which it is economically underdeveloped.

In the qualitative tradition, by contrast, this symmetry often does not apply. In fact, neither of the relationships between the Polity measure and membership in the set of democracies given in figure 13.1 would be a good choice in this culture. Instead, figure 13.2 illustrates a more typical approach when one is centrally concerned with semantics and meaning. One might argue that a case has 100 percent membership in the set of democracies only if it achieves a Polity score of 10 (Goertz 2008). The dichotomous standard in the literature scores cases with scores below 7 as completely not-democracy. Once one is thinking in terms of a fuzzy-set view of democracy, however, it seems reasonable to start at a lower level, e.g., +4 in figure 13.2. Thus, cases with scores between 4 and 10 are partly members of the set of democracies and partly members of the set of non-democracies.[3]

In fuzzy-set analysis, where $X$ is coded from 1 to 0, the negation of $X$ is 1 minus the membership score of $X$. Thus, in figure 13.2, the values for the dashed line representing not-democracy are equal to 1 minus the value for democracy (i.e., $\neg X = 1 - X$). Negation in fuzzy-set analysis is quite literal: one negates the original membership value.

However, not-democracy and authoritarianism are not the same concept. In concrete terms, they do not have the same membership functions. For instance, one would likely relate the Polity data to authoritarianism in a significantly different way than to democracy. For example, cases with Polity scores from $-10$ to $-4$ might be considered full members of the category authoritarianism; cases with scores more than $-4$ but less than $+2$ might be regarded as having partial membership in this category; and cases with scores of $+2$ or higher could be treated as having no membership in the category.

The key point is that, in this tradition, the concepts of democracy and authoritarianism are not symmetric. They are different concepts, and thus they have different membership functions. Of course, not-democracy is related to authoritarianism, which is as it should be. However, they are not the same thing. From a semantic point of view, this is true of many pairs of opposing concepts. For example, most would agree that not-war and peace are different concepts. Israel and Egypt are in a state of not-war; it is less clear that they are at peace with each other.

In short, because a negated concept is different in meaning from the opposite of that concept, the semantic approach assumes that the

---

[3] The Polity concept has separate scales for democracy and authoritarianism. Thus, although most scholars calculate the Polity scale by subtracting the authoritarian variable from the democracy variable, one could separate them and code democracy differently from authoritarianism.

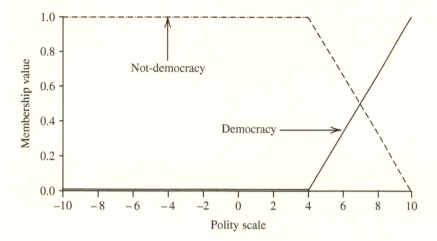

**Figure 13.2.** Conceptualizing democracy and its negation in the qualitative tradition

measurement of a concept and its opposite will often not be symmetric. They each require measurement on their own terms, in light of their own definitions and meanings. We call this the Principle of Conceptual Opposites in qualitative research:

> Principle of Conceptual Opposites: The meaning and measurement of a concept and its opposite are not symmetric.

## Overlapping versus Exclusive Typologies

Qualitative researchers often reject the view that the categories in a typology must be mutually exclusive. For example, the fuzzy-set coding of democracy and not-democracy in figure 13.2 clearly violates the principle of exclusive categories. Some cases (i.e., cases with a Polity score greater than 4 but less than 10) are simultaneously members of the categories democracy and not-democracy. The same non-exclusivity applies to typologies with three or more categories, such as democracy–anocracy–authoritarian or lower class–middle class–upper class. Some cases will belong to multiple categories at the same time.

To continue with the democracy example, many scholars focus centrally on the middle category between authoritarianism and democracy, which

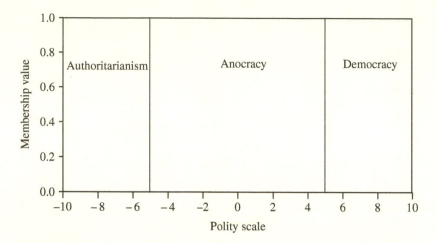

**Figure 13.3.** Democracy-anocracy-authoritarianism: mutually exclusive categories

is sometimes designated as anocracy.[4] When coding cases, one procedure used in the statistical literature is to treat the middle of the Polity scale (e.g., –5 to 5) as anocracy and the two extremes as not-anocracy (i.e., as authoritarianism and democracy). This was the approach used by Fearon and Laitin (2003) in their influential work on civil war, and it seems to have become common. Scholars using this trichotomous approach normally code dummy variables to cover the three categories. Figure 13.3 illustrates the standard trichotomous coding of the dummy variables. Each country-year falls into one—and only one—of the three categories.

A fuzzy-set coding of these concepts using the Polity data would look quite different from the coding in figure 13.3. Fuzzy-set analysis normally does not use sharp break points; the fuzzy-set approach does not follow the mutually exclusive category rule. Instead of abrupt breaks, transitions between categories are gradual and partial. As figure 13.4 suggests, the categories of authoritarianism, anocracy, and democracy are allowed to overlap to greater or lesser degrees. Some countries are simultaneously authoritarian and anocratic, and some are simultaneously anocratic and democratic.

There is no inherent reason why one could not use these fuzzy-set codings in a statistical analysis. Within the statistical framework, they are just three

---

[4] The large literature on hybrid regimes (e.g., Schedler 2002; Levitsky and Way 2010) looks intensively at this middle category. The middle category is also important for the study of civil war (e.g., Vreeland 2008) and interstate war (Goemans 2000).

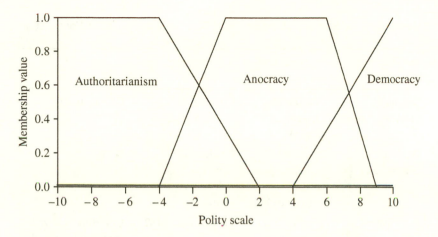

**Figure 13.4.** Overlapping categories: democracy, anocracy, and authoritarianism

variables that range from zero to one. However, the more common approach is the mutually exclusive setup of figure 13.3, which many qualitative researchers also use. This is not wrong per se, but rather reflects a different decision about how boundary lines between categories should be drawn. Fuzzy-set analysis prefers a gradual transition, while the mutually exclusive scheme implicitly sees abrupt shifts.

In summary, while typologies in quantitative research are normally understood to be made up of mutually exclusive categories, a semantic approach to concepts requires an opposing view. We call this qualitative alternative the Principle of Conceptual Overlap:

> Principle of Conceptual Overlap: Adjacent categories in typologies can overlap and not be mutually exclusive.

This principle is central to fuzzy-set analysis both when employed in the social sciences and when applied in the real world to design many of the machines that we use on a daily basis.

## Semantics and Nominal Typologies

It is interesting to consider the history of the concepts used to characterize political regimes. The original trichotomous formulation of political systems by Gurr (1974), reproduced in table 13.1, suggested three nominal

**Table 13.1**

Democracy-Anocracy-Authoritarianism: The Original Gurr 1974 Formulation

| Authority variable | Autocracy | Democracy | Anarchy |
|---|---|---|---|
| Executive recruitment | Ascription=1 Designation=1 Dual=1 | Competitive elections=2 | Ceasaristic=1 |
| Decision constraints | Unlimited authority=2 Slightly limited=1 | Legislative parity=2 Substantial limits=1 | None |
| Participation | Suppressed=2 Restricted=2 | Institutionalized=2 | Uninstitutionalized=2 Factional/restricted=1 |
| Directiveness | Totalitarian=2 Segmental plus=1 | None | Minimal=2 |
| Centralization | None | Decentralized=1 | Decentralized=2 |
| Maximum score | 7 | 7 | 7 |

*Source:* Gurr 1974.

categories. These original categories were autocracy, democracy, and anarchy, and they each had their own distinctive combination of defining traits. Presumably, Gurr intended these categories to be mutually exclusive types. However, given that he used at least five defining dimensions (i.e., the authority variables in table 13.1), each with at least two possible values, the three types clearly do not exhaust the realm of possible political systems. Some political systems likely have characteristics from at least two of Gurr's types.

How should one deal with cases that do not fit available categories if the goal is to have useful nominal categories? One possibility is to simply treat them as "missing data" or otherwise exclude them from the empirical analysis. Yet this solution seems problematic unless one has explicit and justifiable reasons for throwing out these cases. An alternative, semantic solution is to ask whether the cases can be accommodated within the existing categories of the typology or whether they require their own new category. This semantic approach allows the analyst to include all relevant cases in the analysis, either with existing categories or new ones.

To illustrate, we return once more to the Polity dataset. This dataset is quite (in)famous for the way that it codes certain special cases. These cases have received considerable attention lately (e.g., Vreeland 2008) because they influence findings in the analysis of outcomes related to civil wars and human rights violations. Here is the official Polity statement (omitting some details) on the coding of three kinds of special cases:

Interruption Periods (– 66): A score of "– 66" for component variables represents a period of "interruption." Operationally, if a country is occupied by foreign powers during war, thereby terminating the old political system, Polity codes the case as an interruption until an independent government is reestablished.

Interregnum Periods (–77): A "–77" code for the Polity component variables indicates periods of "interregnum," during which there is a complete collapse of central political authority. This is most likely to occur during periods of internal war (e.g., Lebanon between 1978 and 1986).

Transition Periods (–88): A score of "– 88" indicates a period of transition. Some new polities are preceded by a "transition period" during which new institutions are planned, legally constituted, and put into effect. Democratic and quasi-democratic polities are particularly likely to be established in a procedure involving constitutional conventions and referenda. During this period of transition, all indicators are scored "– 88." (Marshall and Jaggers 2002, 16)

In the quantitative culture, these codes are usually treated as a problem of missing data. A standard practice is to drop cases with these codes from the statistical analysis. Given this practice, some scholars naturally have sought to estimate the "missing values." Polity itself now has a procedure to give Polity scores to the –77 and – 88 cases.[5]

By contrast, a qualitative, semantic approach to this issue starts with an examination of the concepts embodied in the – 66, –77, and – 88 codes. The cases of – 66 involve "foreign occupation," the –77 cases are related to "anarchy," and the – 88 cases are kinds of "transition." One might ask how the features of these types match (or not) the concepts of democracy, anocracy, and authoritarianism. One possibility is that they are simply different concepts, and thus they might not fit on the list of democracy, anocracy, and authoritarianism.

The –77 cases of anarchy are a good place to start. In the original Gurr coding, anarchy was one of the nominal types. Over time, Gurr's anarchy became anocracy for some cases and –77 for others. The problem is that the Polity scale is a measure of *regime type*, and it is unclear how one should

[5] Plümper and Neumayer (2010) critique the Polity approach, but they too assume that the problem is one of missing data and that these cases should be coded on the –10 to 10 Polity scale.

approach cases with no functioning government at all, e.g., failed states or situations of large-scale civil war. Polity now codes these cases as zero on its scale, but that seems to confuse anocracy with the absence or breakdown of the central government. Since "type of government" is separate from "existence of government," the natural thing to do from a conceptual point of view is to have a new variable, "anarchy." Anarchy is not a problem of missing data, it is a conceptually separate issue.[6] For many empirical projects, one might define the population of relevant observations to be all states that have governments. Under this definition of the population, cases of anarchy would be excluded, but not because they are missing data, but rather because they do not meet the criteria defining the relevant universe of cases.

The – 66, foreign occupation cases are also worth thinking about from a conceptual point of view. Unlike anarchy, countries under foreign occupation do have a government. Most foreign occupations are "military dictatorships." The German occupation of France during World War II did not result in anarchy, but a military government run by the Germans. From a conceptual point of view, therefore, one option would be to code these cases like other military dictatorships, i.e., as authoritarian regimes. Some of them might be cases of partial military occupations, like the United States in Iraq and Afghanistan. Another option would be to argue that all domestic regimes require a self-governing and fully sovereign state. Thus, cases of military occupation fall into a separate category, such as "non-sovereign polity," which might also include all colonial cases. Either way, these foreign occupation cases raise a conceptual issue that has little to do with missing data.

Finally, similar points could be made about the – 88, transition cases. The problem with these cases is not really missing data; one often has excellent information about them. The problem is that their political institutions are still in the process of being formulated, and it is unclear how nascent institutions should be matched with a category like democracy, which requires clear, explicit, and stable political rules. One possible approach would be to argue that these transition cases, too, belong in the category of "anarchy," given that they lack a functioning government structure. Some may disagree, but the nature of that disagreement involves conceptual issues rather than a dispute about the empirical features of the cases.

---

[6] Many have analyzed civil war as a situation of anarchy (e.g., Walter 1997). The same sort of issue arises in the international conflict literature. For example, Klein et al. (2006) conceptualize the nature, friendly to hostile, of relationships between two states. The question is what to do with states with no relationship, e.g., Bolivia and Burma.

## Conclusion

Qualitative researchers frequently make use of opposing pairs of categories (e.g., democracy versus authoritarianism) and typologies (e.g., democratic, anocratic, and authoritarian regimes). However, their semantic approach leads them to use these categorical devices in ways that deviate quite substantially from the norms of quantitative research. They do not necessarily treat a positive concept and its opposite as symmetric inverses. A measure of development is not necessarily the inverse of a measure of underdevelopment. Hence, when qualitative researchers analyze developed countries and underdeveloped countries, they do not view them as mirror images of one another. This may seem odd to quantitative researchers, whose natural default option is to assume the full symmetry of a concept and its opposite. In the quantitative culture, a case that increases its level of development is understood to simultaneously and in equal measure decrease its level of underdevelopment.

In actual research practice, qualitative researchers sometimes also reject the related idea that the categories of a typology must be mutually exclusive. They often allow adjacent categories to partially overlap with one another, since this is how we use concepts in ordinary language. Again, this may well seem strange from a quantitative standpoint, since typologies are viewed in this culture as being made up of nominal categories that are inherently mutually exclusive. From the semantic perspective, however, the world is not neatly divided into fully separate categories. The clear boundaries assumed in nominal scales are inadequate to capture the simultaneous membership in multiple categories of a typology exhibited by many real world cases.

## References and Suggested Readings

Quantitative skepticism about qualitative categories and typologies is well expressed by King, Keohane, and Verba: "Constructs such as typologies, frameworks, and all manner of classifications, are useful as temporary devices [for] collecting data ... However, in general, we encourage researchers *not* to organize their data this way" (1994, 48). Other quantitative expressions of skepticism based on the idea that typologies disguise underlying variation include Blalock (1982, 109), Jackman (1985, 169), and Shively (2005, 32). For a critique of this skepticism, see Collier, LaPorte, and Seawright (2012). The understanding of nominal scales as representing mutually exclusive types goes back to Stevens's (1946) original formulation. On the use of mutually exclusive typologies for descriptive and explanatory analysis in qualitative research, see Collier, LaPorte, and Seawright (2008), Elman (2005), and George and Bennett (2005). The use of nonmutually exclusive typologies in fuzzy-set analysis is widely discussed in texts focused on engineering applications, including the excellent introductions by Kosko (1993) and by McNeill and Freiberger (1994). However, the point is not well-developed in the qualitative social science literature on typologies. But in research practice, we can often observe the use of non-exclusive typologies (e.g., in the literature on hybrid regimes).

Blalock, H. 1982. *Conceptualization and measurement in the social sciences.* Beverly Hills: Sage.

Collier, D., J. LaPorte, and J. Seawright. 2008. Typologies: forming concepts and creating categorical variables. In *The Oxford handbook of political methodology*, edited by J. Box-Steffensmier, H. Brady, and D. Collier. Oxford: Oxford University Press.

Collier, D., J. LaPorte, and J. Seawright. 2012. Putting typologies to work: concept formation, measurement, and analytic rigor. *Political Research Quarterly* 65: 217–32.

Elman, C. 2005. Explanatory typologies in qualitative studies of international politics. *International Organization* 59:293–326.

Fearon, J., and D. Laitin. 2003. Ethnicity, insurgency and civil war. *American Political Science Review* 97:75–90.

George, A. L., and A. Bennett. 2005. *Case studies and theory development.* Cambridge: MIT Press.

Goemans, H. 2000. Fighting for survival: the fate of leaders and the duration of war. *Journal of Conflict Resolution* 44:555–79.

Goertz, G. 2008. A checklist for constructing, evaluating, and using concepts or quantitative measures. In *The Oxford handbook of political methodology*, edited by J. Box-Steffensmier, H. Brady, and D. Collier. Oxford: Oxford University Press.

Gurr, T. 1974. Persistence and change in political systems, 1800–1971. *American Political Science Review* 68:1482–504.

Jackman, R. W. 1985. Cross-national statistical research and the study of comparative politics. *American Journal of Political Science* 29:161–82.

King, G., R. Keohane, and S. Verba. 1994. *Designing social inquiry: scientific inference in qualitative research.* Princeton: Princeton University Press.

Klein, J., G. Goertz, and P. Diehl. 2006. The new rivalry data set: procedures and patterns. *Journal of Peace Research* 43:331–48.

Kosko, B. 1993. *Fuzzy thinking: the new science of fuzzy logic.* New York: Hyperion.

Levitsky, S., and L. A. Way. 2010. *Competitive authoritarianism: hybrid regimes after the Cold War.* Cambridge: Cambridge University Press.

Marshall, M., and K. Jaggers. 2002. Polity IV project dataset users' manual. Unpublished manuscript, University of Maryland.

Marshall, M. G., K. Jaggars, and T. R. Gurr. 2010. *Polity IV project: political regime characteristics and transitions, 1800–2010.* Retrieved from http://www.systemicpeace.org/polity/polity4.htm.

McNeill, D., and P. Freiberger. 1994. *Fuzzy logic.* New York: Simon and Schuster.

Plümper, T., and E. Neumayer. 2010. The level of democracy during interregnum periods: recoding the Polity2 score. *Political Analysis* 18:206–26.

Schedler, A. 2002. Elections without democracy: the menu of manipulation. *Journal of Democracy* 13:36–50.

Shively, W. P. 2005. *The craft of political research.* Upper Saddle River, NJ: Prentice Hall.

Stevens, S. S. 1946. On the theory of scales of measurement. *Science* 103:677–80.

Vreeland, J. 2008. The effect of political regime on civil war: unpacking anocracy. *Journal of Conflict Resolution* 52:401–25.

Walter, B. 1997. The critical barrier to civil war settlement. *International Organization* 51:335–64.

# PART IV

Research Design and Generalization

# Chapter 14

# Case Selection and Hypothesis Testing

When observations are selected on the basis of a particular value
of the dependent variable, nothing whatsoever can be learned
about the causes of dependent variable without taking into account
other instances when the dependent variable takes on other values.
—*Gary King, Robert O. Keohane, and Sidney Verba*

## Introduction

There are various reasons why one might choose certain cases for intensive analysis (Eckstein 1975). In this chapter, we examine quantitative and qualitative practices of case-study selection when the goal of the analysis is to evaluate causal hypotheses. We explore how the different causal models used in the two cultures shape the kind of cases that provide the most leverage for hypothesis testing. What is a good case for testing a hypothesis about an average treatment effect may not be a good case for testing a hypothesis about a necessary condition or an INUS condition. Unfortunately, the literature on case selection often does not pay attention to the form of the causal model under investigation or simply assumes that the investigator is testing an additive-linear statistical model. As a result, much of the advice about case selection in the literature makes sense if the goal is to estimate an average treatment effect but not if the goal is to test a set-theoretic hypothesis.

We split this discussion of case selection and hypothesis testing into two parts. The first explores what we believe is one of the most confusing issues in the literature: should one select cases based on their value on the dependent variable? The idea that qualitative researchers should avoid selection on the dependent variable is a memorable suggestion from King, Keohane, and Verba (1994). However, this advice has been held up by qualitative methodologists as a classic example of inappropriately extending insights from statistical research to qualitative research (e.g., Collier and Mahoney 1996). We show how the advice makes sense when the causal model is an additive-linear one (in a large-N context) but not when it is a set-theoretic one. Before deciding whether selecting cases on the dependent variable is a good idea, one must first ask about the kind of causal model under investigation.

The second part concerns the kinds of cases that provide the most leverage for causal inference when conducting case-study research. This issue has generated a new literature among multimethod researchers (e.g., Lieberman 2005; Seawright and Gerring 2008). Scholars who seek to supplement their regression results with case-study analyses now often follow ideas in this literature. We believe, however, that some of the suggestions in this literature are misleading for qualitative researchers who seek to test a set-theoretic model. We develop our argument by using a simple 2×2 table and asking which cells each culture prioritizes when doing case-study research. The qualitative culture has a preference for the (1,1) cell, the one in which both the cause and the outcome are present. This culture also has an aversion to choosing cases from the (0,0) cell, which provides limited leverage for assessing set-theoretic hypotheses. By contrast, the quantitative culture typically finds all cells important (Seawright 2002).

## Selecting on the Dependent Variable

One of the most vivid and well-known pieces of advice that quantitative scholars have offered to qualitative researchers concerns the dangers of selecting cases based on their extreme values on the dependent variable. Achen and Snidal (1989, 160–61) view the selection of these extreme cases—such as George and Smoke's (1974) decision to focus mainly on cases of war rather than peace—as posing the risk of "inferential fallacies" that have "devastating consequences" to the validity of one's findings. Geddes (1991; see also Geddes 2003) argues that selecting cases on the dependent variable is a "taboo" that "bedevils" several major qualitative studies, including Skocpol's (1979) analysis of social revolutions. These concerns about selection on the dependent variable culminated in King, Keohane, and Verba's discussion of the problem that we have used as an epigraph to this chapter.

The statistical basis of this critique is well established in the literature, notably in Heckman's work (1976; 1979). With a bivariate relationship, selecting a sample of cases truncated on the dependent variable produces a flatter slope than if the full range of variation on the dependent variable is used. As a result, the estimate of the regression line with the truncated sample is subject to systematic error (i.e., bias). The moral of the story is that one should not select a sample of cases that all are within a limited range of values on the dependent variable. This advice is not controversial in the quantitative culture, and it makes good sense if one is working with a typical linear regression model.

If one is working with a causal model more characteristic of qualitative research, however, this advice is no longer appropriate. For example, consider the following causal model: $Y = (A * B * c) + (A * C * D * E)$. In this equation, $A$ is a hypothesized necessary condition for $Y$. If one wishes to test this hypothesis about $A$, what would be the appropriate case selection strategy?

To answer this question, recall from the "Mathematical Prelude" the following definition of a necessary cause:

$$P(X = 1|Y = 1) = 1. \tag{14.1}$$

Notice what this equation says: look at all the cases of $Y = 1$ and see if they also have $X = 1$. If they do, then the evidence supports the necessary condition hypothesis. Of course, this means selecting on the dependent variable; it means choosing cases precisely because they are $Y = 1$.

A traditional way to think about such designs is J. S. Mill's (1843/1974) method of agreement, which is a strategy for examining hypotheses about necessary conditions. More recently, methodologists have explored how many consistent cases (i.e., cases of $Y = 1$ that are also cases of $X = 1$) one must examine to become confident that the hypothesis is valid (Dion 1998; Braumoeller and Goertz 2000; Ragin 2000). For our purposes here, the key point is that, in qualitative research, selection on the dependent variable when testing necessary conditions follows directly from the definition of a necessary condition.[1]

To see the clash between qualitative case selection norms and the statistical culture, consider Geddes's (1991; 2003) work on selection bias. Geddes takes issue with the qualitative literature on the causes of sustained rapid economic growth in East Asia (e.g., South Korea, Taiwan, and Singapore). She observes that analysts often emphasize the role of government in creating a disciplined and quiescent labor force (i.e., "labor repression") when explaining high growth. However, these scholars make this causal inference using evidence from only a set of countries that have sustained

---

[1] While it exceeds the scope of this discussion, the $Y = 0$ cases do play a role in evaluating necessary condition hypotheses. In particular, they help scholars distinguish trivial from nontrivial necessary conditions (see Braumoeller and Goertz 2000; Goertz 2006; Ragin 2008).

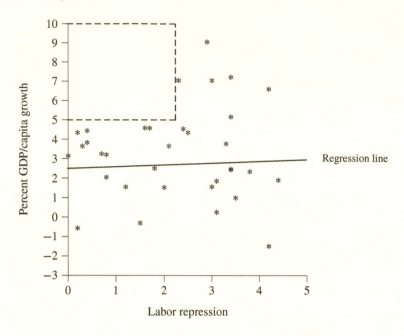

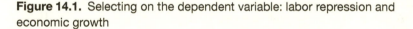

*Data source*: Geddes 2003, 104.

**Figure 14.1.** Selecting on the dependent variable: labor repression and economic growth

high growth. She suggests that, because these scholars select only extreme cases (i.e., only high growth cases), their findings are subject to selection bias. She argues that a different relationship between labor repression and growth might emerge if cases were selected without reference to their value on the dependent variable.

To make the point empirically, she presents bivariate data on the relationship between GDP per capita growth and labor repression using a larger sample of developing countries. Figure 14.1 reproduces her data for 32 developing countries whose GDP per capita in 1970 was greater than South Korea (Geddes 2003, 104). As the flat regression line in the figure illustrates, there is no linear relationship with these data (the slope is .09 and $R^2 = .003$). Hence, when Geddes looks at the scatterplot in figure 14.1, she *sees* no relationship between labor repression and economic growth.[2]

---

[2] One immediate source of concern is that Geddes's example suggests that selection bias leads qualitative researchers to *overestimate* the strength of the true relationship in their truncated sample. Yet, with bivariate data, selection bias should yield a weaker relationship in the truncated sample.

However, the data do suggest the possibility of an important relationship between labor repression and growth when viewed from a set-theoretic perspective. The data have an empty region, a fact we call attention to by emphasizing the region with no observations in the upper left quadrant of figure 14.1. This empty space is what one would expect to see if the following hypothesis were true: labor repression is a necessary condition for high economic growth. Thus, while the data do not support a linear relationship hypothesis, they do seem consistent with a necessary condition one. All cases of exceptional growth have at least moderate levels of labor repression (Mexico is the one case that has slightly below average labor repression but high growth). Thus, at least moderate levels of labor repression may be necessary for sustained high growth in this population. Qualitative scholars who have a set-theoretic causal model in mind cannot help but notice this aspect of the data.

Interestingly, if one goes back to the original scholars who proposed labor repression as a cause of sustained high growth, one finds that they tended to think of the relationship in terms of a necessary condition, not a pattern of linear covariation. For example, Deyo (1987, 182) wrote that "disciplined and low-cost labor . . . has been a prerequisite of development." Koo (1987, 174) asserted that "the control and discipline of industrial labor . . . is one of the conditions that peripheral states must provide to promote a favorable investment climate for foreign capital while enhancing business confidence for domestic capital." These quotations use classic necessary condition language (e.g., "prerequisite"; "must provide"). Geddes's data thus seem consistent with the actual hypotheses proposed by several scholars of the newly industrializing countries.

In summary, case selection is a model-dependent issue; one must select cases that allow one to test the empirical implications of the hypothesis being investigated. If the model proposes a necessary condition, a good strategy is to select $Y = 1$ cases. If the hypothesis concerns a sufficient condition, the best cases are usually the $X = 1$ ones. If the hypothesis assumes an additive-linear model, these modes of case selection are not appropriate.

## Strategies for Selecting Cases

In this section, we shall use table 14.1 as a stylized example for illustrating points. This table has two binary variables, the causal variable $X$ and the outcome variable $Y$. The $(0,1)$ cell where the cause is absent but the outcome is present can be thought of as the necessary condition cell, since this cell must be empty if a necessary condition is present. The $(1,0)$ cell where the cause is present but the outcome is absent is the sufficient condition cell, since this cell must be empty if a sufficient condition is present. The $(1,1)$

**Table 14.1**

Cells for Case-Study Selection

|        | $X = 0$ | $X = 1$ |
|--------|---------|---------|
| $Y = 1$ | (0,1)  | (1,1)  |
| $Y = 0$ | (0,0)  | (1,0)  |

cell contains cases with positive values on both the cause and the outcome; the (0,0) cell contains cases that lack both the cause and the outcome.

## Random Selection

The standard strategy for choosing cases in the quantitative culture is random selection. There are many advantages to this strategy if one is selecting a large number of cases. Most basically, random selection ensures that the case selection procedure is not correlated with any variables in the causal model. In terms of table 14.1, the random selection of a large number of cases ensures that no cell is given priority. When testing a statistical model, this is precisely the kind of data that one desires.

As one moves to a small-N sample of case studies, however, the utility of random selection is debated. Fearon and Laitin (2008) advocate the random selection of a small number of case studies when assessing the causal mechanisms of regression results. They argue that the nonrandom selection of case studies is rarely convincing because one cannot know for certain if researchers are simply "cherry picking" cases that are known in advance to support the hypothesis. In addition, selecting cases simply because one has good data or knowledge about those cases raises questions of representativeness. They believe that this problem of representativeness also applies to strategies in which one chooses observations because of their values on the independent and/or dependent variables. To get around these problems, and to carry out a more objective test, they urge case-study researchers to select their case studies using a random number generator.[3]

Not surprisingly, the strategy of random selection is virtually never used by qualitative scholars.[4] These researchers purposively select cases based in part on their values on particular variables. One big reason why they do so is because certain kinds of cases provide more leverage for testing their causal models than others.

---

[3] In an evaluation of different case selection strategies, Herron and Quinn (2011) find that random selection performs quite well compared to most purposive case selection strategies.

[4] As King, Keohane, and Verba (1994, 125) put it, "Qualitative researchers often balk (appropriately) at the notion of random selection, refusing to risk missing important cases that might not have been chosen by random selection."

Imagine a researcher who is testing a hypothesis about a necessary cause. Here the (0,1) cell in table 14.1 would be very important. Any cases in this cell would be disconfirming ones. No doubt, the researcher would want to look closely at these cases and see if they really do challenge the hypothesis. He or she would explore if there is measurement error or if there is an unanticipated causal mechanism.

The other crucial cell is the (1,1) one. Here are the cases where the researcher expects to see the causal mechanism linking the necessary condition to the outcome. Qualitative researchers intensively investigate (1,1) cases to discover if this expectation is met. In qualitative analysis, the main purpose of the analysis often is to explain $Y = 1$ cases, and thus it is completely natural for these researchers to look very closely at $Y = 1$ cases that also possess a purported necessary cause.

The (1,0) cell where the necessary condition is present but the outcome is absent is less useful but still can help the researcher explore the causal mechanism of interest. With these cases, the researcher may expect the necessary condition to do its causal work—that is, to enable or make possible the outcome of interest by removing blockages or opening up opportunities. Although these possibilities presented by the necessary cause do not culminate in the outcome, it is still appropriate to check and see if they are present. The difficulty is that the causal mechanism of the necessary condition may be hard to see because the absence of other important causes prevents the outcome from actually happening.

Finally, the qualitative researcher's opinion about the (0,0) cell is deeply ambivalent. He or she is pulled in two different directions by this cell. On the one hand, choosing $X = 0$ can be a good way to test a necessary condition hypothesis. Such a hypothesis makes a clear prediction about these cases: $Y$ will not occur. On the other hand, most of these cases are not very relevant for testing hypotheses about necessary conditions (Braumoeller and Goertz 2002; Clarke 2002; see also Seawright 2002). For example, the (0,0) cell can prove especially problematic under random selection rules. In qualitative research, this cell is often quite populated with cases, and thus random selection will choose many of these (0,0) cases. There are a lot of cases in this cell because qualitative researchers typically study rare outcomes, such that the number of $Y = 0$ cases is much larger than the number of $Y = 1$ cases. The total number of cases in the problematic (0,0) cell will depend on the distribution of the necessary cause $X$, but usually the (0,0) cell will be the most populated one, since normally scholars study necessary causes that are not commonly present.[5]

---

[5] When qualitative researchers study sufficient conditions, the cells that provide the most leverage are somewhat different. For these hypotheses, the (1,0) cell is now very important, because any observations in this cell will disconfirm the hypothesis. Confirming

In contrast to the practices of the qualitative culture, Herron and Quinn (2011) find that strategies that select cases because of their extreme or unusual values are actually the most unhelpful ones for evaluating statistical hypotheses. Using a 2×2 table like table 14.1, they conclude that strategies that select cases from sparsely populated cells should be avoided. "From a purely statistical sampling perspective, focusing attention on cases that are not representative of the population as a whole is a huge waste of resources. While such cases may be useful for exploratory analysis and/or theory construction, the amount of information they can provide about population-level average causal effects is, by definition, limited" (Herron and Quinn 2011, 13). Yet, as we saw, the most useful cells for evaluating set-theoretic hypotheses will ordinarily be sparsely populated. For instance, with a necessary condition hypotheses, the highly useful (0,1) cell is not "representative of the population as whole" because the necessary condition hypothesis says this cell should be empty. And the cell that often has the most observations (i.e., the (0,0) cell) is the least useful.

Our point here is that case selection depends on causal models and research goals. Herron and Quinn (2011) explicitly frame their analysis around the idea that one is studying average treatment effects. Hence, their conclusions and advice cannot be separated from that specific research goal. Similarly, our discussion of case selection practices in the qualitative tradition assumes that one is working with set-theoretic hypotheses. Qualitative selection practices make sense only in that context.

## Substantively Important Cases

A separate consideration involves the specific cases that the researcher should select once it has been determined that a group of cases is useful. For example, of the (1,1) cases, which ones should the qualitative researcher select? Following Fearon and Laitin (2008), one might suggest random selection among these cases. This advice again builds on ideas from large-N analysis, where there are no *ex ante* important cases. Random selection helps one avoid consciously or unconsciously cherry picking only those cases that support a favored result.

Yet qualitative researchers would never use random selection even among cases from a useful cell (e.g., the (1,1) cases). Instead, they will often select cases about which they have excellent knowledge or can readily obtain such knowledge. In this culture, knowing a great deal about a case contributes

---

observations in the (1,1) cell remain quite important. Cases in the (0,0) cell are largely irrelevant for testing hypotheses about sufficient conditions and not normally selected for case-study analysis.

significantly to within-case analysis (see part II) and can improve one's chances of carrying out valid inference.

Beyond the value of case expertise, qualitative researchers believe that some cases are more "substantively important" than others. If random selection is used, the odds of choosing these substantively important cases are usually low. Substantively important cases are often "ideal types" or well-known exemplars of a phenomenon. Likewise, cases that are of special normative interest or that played a major political role may be treated as substantively important.

Good qualitative theories must be able to explain substantively important cases. When they cannot, it counts against them. After all, if the point of research is precisely to explain cases, then the ability of a theory to explain important cases should be highly valued. Theories that can only explain minor cases are less valued. Goldstone (2003, 45–46) offers a nice example in his discussion of the consequences for Marxist theory of a failure to adequately explain the French Revolution: "It might still be that the Marxist view held in other cases, but finding that it did not hold in one of the historically most important revolutions (that is, a revolution in one of the largest, most influential, and most imitated states of its day and frequent exemplar for Marxist theories) would certainly shake one's faith in the value of the theory."

From a statistical perspective, by contrast, the norm is that all cases should be a priori weighted equally when testing a hypothesis. Since the goal is not to explain specific cases, but rather to generalize about causal effects for large populations, there is no reason to give special consideration to particular cases. The French Revolution should not count extra when estimating the effect of a variable on social revolution. If many other cases conform, the nonconformity of the French Revolution is not a special problem (or at least no more of a problem than, say, the Bolivian Revolution would be). Hence, the qualitative concern with substantively important cases seems puzzling from the perspective of the quantitative culture.

## Using Cross-Case Evidence to Select Case Studies

In multimethod research, standard strategies for selecting case studies involve using cross-case evidence to identify especially useful cases. Most of this literature assumes that the researcher first carries out a large-N statistical analysis and then uses the results to identify case studies (e.g., Lieberman 2005; Seawright and Gerring 2007; 2008). Case studies are selected for the same reasons as a random sample: representativeness and variation on dimensions of interest. It is assumed that one is seeking to use case studies to help generalize about a well-defined, large population of cases. In this context, case studies can help both to refine and to test the statistical model.

The menu of case selection strategies offered in the multimethod literature includes many different options (e.g., Seawright and Gerring 2007 propose nine). The assumption is that the analysis of the case studies will involve qualitative research. However, it is also assumed that the starting and ending points of the analysis are the estimates of the effects of variables in a statistical model. Hence, the process of *case selection* is fully dependent on the statistical model. For example, the strategy of selecting a "typical" or "on-line" case involves finding a low-residual observation whose value on the dependent variable more or less matches its regression predicted value. A "deviant" or "off-line" case is a high-residual case that has a value on the dependent variable that is not close to its regression predicted value. We believe that these kinds of case studies can be essential as a supplement to regression studies, and the multimethod literature does a good job explaining why (Collier, Brady, and Seawright 2010).

Which quantitative multimethod strategies of case selection are most useful to qualitative research that explores set-theoretic hypotheses? On the one hand, the strategies could be seen as simply irrelevant to this research. Most of these techniques have little resonance with hypotheses about necessary conditions and INUS conditions. Furthermore, some qualitative studies are not even intended to generalize about large populations. Given their limited scope (see the chapter "Scope"), qualitative researchers sometimes conduct case studies on much or all of the relevant population. Hence, the very idea of choosing case studies from a large population may not apply.

On the other hand, however, some of the techniques can be extended to qualitative studies that evaluate set-theoretic hypotheses. The basic rule of using on- or off-line cases can be applied in modified form to a set-theoretic context (see Schneider and Rohlfing 2010). As an example, we can return to Geddes's data in figure 14.1. With respect to the hypothesis that at least moderate labor repression is necessary for high growth, all of the cases are "consistent," with the possible exception of Mexico. Of these consistent cases, however, not all should be treated as examples of on-liers. The real on-liers are those that are strong instances of the cause and outcome. Thus, cases located toward the upper right quadrant are the best candidates for "typical cases." With Geddes's data, Brazil, Malaysia, Singapore, South Korea, Syria, and Taiwan are the six high labor repression/high growth countries and the best on-liers. With the exception of Syria, these are also commonly selected cases in the literature on the NICs.[6]

Of the strategies discussed by Seawright and Gerring (2007), the two that are most readily applicable to qualitative research are probably the "crucial

---

[6] By contrast, the off-line or deviant cases would be those located in the upper left quadrant of the scattergram (there are no major off-line cases in Geddes's data).

case" and "pathway case" strategies (see also Gerring 2007).[7] Crucial cases are defined as those that "are most- or least-likely to exhibit a given outcome" (Seawright and Gerring 2007, 89). In our discussion of table 14.1, we noted that a particular cell has major consequences for hypotheses about necessary or sufficient conditions. Cases in these cells are crucial because they are the least likely to exhibit the outcome of interest (i.e., cases that lack a necessary condition) or the most likely to exhibit the outcome of interest (i.e., cases that possess a sufficient condition).[8]

Pathway cases, by contrast, are defined as cases "where $X_1$ and not $X_2$ is likely to have caused a positive outcome ($Y = 1$)." The purpose of these case studies is to probe causal mechanisms rather than test general propositions. We believe that this kind of case study is common throughout qualitative research. The central goal of case studies is often to evaluate alternative arguments by using process tracing to explore causal mechanisms. In terms of table 14.1, pathway cases are normally found in the (1,1) cell. The researcher analyzes cases that have the cause/s and outcome of interest with the goal of determining whether the causal process works as expected within individual observations. Because this kind of case study is extremely common, it receives substantial attention in its own right in the chapter "Causal Mechanisms and Process Tracing."

## Conclusion

The discussion in this chapter suggests that the rules of case selection follow from research goals. Differences in research goals between quantitative and qualitative analysts yield distinct ideas about best strategies of case selection.

First, in the quantitative culture, random selection is a highly desired and fully appropriate mode of selecting a large-N sample of cases. This selection strategy has no particular preference about cells in a 2×2 table and avoids biases in statistical analysis. However, if one is working with a set-theoretic hypothesis, certain kinds of cases are more useful than others; not all cells in a 2×2 table provide equal leverage. Hence, in qualitative research, one often has a strong preference for sampling certain cells and not others.

Second, once a group of cases is deemed analytically useful, qualitative scholars are often drawn to those cases for which they have expertise and can

---

[7] Seawright and Gerring drop these two strategies in their subsequent work that makes explicit the goal of generalizing about a large-N population (see Seawright and Gerring 2008).

[8] Though common in qualitative research, the crucial case strategy may not always be a good supplement to statistical analysis. In their evaluation of Seawright and Gerring's strategies, Herron and Quinn (2011) have a negative view of one version of the crucial case strategy, regarding it as "nonstarter" because it requires strong prior knowledge of outcomes.

most effectively carry out within-case analysis. Beyond that, they often focus heavily on the substantively important cases. This is a big difference with quantitative research, which does not assign particular cases special weight based on their normative or historical standing. The difference is rooted in the contrasting research goals of the two traditions: qualitative researchers seek to explain particular cases and thus care a great deal about certain special cases; quantitative researchers seek to estimate average effects within large populations and thus do not focus on particular cases for their own sake.

Finally, the quantitative multimethod literature on selecting cases offers a range of useful strategies for choosing cases when assessing a large-N hypothesis about an average effect. Many of these strategies, however, cannot be unproblematically extended to qualitative research that examines a set-theoretic relationship. What it means to select a "typical" or "deviant" case will vary, depending on the causal model that is being tested. With a statistical model, these kinds of cases can be defined in relationship to their residuals. But with a set-theoretic hypothesis, a typical case will be an observation in which both the cause (or causal package) and the outcome are present. A deviant case will be an observation in which the outcome is present but the cause is not (for a necessary condition hypothesis) or an observation in which the cause is present but the outcome is not (for a sufficient condition). In this way, the very meaning of typical and deviant depends on whether one is working with a statistical model or a set-theoretic model.

## References and Suggested Readings

For classic readings concerning selection bias in statistical analysis, see Heckman (1976; 1979); Maddala (1983); Achen (1986); and Manski (1995). For a view that selection bias is not as serious a problem in statistical analysis as some have claimed, see Stolzenberg and Relles (1990). For examples of scholars who apply ideas of selection bias to critique qualitative research, see Achen and Snidal (1989); Geddes (1991; 2003); and King, Keohane, and Verba (1994, chapter 4). For rebuttals to these critiques, see Collier and Mahoney (1996) and Collier, Seawright, and Mahoney (2004).

A brief discussion of the advantages of random selection in large-N research can be found in King, Keohane, and Verba (1994, 124). Arguments in favor of randomly selecting a small number of cases are found in Fearon and Laitin (2008) and Herron and Quinn (2011). Key works in the multimethod literature on case selection include Lieberman (2005); Seawright and Gerring (2007; 2008); Rohlfing (2008); and Sekhon (2004). Case selection for testing set-theoretic hypotheses is discussed in Braumoeller and Goertz (2002); Clarke (2002); Freedman (2010); Mahoney and Goertz (2004); Ragin (2000); Schneider and Rohlfing (2010); and Seawright (2002).

Achen, C. H. 1986. *The statistical analysis of quasi-experiments*. Berkeley: University of California Press.

Achen, C. H., and D. Snidal. 1989. Rational deterrence theory and comparative case studies. *World Politics* 41:143–69.

Braumoeller, B., and G. Goertz. 2000. The methodology of necessary conditions. *American Journal of Political Science* 44:844–58.

Braumoeller, B., and G. Goertz. 2002. Watching your posterior: comment on Seawright. *Political Analysis* 10:198–203.

Clarke, K. A. 2002. The reverend and the ravens: comment on Seawright. *Political Analysis* 10:194–97.

Collier, D., H. E. Brady, and J. Seawright. 2010. Introduction to the second edition: a sea change in political methodology. In *Rethinking social inquiry: diverse tools, shared standards*, 2nd edition, edited by H. E. Brady and D. Collier. Lanham, MD: Rowman & Littlefield.

Collier, D., and J. Mahoney. 1996. Insights and pitfalls: selection bias in qualitative research. *World Politics* 49:56–91.

Collier, D., J. Seawright, and J. Mahoney. 2004. Claiming too much: warnings about selection bias. In *Rethinking social inquiry: diverse tools, shared standards*, edited by H. E. Brady and D. Collier. Lanham, MD: Rowman & Littlefield.

Deyo, F. C. 1987. State and labor: modes of political exclusion in East Asian development. In *The political economy of the new Asian industrialism*, edited by F. C. Deyo. Ithaca: Cornell University Press.

Dion, D. 1998. Evidence and inference in the comparative case study. *Comparative Politics* 30:127–45.

Eckstein, H. 1975. Case study and theory in political science. In *Handbook of political science*, vol. 7, edited by F. I. Greenstein and N. W. Polsby. Reading, MA: Addison-Wesley.

Fearon, J. D., and D. D. Laitin. 2008. Integrating qualitative and quantitative methods. In *Oxford handbook of political methodology*, edited by J. M. Box-Steffensmeier, H. E. Brady, and D. Collier. Oxford: Oxford University Press.

Freedman, D. A. 2010. Black ravens, white shoes, and case selection. In *Statistical models and causal inference: a dialogue with the social sciences*, by David Freedman and edited by D. Collier, J. Sekhon, and P. Stark. Cambridge: Cambridge University Press.

Geddes, B. 1991. How the cases you choose affect the answers you get: selection bias in comparative politics. In *Political Analysis*, vol. 2, edited by J. A. Stimson. Ann Arbor: University of Michigan Press.

Geddes, B. 2003. *Paradigms and sand castles: theory building and research design in comparative politics*. Ann Arbor: University of Michigan Press.

George, A. L., and R. Smoke. 1974. *Deterrence in American foreign policy: theory and practice*. New York: Columbia University Press.

Gerring, J. 2007. Is there a (viable) crucial-case method? *Comparative Political Studies* 40:231–53.

Goertz, G. 2006. Assessing the trivialness, relevance, and relative importance of necessary or sufficient conditions in social science. *Studies in Comparative International Development* 41:88–109.

Goldstone, J. A. 2003. Comparative historical analysis and knowledge accumulation in the study of revolutions. In *Comparative historical analysis in the social sciences*, edited by J. Mahoney and D. Rueschemeyer. Cambridge: Cambridge University Press.

Heckman, J. J. 1976. The common structure of statistical models of truncation, sample selection and limited dependent variables and a simple estimator for such models. *Annals of Economic and Social Measurement* 5:475–92.

Heckman, J. J. 1979. Sample selection bias as a specification error. *Econometrica* 47:153–61.

Herron, M. C., and K. M. Quinn. 2011. A careful look at modern qualitative case selection methods. Paper presented at the annual meeting of the Midwest Political Science Association, Palmer House Hilton, Chicago, IL.

King, G., R. Keohane, and S. Verba. 1994. *Designing social inquiry: scientific inference in qualitative research.* Princeton: Princeton University Press.

Koo, H. 1987. The interplay of state, social class, and world system in East Asian development: the cases of South Korea and Taiwan. In *The political economy of the new Asian industrialism*, edited by F. C. Deyo. Ithaca: Cornell University Press.

Lieberman, E. 2005. Nested analysis as a mixed-method strategy for comparative research. *American Political Science Review* 99:435–52.

Maddala, G. S. 1983. *Limited-dependent and qualitative variables in economics.* Cambridge: Cambridge University Press.

Mahoney, J., and G. Goertz. 2004. The Possibility Principle: choosing negative cases in comparative research. *American Political Science Review* 98:653–69.

Manski, C. F. 1995. *Identification problems in social sciences.* Cambridge: Harvard University Press.

Mill, J. S. 1843, 1974. Of the four methods of experimental inquiry. In *A system of logic*, book 3, chap. 8. Toronto: University of Toronto Press.

Ragin, C. 2000. *Fuzzy-set social science.* Chicago: University of Chicago Press.

Ragin, C. 2008. *Redesigning social inquiry: fuzzy sets and beyond.* Chicago: University of Chicago Press.

Rohlfing, I. 2008. What you see and what you get: pitfalls and principles of nested analysis in comparative research. *Comparative Political Studies* 41:1492–514.

Schneider, C. Q., and I. Rohlfing. 2010. It's complex! Combining set-theoretic methods and case studies in multimethod research. Manuscript.

Seawright, J. 2002. Testing for necessary and/or sufficient causation: which cases are relevant? *Political Analysis* 10:178–207.

Seawright, J., and J. Gerring. 2007. Techniques for choosing cases. In *Case study research: principles and practices*, by J. Gerring. Cambridge: Cambridge University Press.

Seawright, J., and J. Gerring. 2008. Case-selection techniques in case study research: a menu of qualitative and quantitative options. *Political Research Quarterly* 61:294–308.

Sekhon, J. 2004. Quality meets quantity: case studies, conditional probability, and counterfactuals. *Perspectives on Politics* 2:281–93.

Skocpol, T. 1979. *States and social revolutions: a comparative analysis of France, Russia, and China.* Cambridge: Cambridge University Press.

Stolzenberg, R. M., and D. A. Relles. 1990. Theory testing in a world constrained by research design: the significance of Heckman's censored sampling bias correction for nonexperimental research. *Sociological Methods and Research* 18:395–415.

# Chapter 15

## Generalizations

**Generalize**: 1. a. To reduce to a general form, class, or law. b. To render indefinite or unspecific. 2. a. To infer from particulars. b. To draw inferences or a general conclusion from. 3. a. To make generally or universally applicable. b. To popularize.
> —*The American Heritage Dictionary of the English Language*

There is an embarrassing scarcity of covering laws; in sciences such as biology, psychology, and the social sciences, there are hardly any observable empirical regularities that could be considered explanatory.
> —*Peter Hedström and Petri Ylikoski*

### Introduction

Most social scientists want to produce generalizations about the world. A central goal of the research enterprise is to generate concepts, models, and theories that can travel across time and space. However, neither the literature in philosophy nor works in social science methodology say much about the specific forms that generalizations can take. In this chapter, we compare the typical modes of generalization used in the quantitative and qualitative cultures.

The first question to ask is what does one mean by "generalization"? Most will recognize the difference between a descriptive generalization and a causal generalization (e.g., King, Keohane, and Verba 1994). A descriptive generalization often involves one variable that "describes" some state of affairs within a population of cases. For example, one might conduct a survey and use its findings to make the generalization that 50 percent of all Americans have a favorable opinion of President Obama on a given day.

By contrast, causal generalizations always involve at least two variables, *A* and *B*. Causal generalizations ideally specify the *form* and *strength* of the relationship between *A* and *B* within a population of cases.

In the qualitative and quantitative cultures, scholars make causal general-izations that assume different forms, and they adopt contrasting understand-ings of what counts as a strong generalization. Quantitative researchers think about generalizations using notions of association and average treatment effects. Correspondingly, the strength of a generalization is tied to the degree of association and the size of the treatment effect.

In the qualitative culture, by contrast, causal generalizations often assume a set-theoretic form: "All/none *A* are *B*." Of course, sometimes there are a few counterexamples, so one may use language like "almost" or "virtually" all or none of *A* are *B*. For example, one might notice that genocides never occur in countries with democratic regimes. This could lead to the generalization that "all cases of genocide are cases of nondemocracy."

Hence, a strong (causal) generalization means different things in each culture. In the quantitative culture, it means a strong association or treatment effect between variables. In the qualitative culture, it means membership in one category is nearly essential for or nearly ensures membership in another category.

The two cultures have trouble seeing and analyzing each other's typical kind of generalization. Qualitative methods are not designed to find corre-lations, associations, or average treatment effects. For their part, standard statistical methods are not designed to study set-theoretic generalizations. In this chapter, we show that quite a few examples of almost perfect set-theoretic generalizations exist in the literature. Although this finding may be surprising to some readers, it makes sense in the context of qualitative research.

## Qualitative Generalizations

In qualitative research, set-theoretic relationships have a close affinity with necessary and sufficient conditions. "All *A* are *B*" in set-theoretic language means that *A* is a subset of *B*. When stated in terms of logic, *B* is a necessary condition for *A*. Interestingly, these generalizations have the basic form of covering laws. For instance, the causal generalization entailed in the democratic peace can easily be converted into the canonical covering law form (e.g., Hempel 1942; Hitchcock and Woodward 2003):

No wars between democracies.

The United States and Canada are two democracies.

*therefore*

No war between the Unites States and Canada.

In the philosophy of science, laws often take the form of set-theoretic generalizations. For example, Armstrong's (1983) influential analysis of the "laws of nature" focuses most of its attention on the idea that covering laws mean that all *F*s are *G*. It is accurate to say that strong generalizations of the "all/none *A* are *B*" stand as potential candidates for covering laws.

Some readers are no doubt concerned that generalizations as strong as all/none *A* are *B* are rare or nonexistent in the social sciences (though perhaps not in the natural sciences). Yet, in the course of our research and reading, we routinely find examples of these set-theoretic empirical generalizations. The following list reflects our interest in topics such as international conflict, civil war, democracy, and economic development. To emphasize the all or none language of these generalizations, we have put the relevant language in boldface.

> The introduction of universal suffrage led **almost everywhere** (the United States excepted) to the development of Socialist parties. (Duverger 1954, 66)

> **No** famines in democracies. (Our version of Drèze and Sen 1989.)

> **(Almost) no** wealthy democracies transition to authoritarianism. (Our statement of Przeworski et al.'s (2000) well-known finding.)

> There are **no instances** of an *incomplete democratizer with [i.e., AND] weak institutions* participating in, let alone initiating, an external war since World War I .... Out of these sixty-three states with weak institutions that have undergone incomplete democratic transitions since 1945, **not a single one** has either initiated or participated in the outbreak of an external war. (Narang and Nelson 2009, 363, emphasis added)

> The final generalization is a statement of that sequence of changes in attitude which occurred in **every case** known to me in which the person came to use marihuana for pleasure. (Becker 1953, 236)

> We show that, at least in Latin America, there is **not a single case** of a country where democracy has been undermined because of the choice to use [human rights] trials. (Sikkink and Walling 2007, 442)

> The organized working class appeared as a key actor in the development of full democracy **almost everywhere**, the only exception being the few cases of agrarian democracy in some of the small-holding countries. (Rueschemeyer, Stephens, and Stephens 1992, 270)

> It is surely not coincidental that economic crises accompanied **every** transformation reviewed here. The pattern suggests that economic crises might be a necessary though not a sufficient incentive for the breakdown of authoritarian regimes. (Bermeo 1990, 366)

Indeed, the effect of presidential partisanship on income inequality turns out to have been remarkably consistent since the end of World War II. The 80/20 income ratio increased under **each of the six** Republican presidents in this period.... In contrast, four of the five Democratic presidents—**all except** Jimmy Carter—presided over declines in income inequality. (Bartels 2008, cited in Tomasky 2008, 45)

First, **only** staunch opponents of internationalization pursued nuclear weapons in East Asia, ... Second, **all** nuclear programs in the Middle East were launched by leaders steering import-substitution and relatively closed political economies. (Solingen 2008, 18)

**Every group** mounting a suicide campaign over the past two decades has had as a major objective ... coercing a foreign state that has military forces in what the terrorists see as their homeland to take those forces out. (Pape 2005, 21)

**Only one** of the 38 active armed conflicts in the 2001–2005 period took place in the richest quartile of the world's countries; the al-Qaeda strikes on the United States on September 11, 2001. (Buhaung and Gleditsch 2008, 218)

Some of these generalizations are quite famous; in fact, many of the most important findings in the social sciences are set-theoretic generalizations. If one is attentive to the form of these generalizations, it is not hard to find more.

In qualitative methodology, Mill's methods of agreement and difference are tools for studying set-theoretic relationships among individual variables. When formulating causal generalizations, it is natural to examine all cases of $Y = 1$ and see if there is some common factor, $X$, which is always present when $Y$ occurs. This is the standard setup for the method of agreement. In our terms, the method of agreement is used to look for $X$s such that "all $Y = 1$ are $X = 1$." For example, Becker's famous article is a classic example of this at work. He focused his attention on individuals who smoked marihuana for pleasure and found a sequence of behavior common to all of them.

In many of these examples, the author interprets the set-theoretic generalization as reflecting a causal relationship. For example, Bermeo believes there is a causal relationship between crises and the breakdown of authoritarian regimes. She uses the set-theoretic empirical generalization as support for that view. Obviously, to confirm this causal interpretation, she would need to carry out additional analysis, such as within-case analysis and process tracing. But the generalization itself lends support to the idea that one variable causes the other.

Finally, it bears emphasis that the scholars making these generalizations assume that they apply in some contexts and not others. Indeed, the

**Table 15.1**
Set-Theoretic Generalizations:
Fate of Leaders after Imposed Regime Change

|  | Domestic-imposed change | Foreign-imposed change |
|---|---|---|
| Punished | 27 | 22 |
| Not punished | 182 | 0 |

*Source:* Goemans 2000.

scope of qualitative generalizations is often quite restricted (see the chapter "Scope"). In addition, it is clear that many of these generalizations have some exceptions. Thus, while the scholars offer a generalization that closely follows a set-theoretic form, they do not believe that the generalization is a law of the universe that cannot be violated.

## Set-Theoretic Generalizations and Two by Two Tables

Since set-theoretic (causal) generalization involves two variables, it is easy to present these generalizations with 2×2 tables (assuming for the purposes of this section that the variables or concepts are dichotomous). Table 15.1 uses an example that we continue with in the next section; it involves a study by Goemans (2000) on the fate of leaders at the end of international crises and wars. One dependent variable is whether the leader is "punished" (i.e., exiled, imprisoned, or killed) at the end of the war. A key independent variable of interest is whether foreign forces overthrow the antecedent regime. We summarize the bivariate findings in table 15.1.

The table illustrates that one easy way to find strong qualitative generalizations is by looking for an empty (or nearly empty) cell in a 2×2 or $N \times N$ table. If such a cell exists, then one can reformulate the core relationship of the table in the form "all/none $A$ are $B$." In the case of Goemans's analysis, we arrive at "all foreign-imposed regime changes led to the punishment of the previous leader."

Since we discussed set-theoretic versus statistical analyses of 2×2 tables at some length in the "Mathematical Prelude," here we merely summarize two key points.

1. When confronted with a set-theoretic relationship, different statistical measures of association will vary in how they interpret the relationship. Some common 2×2 measures of association, e.g., $\chi^2$, $\tau_\beta$, would see the relationship as significant but not very strong. By contrast, an

odds ratio measure of association would indicate a very strong and significant relationship.

2. Statistical measures do not usually differentiate between the generalization "All $X$ are $Y$" and "All $Y$ are $X$." For example, an odds ratio does not distinguish between a sufficient condition and a necessary condition.

·The point is not that statistical tests fail to accurately report certain features of the data. Rather the point is that these tests are not designed to analyze set-theoretic generalizations. By the same token, of course, set-theoretic tools are not designed to analyze the kind of symmetric associations normally studied in the quantitative culture.

## Statistical Models, Perfect Predictors, and Set-Theoretic Generalizations

A well-known problem in statistical analysis involves what we call "perfect predictors."[1] Basically, in maximum likelihood estimation, if an independent variable perfectly predicts the outcome, then the statistical equation cannot be estimated (see Zorn (2005) for a nice discussion). In the 1990s, popular software packages such as SAS version 6 ignored this problem and produced meaningless results when it was present. Current statistical software will issue warnings (e.g., SAS) or remove the offending variable from the model with a warning (e.g., Stata). In the case of R, the software will estimate the model and leave it up to the researcher to discover the problem by noticing that the standard errors are unusually large.

Once the problem is discovered, most scholars simply eliminate the offending variable from the model (as Stata does automatically). This solution leads to what we call the Paradox of the Perfect Predictor:

*Paradox of the Perfect Predictor.* The variable with the strongest, usually by far, causal effect is removed from the model.

Instead of drawing attention to an unusually strong relationship, the scholar views it as a statistical problem that needs to be fixed. While there are

---

[1] In statistics, this is usually called the problem of "separation," e.g., Heinze and Schemper (2002). The perfect predictor completely separates the outcome variable into zero and one groups. Generally, this occurs when there is a zero in a given cell.

**Table 15.2**

Perfect Predictors: Foreign-Imposed Regime Change

| Variable | MLEs | | MPLEs | |
|---|---|---|---|---|
| | $\hat{\beta}$ | Odds ratio | $\hat{\beta}$ | Odds ratio |
| Constant | −2.96 | – | −2.87 | – |
| | (.46) | | (.44) | |
| Other small loser | .85 | 2.3 | .85 | 2.3 |
| | (.66) | | (.63) | |
| Other big loser | 3.36 | 28.8 | 3.20 | 24.5 |
| | (1.02) | | (1.00) | |
| Mixed regime | 2.69 | 14.8 | 2.61 | 13.7 |
| small loser | (.62) | | (.61) | |
| Mixed regime | 3.24 | 25.6 | 3.12 | 22.5 |
| big loser | (.89) | | (.87) | |
| Foreign-imposed | 22.85 | $8.4 \times 10^9$ | 5.49 | 243.0 |
| regime change | (4840.20) | | (1.51) | |

*Source:* Zorn 2005, 167.

methods to deal with this "problem,"[2] by far the most common solution is to remove the offending variable from the model. For example, consider the following justification for removing a term from a statistical model: "Use of the ICOW data requires some changes to the model specification. The interaction term between nuclear status is excluded from the model since its zero values perfectly determine zero values of the dependent variable" (Gartzke and Jo 2009, 224).

Table 15.2 presents Zorn's (2005) analysis of Goemans's data. As we saw in table 15.1, the perfect predictor is "foreign-imposed regime change." The parameter estimate is $8.4 \times 10^9$, i.e., the odds of punishment for such leaders are roughly 8,400,000,000 times greater than those who are removed without foreign intervention. Zorn finds infinity—what $8.4 \times 10^9$ basically is mathematically—to be an unreasonable estimate and shows ways to arrive at smaller values. He argues that his correction methods "present a far more credible picture of the influence of foreign-imposed regime change on postwar leaders' fates" (Zorn 2005, 167). In the more "realistic" model, the odds ratio is "only" 243 (see table 15.2). However, while 243 is less than

---

[2] Zorn (2005) discusses several ways to get "more reasonable" parameter estimates for these variables. Bayesian techniques address the issue by using priors to make it possible to estimate the likelihood equations.

8.4 billion, the coefficient is still so high that the results mean the same for almost all practical purposes.[3]

Perfect predictors suggest how the two cultures can have differing reactions to the same data. The qualitative scholar is likely to make a perfect predictor the centerpiece of his or her analysis. This scholar is drawn to perfect predictors because his or her goal is to offer a comprehensive explanation of the outcome of interest. By contrast, in the quantitative school, the goal of the analysis may well be to estimate the effect of some other variable besides the perfect predictor. Given this goal, the presence of a perfect predictor becomes a statistical problem, one that may require throwing out the variable or introducing other solutions to get around it.

## Control Variables and Perfect Predictors

Much of the literature on causal inference with observational data focuses on the problem of confounding variables. It is always possible that if one includes a new control variable, a key statistical finding will disappear. Skeptical reviewers are quick to point out that an author may have failed to include a key control variable. Economists can be obsessed with these issues of omitted variable bias, including controls and fixed effects for the cross-section, for each year, and for each region. As Lieberson and Lynn say:

> There are an almost infinite number of conditions or influences on the dependent variable (to use the contemporary language of sociology). If a survey generates a complex analysis where, say, fifteen variables are taken into account, it is perfectly acceptable in contemporary analysis to propose that a sixteenth variable should also be considered. There is always the possibility that "controlling" for an additional attribute might completely alter the conclusions previously reached. (Lieberson and Lynn 2002, 8)

Given the sensitivity of statistical findings to particular model specifications, it has become common in recent years in social science journals for authors to devote (precious) journal pages to "robustness" analyses. These discussions, often shadowed by significant websites, deal with the fragility of statistical findings by varying many of the core features of the analysis in order to see if the main variables retain their sign and remain statistically significant.

---

[3] Another way that perfect predictors can be identified is when the standard errors are massive. For example, notice that the standard error is more than 4,800 in table 15.2 for the offending variable.

In contrast, the set-theoretic generalizations developed in the qualitative culture are fundamentally bivariate in nature and do not require the inclusion of control variables. The hypothesis entailed in a claim about necessity or sufficiency is that no other variable or combination of variables can overcome the effects of a necessary and/or sufficient cause (Seawright 2002, 181). In fact, set-theoretic generalizations are robust to the problem of spurious correlation. In general, one does not have to worry about the introduction of additional variables removing the relationship:

> No control or confounding variables can defeat a strong set-theoretic generalization.[4]

To see why this is true, recall that control variables look for differing relationships within subgroups of an overall population of cases. But set-theoretic generalizations remain stable when moving from the full population to subpopulations. If all $A$ are $B$ for population $Z$, the same generalization will hold for all subpopulations of $Z$. A perfect predictor in the population as a whole will always be a perfect predictor in a subpopulation.

We can also see this intuitively by looking at the causal impact of the perfect predictor in table 15.2. The odds ratio is either essentially infinity or the very large 243. Although one could introduce different control variables, use fixed effects, or make other model adjustments, it is very unlikely that the causal effect will go away. With actual perfect prediction, the addition of control variables will have no effect. If there are a few counterexamples to the set-theoretic generalization, the estimated parameter may well decrease in size (because of multicollinearity), but even here the control variables are in general not likely to have much impact.

## Conclusion

The notion of a strong generalization means something different in the qualitative and quantitative cultures. For the qualitative culture, it implies a set-theoretic relationship that approximates the form: "All/none $A$ are $B$." For the quantitative culture, by contrast, the notion of a strong generalization suggests a powerful statistical association between two variables or a substantively and statistically significant average treatment effect.

These different kinds of generalizations are closely related to the overall goals of the two traditions. Qualitative researchers often seek to comprehensively explain outcomes, including by identifying factors that are necessary

---

[4] The exception to this rule is if the control variable itself is perfectly correlated with the generalization variable.

for these outcomes. This orientation lends itself quite naturally to the quest of finding strong set-theoretic generalizations. By contrast, in the quantitative culture, researchers seek to estimate average effects for particular variables. Given this goal, a strong generalization will often involve a statement about the size of a causal effect or the robustness of a finding about a causal effect.

## References and Suggested Readings

King, Keohane, and Verba (1994) provide a good discussion of both descriptive and causal generalization from a quantitative perspective. On the connection between set-theoretic generalizations and qualitative research, see Ragin (2000). Goertz (2003) offers a long list of examples of necessary condition theoretical generalizations and hypotheses. The challenge of studying these generalizations with standard statistical tools is discussed by Dion (1998) and Braumoeller and Goertz (2000). Pearl (2000, chapter 1) provides a discussion of how exceptions to set-theoretic generalizations often lead scholars to focus on probabilities.

Armstrong, D. M. 1983. *What is a law of nature?* Cambridge: Cambridge University Press.

Ashworth, S., J. Clinton, A. Meirowitz, and K. Romsay. 2008. Design, inference, and the strategic logic of suicide terrorism. *American Political Science Review* 102:269–73.

Bartels, L. 2008. *Unequal democracy: the political economy of the new Gilded Age.* Princeton: Princeton University Press.

Baumgartner, F., C. Breunig, C. Green-Federsen, et al. 2009. Punctuated equilibrium in comparative perspective. *American Journal of Political Science* 53:603–20.

Becker, H. 1953. Becoming a marihuana user. *American Journal of Sociology* 59:235–42.

Bermeo, N. 1990. Rethinking regime change. *Comparative Politics* 22:359–77.

Braumoeller, B., and G. Goertz. 2000. The methodology of necessary conditions. *American Journal of Political Science* 44:844–58.

Buhaung, H., and C. Gleditsch. 2008. Contagion or confusion? why conflicts cluster in space. *International Studies Quarterly* 52:215–33.

Chapman, T., and P. Roeder. 2007. Partition as a solution to wars of nationalism: the importance of institutions. *American Political Science Review* 101:677–91.

Cooper, G. 1998. Generalization in ecology: a philosophical taxonomy. *Biology and Philosophy* 13:555–86.

Dion, D. 1998. Evidence and inference in the comparative case study. *Comparative Politics* 30:127–45.

Doyle, M. 1983a. Kant, liberal legacies, and foreign affairs, part I. *Philosophy and Public Affairs* 12:205–35.

Doyle, M. 1983b. Kant, liberal legacies, and foreign affairs, part II. *Philosophy and Public Affairs* 12:323–53.

Drèze, J., and A. Sen. 1989. *Hunger and public action.* Oxford: Oxford University Press.

Duverger, M. 1954. *Political parties: their organization and activity in the modern state.* London: Methuen.

Gartzke, E., and D. Jo. 2009. Bargaining, nuclear proliferation, and interstate disputes. *Journal of Conflict Resolution* 53:209–33.

Geddes, B. 2003. *Paradigms and sand castles: theory building and research design in comparative politics.* Ann Arbor: University of Michigan Press.

Goemans, H. 2000. Fighting for survival: the fate of leaders and the duration of war. *Journal of Conflict Resolution* 44:555–79.

Goertz, G. 1994. *Contexts of international politics.* Cambridge: Cambridge University Press.

Goertz, G. 2003. The substantive importance of necessary condition hypotheses. In *Necessary conditions: theory, methodology, and applications*, edited by G. Goertz and H. Starr. Lanham, MD: Rowman & Littlefield.

Goertz, G., T. Hak, and J. Dul. Forthcoming. Ceilings and floors: theoretical and statistical considerations when the goal is to draw boundaries of data, not lines through the middle. *Sociological Methods and Research.*

Hale, H. 2004. Divided we stand: institutional sources of ethnofederal state survival and collapse. *World Politics* 56:165–93.

Hansen, H., S. Mitchell, and S. Nemeth. 2008. International organization mediation of interstate conflicts: moving beyond the global vs. regional dichotomy. *Journal of Conflict Resolution* 52:295–325.

Harff, B. 2003. No lessons learned from the Holocaust? Assessing risks of genocide and political mass murder since 1955. *American Political Science Review* 97:57–73.

Heinze, G., and M. Schemper. 2002. Solution to the problem of separation in logistic regression. *Statistics in Medicine* 21:2409–19.

Hempel, C. 1942. The function of general laws in history. *Journal of Philosophy* 39:35–48.

Hitchcock, C., and J. Woodward. 2003. Explanatory generalizations, part I: a counterfactual account. *Noûs* 37:1–24.

Jones, B., F. Baumgartner, C. Breunig, et al. 2009. A general empirical law of public budgets: a comparative analysis. *American Journal of Political Science* 53:855–73.

King, G., R. Keohane, and S. Verba. 1994. *Designing social inquiry: scientific inference in qualitative research.* Princeton: Princeton University Press.

Levy, J. S. 1988. Domestic politics and war. *Journal of Interdisciplinary History* 18:653–73.

Lieberson, S., and F. Lynn. 2002. Barking up the wrong branch: alternatives to the current model of sociological science. *Annual Review of Sociology* 28:1–19.

Lipset, S. 1959. Some social requisites of democracy: economic development and political legitimacy. *American Political Science Review* 53:69–105.

Narang, V., and R. M. Nelson. 2009. Who are these belligerent democratizers? Reassessing the impact of democratization on war. *International Organization* 63:357–79.

Ostrom, E. 2005. *Understanding institutional diversity.* Princeton: Princeton University Press.

Pape, R. 2005. *Dying to win: the strategic logic of suicide terrorism.* New York: Random House.

Pearl, J. 2000. *Causality: models, reasoning, and inference.* Cambridge: Cambridge University Press.

Przeworski, A., M. Alvarez, J. Chelbub, and F. Limongi. 2000. *Democracy and development: political institutions and well-being in the world, 1950–1990.* Cambridge: Cambridge University Press.

Ragin, C. 1987. *The comparative method: moving beyond qualitative and quantitative strategies.* Berkeley: University of California Press.

Ragin, C. 2000. *Fuzzy-set social science.* Chicago: University of Chicago Press.

Ragin, C. 2008. *Redesigning social inquiry: fuzzy sets and beyond.* Chicago: University of Chicago Press.

Ragin, C., and G. Schneider. 2009. Case-oriented versus variable-oriented theory building and testing. Manuscript, University of Arizona.

Ramirez, F., Y. Soysal, and S. Shanahan. 1997. The changing logic of political citizenship: cross-national acquisition of women's suffrage rights, 1890 to 1990. *American Sociological Review* 62:735–45.

Ray, J. 1993. Wars between democracies: rare or nonexistent? *International Interactions* 18:251–76.

Rodrik, D. 2006. Industrial development: stylized facts and policies. Manuscript, Harvard University.

Rueschemeyer, D., E. H. Stephens, and J. D. Stephens. 1992. *Capitalist development and democracy.* Chicago: University of Chicago Press.

Russett, B. 1995. The democratic peace: "and yet it moves." *International Security* 19:164–75.

Russett, B., and H. Starr. 2000. From democratic peace to Kantian peace: democracy and conflict in the international system. In *Handbook of war studies*, 2nd edition, edited by M. Midlarsky. Ann Arbor: University of Michigan Press.

Ryckman, M., and G. Goertz. 2009. Rethinking and re-estimating the impact of wealth (GDP/capita) on civil war onset. Paper presented at Peace Science Society Meetings.

Sambanis, N. 2008. Terrorism and civil war. In *Terrorism and development*, edited by P. Keefer and N. Loayza. Cambridge: Cambridge University Press.

Seawright, J. 2002. Testing for necessary and/or sufficient causation: which cases are relevant? *Political Analysis* 10:178–207.

Sikkink, K., and C. B. Walling. 2007. The impact of human rights trails in Latin America. *Journal of Peace Research* 44:427–45.

Singh, S., and C. Way. 2004. The correlates of nuclear proliferation: a quantitative test. *Journal of Conflict Resolution* 48:859–85.

Solingen, E. 2008. The genesis, design and effects of regional institutions: lessons from East Asia and the Middle East. *International Studies Quarterly* 52:261–94.

Tomasky, M. 2008. How historic a victory? *New York Review of Books* 55:44–47.

Woodward, J., and C. Hitchcock. 2003. Explanatory generalisations, part 1: a counterfactual account. *Noûs* 37:1–24.

Young, J. 2008. Repression, dissent, and the onset of civil war. Ph.D. dissertation, Florida State University.

Zorn, C. 2005. A solution to separation in binary response models. *Political Analysis* 13:157–70.

# Chapter 16

## Scope

The timeworn idea that subjects in a study form a random sample
of some hypothetical superpopulation still deserves a moment of
respectful silence.
            —David Freedman

### Introduction

Since the concept of "scope" often does not appear in methods books, it is
useful to begin with a brief illustration. A simple example from the natural
sciences raises nicely the issues of model fit and model specification that will
concern us in this chapter. The example is Hooke's law from physics, which
states that the strain on a spring is proportional to stress (Freedman (2009)
uses this as a core example). If we hang a $weight_i$ on a spring, and the length
of the spring is $length_i$, the law says:

$$length_i = \beta * weight_i + \epsilon_i. \tag{16.1}$$

In classical physics (e.g., Laplace and Gauss), $\epsilon_i$ is the measurement error,
which is itself a combination of instrument, human, and other factors that
make the observed measurement deviate from its true value.

As it stands, equation (16.1) has no scope limits. Hooke's law thus might
be presumed to be valid for all weights and in all physical settings in the
universe. Scope conditions are introduced only when the analyst imposes
one or more limitations on the applicability of the law.

There are two natural ways to introduce scope limits with Hooke's law.
The first is to assert that the law is valid for only some range of weights. As
physicists know, many "laws of science" break down in extreme conditions.

In this case, the use of large weights requires the analyst to add a quadratic term to equation (16.1). Hence, the scope of Hooke's law as stated above is limited to only weights beneath some threshold. Above that threshold, one needs to modify the law by adjusting the variables in the model.[1]

A second natural way to limit Hooke's law involves asserting that it is valid only when the gravitational forces are equivalent to those of the earth (or assert that the nature of the law will vary depending on distance from the earth's gravitational center). Here one is specifying the "context" or "background conditions" that are necessary for the law to work. This context is really one or more implicit (i.e., omitted) variables not specified in equation (16.1). Unless these variables are present (or assume certain specific values), the relationship as formulated in the law will not apply.

The need for scope conditions thus arises because Hooke's law is limited in its applicability: the parameters of the model are not stable across all subpopulations of units (e.g., springs under very heavy weights work differently) and across all contexts (e.g., alternative gravitational forces). Virtually no physical theory has universal scope. Except perhaps for the basic theories of quantum mechanics, all theories and generalizations are context sensitive, i.e., have scope limits.

It is helpful to think of scope as a set of variables such that:

If scope conditions $S_i$ hold, then the effect of the treatment is $\beta$.

Outside these scope conditions, we may or may not know what the actual relationship is, but we suspect or know that the relationship is different. In short, a scope condition is a claim about causal homogeneity—i.e., about the domain in which causal effects can be expected to be stable.

Unsurprisingly, the scopes of theories in the social sciences are more restricted than in the natural sciences. Whereas Hooke's law is quite general because it holds across a large range of weights and most contexts on earth, models in the social sciences are notoriously fragile across different subpopulations and contexts. Running the same model on a subpopulation or on a new population of cases is quite likely to produce different parameter estimates.

## Within-Model Responses to Causal Heterogeneity Problems

To avoid having to limit the scope, scholars can address problems of model fit and causal heterogeneity by changing the causal model—what we label

---

[1] Eventually all springs will simply break under enough weight. This breaking point is a kind of ultimate limit. When this limit is reached, the law does not apply.

"within-model" responses. We briefly survey some of the most popular of these within-model responses. For reasons that we explore, the option of changing the causal model to address causal heterogeneity issues is more attractive to quantitative scholars than to qualitative scholars. This is one reason why highly restrictive scope limitations are more likely to be found in qualitative than in quantitative research.

## Responses in Quantitative Research

The discussion of Hooke's law suggests a useful way to think about using scope conditions versus within-model solutions when confronted with causal heterogeneity in quantitative research:

$$\text{length} = \beta * \text{weight} + \epsilon, \text{ for weight} < S_1 \tag{16.2}$$

$$\text{length} = \beta * \text{weight} + \gamma * \text{weight}^2 + \epsilon, \text{ for weight} < S_2. \tag{16.3}$$

For a lighter weight, $S_1$, we have a simpler equation. If we want to increase the scope limits to also include heavier weights, i.e., $S_2$, then we need to add a quadratic term. By including the quadratic term (i.e., weight$^2$), we have dealt with the scope problem within the model itself.

Scope decisions involve various forms of what we call Fundamental Tradeoffs. While it is not a law of the universe of which we are aware, it seems almost inevitable, in the social sciences at least, that when one wants to increase the scope of any given theory (without developing a entirely new theory), the modified theory will be more complex (Przeworski and Teune 1970). The Fundamental Tradeoff thus involves asking whether the gain in the scope of generalization is worth the loss in parsimony (i.e., the increase in complexity). As long as the costs incurred by the loss of parsimony are not too high, which they certainly are not with Hooke's law, then a within-model solution is often a good idea.

It is important to note that randomization is not a surefire solution to problems of scope. To take a simple example, suppose there is a treatment (say a drug) which has a positive effect on men but no effect on women. The sex of individuals is thus a scope condition that defines the range of cases within which the treatment works. If we were unaware of this scope and ran an experiment or statistical model on all individuals, we might assume that the treatment has on average an effect for everyone, when in fact it does not.

A natural response would be to include sex as a control variable. As countless philosophers and methodologists have emphasized, adding control variables is critical for producing homogeneous subpopulations, which in turn are essential for good causal inference. Control variables are a classic example of what we mean by a within-model response, because one incorporates the scope variable into the model, thereby making it more complex (i.e., less parsimonious). So one might have the model:

$$Y = \beta_0 + \beta_1 T + \beta_2 S + \epsilon. \tag{16.4}$$

Here one examines the effect of $T$ (treatment) while controlling for $S$ (sex). With this model, we would certainly see that the sex of the subject is an important part of the story.

As is well known, the introduction of control variables can radically change the parameter estimate of the independent variable of interest, i.e., $T$. In the context of scope, the control variable is testing for causal homogeneity within subpopulations defined by the different values of the control variable (see Berk 2004, chapter 1, for a nice intuitive explanation). If the addition of the control variable changes the parameter estimate, then one might suspect that $X$ does not have constant effects across the whole population. In our simple example, $\beta_1$ will change when the sex variable is added. This implies that the treatment effect varies by subpopulations defined by sex.

The addition of a control variable and the changed estimate of $\beta_1$ suggest that causal heterogeneity is a problem. However, adding control variables per se does not solve the problem: it is a diagnostic tool that tells the researcher that causal heterogeneity is an issue.

To capture the heterogeneity, a natural move is to interact sex and treatment. The coefficient for the interaction term picks up the true dependence of the treatment on sex. It allows us to see that the effect of the treatment runs entirely through males. Complexifying a model with an interaction term in this way is a good example of a within-model solution to causal heterogeneity that stops short of directly imposing scope conditions.[2] One models how the effect of $X$ depends on $S$ without having to restrict the analysis to only cases with a particular value on $S$. This kind of solution makes good sense if the potential scope condition interacts with only one independent variable and that impact can be correctly modeled with a simple interaction term.

A different approach is to estimate separately the whole model on the subpopulations defined by a scope variable. For example, one can estimate the effect of $T$ separately for males and females. If one believes that the causal mechanism is quite different for different subpopulations, then this solution can be a good choice. For example, in the international relations conflict literature, analysts sometimes estimate separate models for different time periods, e.g., pre–World War I, post–World War II, and post–Cold War

---

[2] "Estimates of the extent to which a causal relationship holds over variations in persons, settings, treatments, and outcomes are conceptually similar to tests of statistical interactions" (Shadish et al. 2002, 86).

(e.g., Senese and Vasquez 2008). Often the parameter estimates vary quite a bit for many variables across the different time periods.

In summary, we think that there are three common within-model responses to problems of causal heterogeneity that stop short of restricting the scope: (1) control variables, (2) interaction terms, and (3) estimating the whole model in subpopulations. Solutions (1) and (3) are really diagnostic tools for identifying the existence of a problem of causal heterogeneity that may require a scope restriction. Solution (2) can in principle address the substance of a causal heterogeneity problem without imposing scope limitations.

### Responses in Qualitative Research

How can qualitative researchers respond to problems of causal heterogeneity without restricting the scope of their arguments? In this culture, it is also possible to use within-model solutions that stop short of scope restrictions. As in the quantitative culture, however, these solutions typically come at the cost of parsimony and thus raise Fundamental Tradeoffs.

A possible within-model solution in the qualitative culture involves adding one or more additional causal paths to an initial set-theoretic model. For instance, consider a qualitative model such as $Y = AbC + BCD$. To accommodate additional cases, one might need to add a new causal path. Thus, the original model might be modified to: $Y = AbC + BCD + EF$. The extent to which adding new paths for new cases is worthwhile depends on various considerations, including the nature of theory under investigation and the extent to which the new paths apply to more than one new case. One does not want to have to add a new path for each additional case.

The discovery that a model only works within a given context also can lead the researcher to add new variables to the causal paths in the initial model. For instance, consider again the set-theoretic model of $Y = AbC + BCD$. Suppose that the researcher discovers that this model only applies for units that have a certain specific characteristic, $Z$. One can include this characteristic as a part of the model by making it a necessary condition: $Y = Z * (AbC + BCD)$. Unless $Z$ is present, one cannot expect $AbC$ or $BCD$ to be sufficient for $Y$.

For those cases where $Z$ is not present, one needs to identify a different set of causal conditions that generate $Y$. These new causes may be associated with theories that have little to do with those used in the original model. For example, one might find that: $Y = zEF$. These new variables $E$ and $F$ may be unrelated to the variables from the original model. Nevertheless, the new model could be combined with the original one to avoid a scope restriction. The resulting final model would be less parsimonious: $Y = ZAbC + ZBCD + zEF$.

In both quantitative and qualitative research, then, limiting the scope of a theory can, in principle, be avoided by modifying the causal model. If the appropriate modifications are known and they are attractive—i.e., the Fundamental Tradeoff is worthwhile—then scholars have little reason to resort to scope restrictions. If, on the other hand, the within-model changes are unknown or introduce unwieldy complications, then scope restrictions become a sensible alternative.

## Why Use Scope Conditions?

Although scholars can sometimes avoid using highly restrictive scope conditions by modifying their causal models, they nevertheless often end up implicitly or explicitly imposing certain restrictions on the scope of their models. In this section, we consider how the existence of causal complexity and concerns about fit with data can lead scholars to use scope conditions.

### Causal Complexity

As a general rule, we propose:

> If expanding the scope of a causal model requires making the model considerably more complex, then imposing scope restrictions becomes an attractive option.

This proposal grows directly out of the idea that there is a tradeoff between increasing the generality of a causal model and maximizing the parsimony of that model. Scope restrictions are often made when the analyst decides that the gains of extending the generality of the model are outweighed by the loss of parsimony associated with the added complexity that must be introduced. In fact, quite often the analyst will not know how to modify the model such that it can encompass a wider range of cases. Scope restrictions then become an essential tool for specifying the domain in which the model does operate.

In practice, scope restrictions are often quite vague or entirely implicit in the social sciences (in both qualitative and quantitative research). Scholars often implicitly or occasionally explicitly use scope conditions that are about time periods or regions. While restricting the scope to a specific region or time period is relatively precise in an operational sense (e.g., the scope is Africa only), it is not precise in a theoretical sense. Ideally, one would identify abstract scope conditions that transcend specific times and places.

One of the reasons why scope restrictions are vaguely specified in terms of regions and time periods is that *many* important things change from one region or time to another. For example, Africa is different from Latin America in many ways, e.g., climate, population density, culture, colonial history, and so on. The researcher may not know which of these specific differences are most important and why exactly they are important. Thus, while the researcher believes it is essential to adopt an Africa-only scope, he or she may not be able to identify the complex reasons why this scope is appropriate. Within-model solutions are off the table precisely because they would require having already worked out these theoretical complexities.

The fact that qualitative causal models are designed to accommodate every case within a population helps explain why qualitative scholars use scope restrictions more readily than quantitative scholars. With a set-theoretic model, the addition of one or a small number of new cases may well require the analyst to make fundamental changes to the initial model. The resulting causal model may suffer a severe reduction in parsimony. Moreover, the scholar may not even know how to change the model in ways that can accommodate causal patterns in the new cases.

To take a hypothetical example, a qualitative scholar not only needs to learn that $D$ is an important variable when additional cases are added, but also that the missing causal combination for these cases is $BCD$. In her famous theory of social revolutions, Skocpol (1979) restricts the scope to noncolonial states. For her to extend the scope to include postcolonial social revolutions such as Mexico and Iran would require the addition of several new variables. Moreover, she would be faced with putting these new variables into her theory so that everything worked together. The complexities of the resulting theory would not have yielded the relatively elegant argument for which Skocpol is famous. When Skocpol did work to explain social revolutions for postcolonial countries, consequently, she developed a separate theory (Goodwin and Skocpol 1989).

### Better Fit

In quantitative research, the goal of analysis is usually to estimate the effects of individual variables of interest. As such, scope conditions are normally imposed to address problems related to causal heterogeneity. But in qualitative research, scope conditions are often linked to the goal of having causal models that achieve a strong fit with the data. One introduces scope restrictions in order to improve the overall fit of the model.

Table 16.1 illustrates this concern with improving fit in a simple way (see Ragin and Schneider 2010 for an extended analysis of this idea). In this table, we have a relationship between two binary variables: high GDP per capita (independent variable) and democracy (dependent variable). The fit is generally pretty good from a set-theoretic perspective: high GDP per capita is almost sufficient for democracy. However, there are eight cases

**Table 16.1**

Broad Scope: GDP/Capita and Democracy

|  |  | High GDP per capita | |
|---|---|---|---|
|  |  | 0 | 1 |
| Democracy | 1 | 55 | 37 |
|  | 0 | 44 | 8 |

$\chi^2 = 9.5$, $p = .002$, $N = 144$

Year: 1995.

*Source:* Gerring 2007.

that have no democracy but high GDP per capita, thus violating the set-theoretic relationship. Ideally, the qualitative researcher would like to have zero inconsistent cases, i.e., the lower right cell should be empty.

One way to improve fit is to explore whether these "problem" cases have something in common that could become the basis for a scope condition. If so, they could be eliminated from the analysis, leaving behind stronger and clearer results (i.e., a perfect sufficient condition relationship). It turns out that the problem cases are all (except Singapore) heavily dependent on oil, e.g., oil monarchies of the Persian Gulf. Hence, if one introduces a scope restriction that excludes all heavily oil-dependent states, the set-theoretic fit of the model improves significantly.

One might be inclined to believe that this kind of scope restriction is nothing more than removing outliers (defined against some model). However, the scope restriction is an abstract variable (i.e., heavy oil dependence), not simply a set of specific countries (e.g., Saudi Arabia, Yemen). Moreover, there may be good theoretical reasons for excluding oil-dependent states from a test concerning the effect of high GDP per capita on democracy. If one believes that high GDP per capita is a measure of a broader concept such as "economic development," then the inclusion of these cases raises concerns about measurement error—i.e., an oil-dependent economy may have a high GDP per capita without having real economic development.

Another approach would be to argue that oil-dependent countries differ from almost all other states in that they do not depend on taxing their citizens to generate revenue. If one believes that the mechanism through which a high GDP per capita leads to democracy is related to state infrastructural power and presence within society, one might have good reasons to exclude these cases, since they do not display the proposed mechanism.

To explore this idea further, we gathered data on oil exports for 1995 and removed *all* states with high dependence on oil. The resulting population of cases produces table 16.2. Although we still have Singapore in the lower

**Table 16.2**

Narrow Scope: GDP/Capita and Democracy

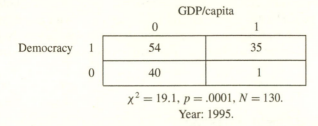

GDP/capita

|  |  | 0 | 1 |
|---|---|---|---|
| Democracy | 1 | 54 | 35 |
|  | 0 | 40 | 1 |

$\chi^2 = 19.1$, $p = .0001$, $N = 130$.
Year: 1995.

right cell, the set-theoretic finding about a sufficiency relationship is much stronger. From a qualitative point of view, this could be regarded as a theoretically motivated scope restriction that addresses problem cases in a methodologically appropriate way. In terms of tradeoffs, we have achieved an almost perfect sufficiency relationship at the cost of a relatively minor and theoretically defensible scope change.

It is important to note that while we have focused on the sufficient condition cell, the application of a scope condition will potentially remove cases from all cells. In this example, the scope condition removes observations from all four cells, 14 cases in total. From a set-theoretic point of view, this is not a big problem, since the upper right-hand cell remains well occupied. If the scope condition had removed all (or nearly all) cases from the upper right-hand cell, the relationship would still be one of near sufficiency, but it would be trivial (Goertz 2006; Ragin 2008).

One can also ask about using scope conditions with table 16.1 from a quantitative perspective. Two things happen if scope conditions work properly: the N goes down and the fit goes up. Significance levels will suffer from the decreased N, but hopefully the increase in fit will more than compensate for that loss. In this example, this is what happens: we arrive at a more substantively and statistically significant $\chi^2$. We see this result by comparing tables 16.1 and 16.2. The N goes down by 14 but $\chi^2$ goes up from 9.5 to 19.1 and the significance level improves quite a bit too.

The larger question remains: is it worth it? In large-N statistical analysis, the answer is often that it is not. The increase in $\chi^2$ is nice.[3] However, the cost is a reduction in the scope of generalization as well as time spent getting the relevant data (not as easy as it seems). The researcher would have to justify why the scope condition is used rather than a within-model solution. Depending on how difficult it is to formulate this justification, the imposition of a scope restriction might not be worth the gains in model fit.

---

[3] Odds ratio increases with this data would be much larger given that they are sensitive to empty cells.

By contrast, in qualitative research, the gains achieved from eliminating a few problem cases via a scope restriction often outweigh the losses in generality. When compared to quantitative researchers, qualitative scholars seek stronger generalizations (i.e., ideally no exceptions). With this culture, the goal of discovering powerful set-theoretic relationships frequently justifies reducing the scope to a population that may include only a small number of cases.


## Scope and Empirical Testing

Occasionally, scholars will argue explicitly that their theories apply to all cases of the phenomenon in question. For example, in the international relations conflict literature, we see prominent scholars arguing that their theories apply virtually everywhere:

> Most rational choice theorists (including structural realists) do not claim that their theories should be limited in time or space, and so would expect the same relationships found in politically relevant dyads, or other subsets, to hold among all dyads. In fact, among formal rational choice theorists, Bueno de Mesquita (1981) explicitly argues that the expected utility theory of war should apply to all regions and periods. Kenneth Waltz, writing in a less mathematical formulation, similarly argues that the constraints and inducements of system structure (as opposed to internal domestic factors) affect all states equally through time. (Bennett and Stam 2000, 555)

While some scholars imply a universal scope at the level of theory, there may be a disjunction between their *proposed scope* and the *empirical scope* of the theory. Empirical scope refers to the scope of a model as established by empirical testing and investigation. In the social sciences, scope restrictions frequently grow out of empirical poking and prodding to see where the theory works and where it does not. There is nothing wrong with this; in fact, it is common in the natural sciences and is a critical part of scientific research. In progressive research programs, there is often a natural back and forward between empirical findings and refinements of scope (and other aspects of theory). Empirical results and discoveries are crucial to the process through which investigators *construct* the full population for which their theory is relevant (Ragin 2000).

Unfortunately, there is often an inverse relationship between the proposed scope of theories and the empirical validity of theories. As a generalization, we suggest that theories with broader scopes are more often empirically false (or not confirmed by strong tests) when compared to theories with more restricted scopes. Scholars thus face a Fundamental Tradeoff between scope and empirical validity (Przeworski and Teune 1970). While they seek to formulate theories with high levels of generality, they often must sacrifice generality in order to arrive at valid explanations.

In the quantitative tradition, this tension between greater generality and empirical validity arises in discussions about using a large number of control variables with statistical models. Although the use of control variables is a within-model solution that can help scholars to avoid restricting the scope of their theories, recent writings have called into question the extent to which one can achieve valid explanation when multiple control variables are included. For example, Achen suggests that only about three independent variables should be included in a statistical model:

> A Rule of Three (ART): A statistical specification with more than three explanatory variables is meaningless. ART may sound draconian, but in fact, it is no more than sound science. With more than three independent variables, no one can do the careful data analysis to ensure that the model specification is accurate and that the assumptions fit as well as the researcher claims. (Achen 2002, 446)

If one takes this advice seriously, then scope limits become an attractive option. Although scope restrictions limit generality, they allow one to work with a statistical model that includes fewer control variables. It is not surprising that Achen argues for more intensive and higher quality analyses with smaller scopes:

> Still more importantly, big, mushy linear regression and probit equations seem to need a great many control variables precisely because they are jamming together all sorts of observations that do not belong together. Countries, wars, racial categories, religious preferences, education levels, and other variables that change people's coefficients are "controlled" with dummy variables that are completely inadequate to modeling their effects. The result is a long list of independent variables, a jumbled bag of nearly unrelated observations, and often a hopelessly bad specification with meaningless (but statistically significant with several asterisks!) results . . .. Instead, the research habits of the profession need greater emphasis on classic skills that generated so much of what we know in quantitative social science: plots, crosstabs, and just plain looking at data. Those methods are simple, but sophisticatedly simple. They often expose failures in the assumptions of the elaborate statistical tools we are using, and thus save us from inferential errors. Doing that kind of work is slow, and it requires limiting ourselves to situations in which the number of explanatory factors is small— typically no more than three. But restricting ourselves to subsets of our data where our assumptions make sense also typically limits us to cases in which we need only a handful of explanatory factors, and thus where our minds can do the

creative thinking that science is all about. Far from being a limitation, therefore, small regression specifications limited to homogeneous subsets of the data (and their probit and logit equivalents) are exactly where our best chances of progress lie. (Achen 2005, 337, 338)

This line of argument is congenial to a qualitative scholar. It fits well with the qualitative researcher's hesitation in using research designs that cover wide temporal and spatial domains.

While not often raised in this context, the use of matching methods in the statistical culture involves a reduction of empirical scope in the service of a better empirical test. When matching methods are used, quantitative scholars discard some cases and focus closely on others. Depending on the nature of the data, a relatively large percentage of cases might be discarded because there is no match. The included cases of matching are not a random subset of all the cases in the population. As a result, the empirical scope of the results generated by matching may be smaller than with a standard statistical analysis of the whole dataset.

The use of experiments also often involves limiting generality in order to carry out strong empirical tests. This tradeoff can be discussed with the language of internal validity versus external validity. While well-designed experiments might achieve a high level of internal validity for the population of subjects that is actually studied, researchers often have difficulty generalizing the findings of these experiments to broader contexts. The external validity of the findings is often a real issue (Morton and Williams 2010, 254–356). While these problems are not necessarily insurmountable, they routinely pose challenges for the generality of experimental findings.

In the qualitative tradition, of course, these same problems and challenges come up all the time. For instance, it is completely standard for case-study researchers to face questions concerning the generality of their work. While the explanation might be convincing for the one case, the scholarly community wants to know if it applies more generally. In this sense, case-study researchers and experimentalists often must address similar questions about external validity.

## Conclusion

Issues of scope raise Fundamental Tradeoffs in social science research. One tradeoff concerns the tension between generality and parsimony. In the effort to increase generality, scholars may expand the scope of their theories. However, increasing scope ordinarily requires complexifying the causal model, such that the theory becomes less parsimonious. Whether or not it makes sense to sacrifice parsimony for greater scope depends on how much complexification is required and how much the scope is expanded. In the qualitative tradition, expanding the scope often does not make sense because even modest expansions frequently involve complicated modifications to the causal model. By contrast, in the quantitative culture, scope extensions are more likely to make sense because analysts sometimes can accommodate many new cases through relatively modest adjustments to the causal model.

Another tradeoff concerns the tension between generality, on the one hand, and issues of model fit on the other. Scope restrictions often make sense if they yield large gains in model fit or empirical validity. In qualitative research, where analysts seek strong generalizations with few exceptions, scope restrictions can significantly improve a model's fit with the data, especially when the restriction can be clearly justified on theoretical grounds. Traditionally, quantitative researchers have been more reluctant to reduce the scope of their arguments in order to achieve a better fit with the data. However, some quantitative methodologists have recently encouraged the greater use of scope restrictions. It is possible that a new trend in quantitative research will be to sacrifice generality in order to carry out stronger tests and improve validity.

## References and Suggested Readings

There are surprisingly few methodological works that offer extended discussions on the topic of scope. The most notable exceptions are probably Cohen (1989) and Walker and Cohen (1985). We discuss conceptual and causal scope in Goertz and Mahoney (2009). Scope issues come up briefly in many leading qualitative methods and research design works, such as Geddes (2003, 95–98; 152–57); George and Bennett (2005, 25–27; 119–20); and Ragin (2000, 61–62). The importance of "abstract" scope conditions is emphasized in Kiser (1996). The relationship between scope conditions and selection bias is discussed in Collier and Mahoney (1996); issues concerning scope conditions and negative case selection are addressed in Mahoney and Goertz (2004).

A good discussion of scope from a quantitative perspective is Bartels (1996). An important early statement concerning outliers and scope restrictions in quantitative research is Bollen (1990). On the movement within quantitative methodology to improve inference through the use of simpler models, see Achen (2002) as well as the special issue of *Conflict Management and Peace Science* with articles by Achen (2005), Clarke (2005), Ray (2005), and others. The Fundamental Tradeoffs considered in this chapter are raised in a different context in Przeworski and Teune (1970, 20–23).

Achen, C. 2002. Toward a new political methodology: microfoundations and ART. *Annual Review of Political Science* 5:423–50.

Achen, C. 2005. Let's put garbage-can regressions and garbage-can probits where they belong. *Conflict Management and Peace Science* 22:327–39.

Bartels, L. 1996. Pooling disparate observations. *American Journal of Political Science* 40:905–42.

Bennett, D., and A. Stam. 2000. A cross-validation of Bueno de Mesquita and Lalman's international interaction game. *British Journal of Political Science* 30:541–60.

Berk, R. 2004. *Regression analysis: a constructive critique.* Newbury Park: Sage Publications.

Bollen, K. 1990. Political democracy: conceptual and measurement traps. *Studies in Comparative International Development* 25:7–24.

Bueno de Mesquita, B. 1981. *The war trap.* New Haven: Yale University Press.

Clarke, K. 2005. The phantom menace: omitted variable bias in econometric research. *Conflict Management and Peace Science* 22:341–52.

Cohen, B. 1989. *Developing sociological knowledge: theory and method,* 2nd edition. Chicago: Nelson-Hall.

Collier, D., and J. Mahoney. 1996. Insights and pitfalls: selection bias in qualitative research. *World Politics* 49:56–91.

Freedman, D. 2009. *Statistical models: theory and practice,* revised edition. Cambridge: Cambridge University Press.

Freedman, D. 2010. *Statistical models and causal inference: a dialogue with the social sciences.* Cambridge: Cambridge University Press.

Geddes, B. 2003. *Paradigms and sand castles: theory building and research design in comparative politics.* Ann Arbor: University of Michigan Press.

George, A., and A. Bennett. 2005. *Case studies and theory development.* Cambridge: MIT Press.

Gerring, J. 2007. *Case study research: principles and practices.* Cambridge: Cambridge University Press.

Goertz, G. 2006. Assessing the trivialness, relevance, and relative importance of necessary or sufficient conditions in social science. *Studies in Comparative International Development* 41:88–109.

Goertz, G., and J. Mahoney. 2009. Scope in case study research. In *Handbook of case-oriented research,* edited by D. Bryne and C. Ragin. Newbury Park: Sage Publications.

Goodwin, J., and T. Skocpol. 1989. Explaining revolutions in the contemporary Third World. *Politics and Society* 17:489–509.

Kiser, E. 1996. The revival of narrative in sociology: what rational choice theory can contribute. *Politics and Society* 24:249–71.

Mahoney, J., and G. Goertz. 2004. The Possibility Principle: choosing negative cases in comparative research. *American Political Science Review* 98:653–69.

Morton, R., and K. Williams. 2010. *Experimental political science and the study of causality: from nature to the lab.* Cambridge: Cambridge University Press.

Przeworski, A., and H. Teune. 1970. *The logic of comparative social inquiry.* New York: John Wiley & Sons.

Ragin, C. 2000. *Fuzzy-set social science.* Chicago: University of Chicago Press.

Ragin, C. 2008. *Redesigning social inquiry: fuzzy sets and beyond.* Chicago: University of Chicago Press.

Ragin, C., and G. Schneider. 2010. Comparative political analysis: six case-oriented strategies. Manuscript, University of Arizona.

Ray, J. 2003. Explaining interstate conflict and war: what should be controlled for? *Conflict Management and Peace Science* 20:1–30.

Ray, J. 2005. Constructing multivariate analyses (of dangerous dyads). *Conflict Management and Peace Science* 22:277–92.

Sambanis, N. 2004. What is civil war? Conceptual and empirical complexities of an operational definition. *Journal of Conflict Resolution* 48:814–58.

Senese, P., and J. Vasquez. 2008. *The steps to war.* Princeton: Princeton University Press.

Shadish, W., T. Cook, and D. Campbell. 2002. *Experimental and quasi-experimental designs for general causal inference.* Boston: Houghton Mifflin.

Skocpol, T. 1979. *States and social revolutions: a comparative analysis of France, Russia, and China.* Cambridge: Cambridge University Press.

Walker, H., and B. Cohen. 1985. Scope statements: imperatives for evaluating theories. *American Sociological Review* 50:288–301.

# Chapter 17

# Conclusion

Dissimilarity, just like resemblance, can be a cause of mutual
attraction ... differences of a certain kind incline us towards one
another. These are those which, instead of opposing and excluding
one another, complement one another.
—*Emile Durkheim*

King, Keohane, and Verba conclude *Designing Social Inquiry* with the
following message: "The appropriate methodological issues for qualitative
researchers to understand are precisely the ones that all other scientific
researchers need to follow. Valid inference is possible only so long as the
inherent logic underlying all social scientific research is understood and
followed" (1994, 230). By contrast, we wish to end this book by again
calling attention to important differences in the nature of qualitative and
quantitative research—differences that extend across research design, data
analysis, concepts, and causal inference. Beyond platitudinous similarities
(e.g., the goal of research is valid inference through the use of systematic
procedures), there is no set of principles that unifies all social scientific work.

Yet we are convinced that there is room for dialogue between the
quantitative and qualitative research paradigms. While their differences are
considerable, the paradigms can nicely complement one another within an
overall project aimed at explaining the social and political world. Like
Durkheim's vision of organic solidarity, we see the real possibility for a
fruitful collaboration between qualitative and quantitative research—one
built around mutual respect and appreciation. Achieving this possibility,
however, requires understanding and acknowledging head-on the many
important differences that exist between the research traditions.

220

**Table 17.1**
Summary of Contrasts I: Individual Cases

| Description | Quantitative | Qualitative | Chapters |
|---|---|---|---|
| (1) Explain outcome in individual case | Rare | Common | 1,3,4,6 |
| (2) Cross-case versus within-case | Cross-case primary | Within-case primary | 1,4,8 |
| (3) Causal mechanism | Optional | Must be identified | 7,8,14 |
| (4) Process tracing | Optional | Standard | 7,8,14 |
| (5) Counterfactual analysis | Primarily cross-case | Primarily within-case | 9 |

**Table 17.2**
Summary of Contrasts II: Causality and Causal Models

| Description | Quantitative | Qualitative | Chapters |
|---|---|---|---|
| (1) Individual variable is focus | Standard | Sometimes | 2,6,8,9 |
| (2) Causal configurations, interaction terms | Sometimes | Common | 2,4,6,8 |
| (3) Causal effects | Average Treatment Effect | Necessary and/or sufficient | 2,3,4,6,8 |
| (4) Purpose of counterfactual | Explicate model and parameter estimates | Within-case causal inference | 9 |
| (5) Equifinality | Implicit, model is the path | Explicit | 2,4 |
| (6) Aggregation in causal model | Addition, log-linear, additive in link function | Maximum, minimum, INUS | 2,4 |

## Summary of Differences

Tables 17.1–17.5 provide a summary of key differences that we have surveyed in this book.[1] These tables are not intended to present all differences but rather to give a sense of the extent and depth of the contrasts between

---

[1] To recall, our argument applies only to research that is centrally interested in causal inference, and thus our summary does not include most interpretive analyses. An entirely different checklist would be needed to compare the interpretive tradition to the kinds of research that we describe.

**Table 17.3**

Summary of Contrasts III: Populations and Data

| Description | Quantitative | Qualitative | Chapters |
|---|---|---|---|
| (1) Scope | Broad | Narrow | 16 |
| (2) Case study selection | Representative, random | (1,1) cell is most important | 14 |
| (3) Select on the dependent variable | No | Sometimes | 14 |
| (4) Data format (e.g., spreadsheet) | Rows are individual observations | Rows are configurations of variables | 2 |
| (5) Triangular data | Heteroskedasticity | Necessary or sufficient condition | 2 |

**Table 17.4**

Summary of Contrasts IV: Concepts and Measurement

| Description | Quantitative | Qualitative | Chapters |
|---|---|---|---|
| (1) Terminology | Variables–indicators | Concepts–data | 10 |
| (2) Ontology | Unobserved variable causes indicator | Defining dimensions of concepts | 10 |
| (3) Variation | All variation is a priori important | Zones where variation in data does not change meaning | 11 |
| (4) Variable transformation rationale | Skewness, better fit in statistical model | Semantics and meaning transformations | 11,12 |
| (5) Typologies | Mutually exclusive | Overlapping or mutually exclusive | 13 |

the two traditions. With about five items per table, we arrive at a list of 25 differences. In some instances the distance between the two practices is quite great and in others less so, but we feel that in every case the difference is significant.

One way to use these tables is as a set of "identity" checks for classifying research (including one's own research). If our two cultures argument is a good description of research practices, then individual research projects

**Table 17.5**
Summary of Contrasts V: Asymmetry

| Description | Quantitative | Qualitative | Chapters |
|---|---|---|---|
| (1) Explaining 0s different than explaining 1s | No | Sometimes | 5,13 |
| (2) Concept and its opposite | Same variable used for concept and its opposite | Different concepts and measures often used | 5,13 |
| (3) Counterfactual $x_i \rightarrow x_j$ different from counterfactual $x_j \rightarrow x_i$ | Implicitly the same | Often different | 9 |
| (4) 2×2 tables when exchanging (0,1) and (1,0) cells | Same value for almost all measures of association | Different because one is necessary condition cell and the other is the sufficient condition cell | 2,5,15 |

should tend to fall on one side or other for the items they address, with relatively few hybrid responses. In the case of mixed-method research, it should be possible to identify the portion of the project that is quantitative and the portion that is qualitative.

## Individual Cases

One core component of our argument is the claim that quantitative and qualitative researchers treat individual cases quite differently. In quantitative research, it is rare for analysts to seek to explain why specific cases have particular outcomes. Instead, these researchers are focused on cross-case analysis and the characteristics of the larger population as a whole. In a good quantitative study, one need not carry out any process tracing or identify causal mechanisms to achieve major research goals. If counterfactual analysis is conducted, it too derives from cross-case comparisons.

In qualitative research, it is quite common for analysts to seek to explain why specific outcomes occurred within particular cases. In this mode of investigation, scholars depend heavily on within-case analysis and usually only secondarily on cross-case analysis for their inferences. Accordingly, they almost always employ process tracing and seek to locate mechanisms within the specific cases under analysis. They also carry out counterfactuals in which they rerun the history of one or more specific cases.

## Causality and Causal Models

Concerning causality and causal models, quantitative researchers typically focus on the effects of individual variables and only sometimes include interaction terms. They understand and define causality in terms of average treatment effects. They sometimes use counterfactuals for the purpose of explicating their statistical models, but counterfactuals are not used as a method of hypothesis testing. The form of aggregation in the typical quantitative model involves addition or at least is additive in the link function. Quantitative researchers do not usually talk about equifinality but instead treat their causal model as representing the path to the dependent variable.

Qualitative researchers often focus more on causal configurations than the effects of individual variables (with the exception of necessary conditions). They understand and define causality in terms of necessary conditions, sufficient conditions, and INUS conditions. They often use individual case counterfactuals as a means of testing hypotheses. Their causal models commonly assume that cases can follow different paths to the same outcome, but there are not many paths. Qualitative models tend to aggregate causal factors by implicitly using Boolean operations such as taking the maximum or minimum values.

## Populations and Data

Quantitative researchers tend to study large populations and develop generalizations that encompass a wide scope. When they select case studies, they try to choose cases that are representative of this larger population. In this tradition, it is usually a bad idea to select cases based on their value on the dependent variable. Quantitative scholars assemble data into standard rectangular spreadsheets in which rows are individual observations and columns are variables. When quantitative analysts are presented with a triangular dataset, a natural thing to do is correct it for heteroskedasticity.

By contrast, qualitative researchers tend to study a small number of cases and develop generalizations with a narrow scope. They focus closely on cases in which the outcome of interest and causes of interest are present. They sometimes select cases precisely because of their value on the dependent variable. In the qualitative tradition, the rows of data sets may be understood to be logical configurations of variable values. When scholars trained in Qualitative Comparative Analysis view triangular data, they naturally interpret it as representing necessary or sufficient conditions.

## Concepts and Measurement

In the quantitative tradition, measurement issues are commonly discussed using the terminology of variables and indicators. The assumption is generally that a latent variable causes its indicators, such that the latter is correlated with the former. In this tradition, one is interested in studying and explaining the full range of variation on variables. Variable transformations are commonly carried out for good statistical reasons (e.g., to correct for skewness). When typologies are used, they refer to mutually exclusive categories.

In the qualitative tradition, measurement issues usually are addressed by exploring the relationship between concepts and data. Measurement is a semantic issue that requires specifying the defining dimensions of concepts. Qualitative scholars often assume that certain zones of variation on a variable may be irrelevant to the measurement of a concept (especially the upper and lower ranges on a variable). Qualitative scholars are leery of variable transformations unless they preserve or increase the meaning of the concept in question. When typologies are used, they may either be mutually exclusive or permit overlapping membership in multiple categories.

### Asymmetry

Quantitative scholars develop symmetric causal arguments in which the same variables and model explain the presence versus absence of an outcome. These scholars also view a concept and its opposite symmetrically, such that the negated concept (e.g., not-development) is the same thing as the opposite concept (e.g., underdevelopment). They likewise implicitly assume a symmetric view of counterfactuals in which a change in one direction (e.g., from authoritarianism to democracy) is as plausible as a change in the other direction. Finally, most statistical measures of $2 \times 2$ tables are symmetric.

By contrast, qualitative scholars often develop asymmetric causal arguments in which different variables and models are needed to explain the presence versus absence of an outcome. They often assume that a concept and its opposite are not symmetric; they may require different definitions and measures. They likewise allow for an asymmetric view of counterfactuals in which a change in one direction may not be as plausible as a change in the other direction. Finally, in the qualitative tradition, $2 \times 2$ tables are inspected for their asymmetric properties, especially the characteristic patterns of necessary conditions and sufficient conditions.

## Methodological Pluralism in the Social Sciences

The existence of differences between the quantitative and qualitative paradigms does not have to be a source of conflict in the social sciences. None of the differences we have listed imply contradictions. They are all in fact quite understandable once one takes into consideration the contrasting goals and purposes of the research paradigms. Both cultures "make sense" in light of these goals and purposes.

Given that the cultures are relatively coherent systems, it is not surprising that many researchers gravitate strongly toward one and not the other. Fortunately, cooperation and mutual respect do not require that all scholars become fully members of both cultures. There is no reason to argue against the existence of a division of labor in which some scholars pursue the specialized tasks for which their methods and tools are best equipped.

Yet it is also true that the two cultures are permeable, loosely bounded systems that influence one another. Quantitative and qualitative analysis do not and need not pursue their research in isolation of one another. Rather, there are many ways in which the methods and findings of one tradition can beneficially spill over into the other tradition. Moreover, we are convinced that mixed-method research is often a viable option.

The extent to which researchers might mix the two cultures can vary. In some cases, the researcher may be primarily quantitative or primarily qualitative, but draw on selected ideas and tools from the other tradition. As we have stressed, there is a tremendous amount to be learned by understanding how scholars in the other culture do things. And it is certainly possible for a given scholar to import certain practices and procedures into her or his study without embracing the other culture wholesale.

Even more thoroughly mixed-method research would entail scholars simultaneously and fully pursuing goals characteristic to both quantitative and qualitative research. Here the researcher would estimate the effects of particular variables in large populations and explain specific outcomes for particular cases within that population. To achieve the former goal, she or he would use cross-case analysis, statistical modeling, and the tools of the quantitative paradigm. To achieve the latter, she or he would pursue within-case analysis, develop configurational causal models, and utilize the full resources of the qualitative paradigm. The final product would thereby encompass two quite different though non-contradictory sets of findings.

If we allow for some division of labor and the possibility of mixing the two cultures, we arrive at a pluralistic vision of social science. On this view, there should be an important and respected place for quantitative research, qualitative research, and various kinds of mixed-method research. We believe that the main obstacle standing in the way of the blossoming of such methodological pluralism is simply a failure to recognize clearly the different—though equally legitimate—purposes and procedures of quantitative and qualitative analysis. By treating the two paradigms as alternative cultures, this book has sought to shed light on these differences while fostering a constructive dialogue between the two.

# Appendix

This appendix presents the results of a survey of methodological practices as carried out in substantive articles in political science and sociology. The survey tracks what scholars are actually doing when producing empirical work that is regarded by the disciplines as excellent, as defined by publication in major journals. While one can debate whether the practices typically used in this work represent "best practices," they are the procedures that scholars employ to produce the best substantive work in these disciplines.

The results in the following tables derive from a stratified random sample of articles published in top journals in political science and sociology. The sampling frame is articles published from 2001 to 2010 in six leading journals: *American Journal of Sociology, American Political Science Review, American Sociological Review, Comparative Politics, International Organization*, and *World Politics*. The sample is stratified by journal and by time period (2001–2005 and 2006–2010). Forty articles were selected per strata, of which eighteen were coded, leading to a total of 216 articles. Review articles and non-empirical theory articles were excluded from the sample. The coding was performed by two Ph.D. candidates at Northwestern University, Khairunnisa Mohamedali and Christoph Nguyen. The spreadsheet with all the data is available upon request.

Table A.1 provides some basic statistics on our sample of articles. As one can see, quantitative methodologies make up the clear majority (72 percent versus 31 percent). Here it is important to keep in mind that we have two journals, *American Political Science Review* and *American Sociological Review*, that publish little qualitative work. The other four journals publish a significant proportion of qualitative work.

The data indicate that explicit multimethod work is almost never carried out in these journals. One of the challenges of multimethod research is conducting it within the confines of a journal length article. Yet in some

**Table A.1**

Methodologies Used

| Methodology | Percent |
|---|---|
| Quantitative | 72 |
| Qualitative | 31 |
| Explicit multimethod | 1 |
| Interpretive | 2 |
| Theoretical/game theory | 8 |

*Note:* Articles can use more than one methodology.

**Table A.2**

Qualitative Methodologies Used

| Methodology | Percent |
|---|---|
| Case study ($N = 1$) | 27 |
| Small-N study ($1 < N < 10$) | 63 |
| Medium-N study ($N > 9$) | 8 |
| Typology | 26 |
| QCA | 1 |
| Equifinality | 13 |
| Counterfactual | 15 |
| New concept | 31 |
| Explicit process tracing | 22 |
| Median number of independent variables | 2 |

*Note:* Articles can use more than one methodology.

subfields and for some journals, e.g., *International Organization*, we observe a tradition of publishing quantitative articles that include a couple of short case studies. Moreover, recent books on comparative politics and international relations are now explicitly cast as multimethod studies.

Table A.2 presents basic information about various qualitative methodologies used in the articles in our survey. It is not surprising that over 90 percent of qualitative articles are individual case studies or small-N studies. Of these, there are many more small-N studies than individual case studies. The data also show that medium-N studies are not common; only 8 percent of the qualitative articles had 10 or more cases.

A fairly common component of qualitative work is the use of typologies, with about one quarter of all articles including an explicit typology. Since qualitative scholars are not constrained by needing data for lots of cases, they can more easily develop typologies for either descriptive or explanatory

**Table A.3**
Quantitative Methodologies used

| Methodology | Percent |
|---|---|
| OLS | 23 |
| Logit/probit | 37 |
| Time series | 2 |
| Panel/TSCS | 18 |
| Interaction terms | 18 |
| $R^2$ discussed | 6 |
| Bayesian | 3 |
| Experimental | 5 |
| Instrumental variables | 3 |

*Note:* Articles can use more than one methodology.

purposes. Often these typologies introduce new concepts, which is not uncommon in qualitative research (i.e., 31 percent of all qualitative articles introduce a new concept).

The percentages for the explicit discussion of counterfactuals and equifinality are lower (15 percent and 13 percent, respectively). As we have discussed, the use of counterfactuals in qualitative research is often implicit and not directly discussed as a method of inference. In turn, this is related to the nonsystematic way in which most qualitative researchers use methodological tools. Similarly, equifinality is often implicit in an analysis, though its limited usage is probably more related to the small N of much qualitative research. A case study almost by definition can only look at one path. Equifinality really comes into play when there are more than one or two cases.

Although process tracing is often used implicitly in qualitative research, it is usually not used explicitly. In our sample, only 22 percent of the articles *explicitly* used process tracing.

One of the big challenges for the field of qualitative methodology involves encouraging scholars to be more aware of methodological issues and more explicit about the procedures they use to make inferences. We hope that this book helps to promote greater methodological self-consciousness among qualitative researchers.

Turning to quantitative research, Table A.3 shows that the mainstream, classical, statistical subculture is still dominant in political science and sociology. If we combine OLS, logit, time series, and panel methodologies, we capture about 80 percent of all quantitative articles.[1] Bayesian techniques

---

[1] It is possible for an article to use multiple methodologies but these categories rarely overlap.

are on the rise, though we found few in our survey, which may be an artifact of the journals that we examined. Similarly, while the potential outcomes framework, aka Neyman-Rubin-Holland model, is very influential in methodological circles, it did not make an explicit appearance in any of the 216 articles that we surveyed. On the other hand, the use of instrumental variables and experiments could be seen as indicators of the potential outcomes framework, and they add up to 8 percent of all articles.

Cultures are always a mix of longstanding practices and rapidly changing ones. The qualitative and quantitative cultures and their subcultures are no exceptions. Our survey reflects research over the last decade, but if one looked over a longer period of time, many of the scores for the items coded would change significantly, and even more importantly some of the items would come and go. In addition to changing over time, cultures also vary across space—be it subfields, disciplines, or geography. Multimethod analysis seems increasingly common and prestigious in comparative work and international relations, but much less so for work on American politics. In sociology, QCA commands more attention and respect than in political science. The same is true if one compares its standing in Europe to the United States.

Ultimately, then, our volume provides a snapshot of methodological practices at a certain time and place. The two cultures argument describes especially well the situation in the United States in the early twenty-first century. The differences between the two cultures are substantial enough that they will likely persist well into the future. Yet, we also think a growing group of scholars will cross boundaries and conduct research that innovatively combines ideas from both cultures. Work at this intersection focused on transcending differences may well represent the most exciting social science in the coming years.

# Name Index

# Subject Index

aggregation techniques, qualitative and quantitative, 29–31

asymmetry: and concept formation, 161–65; contrasted with statistical methods, 23, 28–29, 65–67, 70–72, 197; of explanation, 68; in qualitative research, 7, 23, 28–29, 66–70, 142–43, 197; "static causal," 64

average treatment effect: and case selection, 177, 184, 188; and causal complexity, 57; contrasted with necessary/sufficient conditions, 8; and counterfactual theory of causation, 77–78, 116–17; defined, 52–53; and the effects-of-causes approach, 41–43; and generalization, 193, 201; and scope conditions, 207, 211. *See also* effects-of-causes approach; potential outcomes framework

Bayesian inference, 4, 53, 128, 198n2, 229

Boolean methods, 24, 54, 58, 60, 68. *See also* fuzzy-set analysis; Qualitative Comparative Analysis (QCA)

cases: versus causal-process observations, 92; crucial, 186–87; and degrees of freedom problem, 10, 92; deviant, 186, 188; extreme, 152, 184; number of, 10, 48, 87, 228; on-line, 186; pathway, 187; and random selection, 182–84, 207; and rare outcomes, 183–84; and representativeness, 182, 185; and selection on the dependent variable, 177–81; and substantive importance, 185,

188; typical, 186, 188. *See also* individual case analysis

causal complexity, 56–58; 210–11

causal inference: and counterfactuals, 115–17; cross-case versus within-case modes of, 11, 87–90; in experimental research, 101–2; in quantitative research, 4, 41–47; in qualitative research, 4, 9, 41–42, 46–48; 102–6; standard models for, 51–54. *See also* causal models; causes-of-effects approach; effects-of-causes approach

causal mechanism: defined, 100; and experimental research, 102, 110; and process tracing, 55, 94, 102–6, 183, 187; and statistical research, 101, 104, 106–7, 182; and scope conditions, 208, 212; and "strong" causal inference, 103

causal models: additive-linear, 51–52, 107, 109–10, 177–80; and case selection, 177, 184; and fit with data, 31–36; and individual cases, 46–47; set-theoretic, 51–56, 65–70, 96, 177–78, 181, 184, 193–95, 209, 211. *See also* average treatment effect; INUS condition; necessary condition; sufficient condition

causal-process observation (CPO): defined, 90; examples of, 90–91; and causal mechanisms, 101; and process-tracing tests, 93–96

causes-of-effects approach: contrasted with effects-of-causes approach, 41–44; defined, 41–42; and generalization 46–47